"Thank God I'm Not A Boy!"

THE LETTERS OF DORA WILLATT, DAUGHTER, SWEETHEART AND NURSE 1915-18

LAMPADA PRESS
Cottingham Road
Hull
HU6 7RX

A CIP catalogue record for this book is available from the British Library.

© **Alan Wilkinson**

Published 1997

Paperback ISBN 1 873811 05 5

Printed by
Advanced Laser Press
Digital Park
Longstanton
Cambridge

"Thank God I'm Not A Boy!"

THE LETTERS OF DORA WILLATT, DAUGHTER, SWEETHEART AND NURSE 1915-18

Alan Wilkinson

Acknowledgements

We are grateful to the family of Cecil M Slack for granting permission to publish these letters, also for their kind cooperation at every stage of the production of this volume.

The publishers would also like to thank the Ferens Educational Trust for their support in the completion of this project.

Contents

INTRODUCTION

The Great War of 1914 to 1918 caused immense dislocation within individual families as well as across entire nations. British fighting men were sent abroad, while at home newly drafted servicemen found themselves billeted in unfamiliar places to await postings. Women took up work for the first time as nurses, munitions workers and farm labourers; as drivers, teachers and clerks; some found work abroad or on hospital ships. Individuals were disorientated, families and communities fragmented. It was through word- of-mouth, through some not always reliable newspaper reports, but primarily by letter that these dislocated men and women stayed in touch, and it is through that written correspondence - where it survives - that we can best gain a flavour of those awful years.

The family of Cecil Moorhouse Slack have long treasured a collection of some 700-odd letters and other papers relating to his four years in uniform. Slack himself clearly valued the collection: it was he who gathered it together in 1977 and published a book, Grandfather`s Adventures in the Great War, 1914-18, in which he reproduced the bulk of his letters home. To these he added a commentary, thereby painting a broader picture of trench life and the battles he had experienced. The particular value of that volume is that it contains not only his own regular letters - to his parents, his brothers and sisters, his sweetheart - but also, in many instances, their replies to him. Thus, alongside his graphic portrayal of the appalling conditions under which the war was conducted - added to which are some even more brutal details added in his old age - there are set the mundane events of life on the home front. Thus we are afforded a vivid impression of the pain suffered by those who awaited news from friends and family at war.

However, Slack omitted a great deal. In the main he omitted material which he evidently considered too personal in its nature. In essence, this comprised the hundreds of letters he received from Dora Willatt, the girl he had admired since childhood and whom he courted through the latter part of the war.

Dora`s father, W.H. Willatt, a Director of the Hull firm of Reckitt & Sons Ltd., had been one of 70 Reckitts men to join the services more or less at the outset of the war. He was a volunteer who clearly saw it as his duty to serve his country. From the end of 1915 until June 1917 he was stationed with the East Riding Royal Engineers at Silkstone, near Barnsley. An engineer himself, he was charged with training recruits in the construction of trenches and other earthworks, building pontoon bridges, and so on. Thus it was that he, his wife and two daughters left their Newland Park home to the depredations of the winter damp and the occasional Zeppelin raid, and settled into a cottage on Silkstone Common.

Dora Willatt was a young lady with time on her hands when she arrived at Heath Cottage - too much time. Like her father - and like most people of her age - she wanted to contribute to the war effort, but she was continually thwarted. Late in 1915 she had worked briefly as a VAD nurse at Hull`s Naval Hospital in Argyle Street, but that had come to an end with the move to Silkstone. Duty in any case ordained that she place family first: her mother was prone to sickness and frequently required nursing. Moreover, as Dora makes clear in a number of her letters, her family were not at all keen on her taking steps towards independence. They had already put an embargo on her going to college, as one or two of her contemporaries had done. So she suffered the torpor of village life, and the tiresome company of "coal magnate specimens", as she dreamed of following friends onto hospital ships or into field hospitals on the Continent. And she champed at the bit: sometimes, she wrote in a rare moment of exasperation, she felt "a positive rebel and a suffragette a dozen times over".

Cecil Slack was, at first, one of a number of people with whom Dora corresponded. She clearly remained in touch with her scattered former schoolmates as well as with a large number of friends from Hull. She occasionally visited the town, checking on the house and paying social calls. And Cecil, the eldest son of another Reckitts director resident on Holderness Road, was no more than another friend at first, albeit a close one. The two had known each other since their early days at a local dame`s school, Miss Keen`s, when the seven-year-old Cecil had pushed Dora off her bench and chased her around the desk in an attempt to steal a kiss. They had attended adjoining boarding schools on the coast of North Wales. Their families certainly socialised, as this picture, taken at Hornsea before the war, shows.

In August 1914 Cecil was a junior clerk at Reckitts, where his father, naturally, had plans for his future. He did not join up immediately: he shared the popular view that the war would last no more than a few months. But he was always a restless individual, a man of action, so after waiting all of ten days he took the plunge - twice! He signed as a private with a Hull Commercial Battalion and at the same time applied for a commission with the Territorials. It was the Commercial Battalion which moved first, meaning that when the Territorials (in the shape of the 4th East Yorkshire Battalion) called for him - and he went running - he was briefly in danger of being sued for desertion.

His first tour in France lasted no more than a couple of weeks. He embarked at Folkestone on 17 April 1915, was pitched into the second battle of Ypres, and returned to Blighty on 6 May with wounds to the left arm and shoulder. He was admitted to a London hospital where Mrs Willatt, Dora and her sister Flossie were among his visitors. After a short convalescence, he was passed fit and sent to Dalton Holme camp, near Beverley, where he remained until January 1916.

Quite how often Cecil wrote to Dora during 1915 we cannot tell: no letters to her survive from that period. But he was certainly in touch, for during his time in the `third line` at Dalton he was a frequent caller at "Beech Croft", as a remark in one of Dora`s early letters bears out: "you came to our house a good deal for tennis". To all intents and purposes, however, the correspondence between the two of them dates from the end of 1915, shortly after the Willatts moved to Silkstone.

Cecil`s letters to Dora are fascinating, but they tell a tale familiar to anyone with a basic knowledge of the Great War: mud, boredom, the chaos of battle, the tedium of waiting for leave, for action, for news of peace, the whole enlivened by sporadic bombardments and the occasional arrival of news - and dainties - from home. Dora`s letters, on the other hand, reveal much that is generally overlooked in histories of wars. They reveal, in the earliest days, a view of war as a bit of a lark. This changes radically as successive friends and acquaintances suffer injury, death or bereavement. While at one stage she suggests that Cecil bomb `Old Hunny Dear` with a rather over-cooked cake she has sent him, it is not long before she surrenders to gut feeling: "I don`t care a hang for the nation so long as you come through all right."

The letters also reveal a girl growing into womanhood. For although Dora is twenty years old when we first hear from her, she is very much a young girl recently out of boarding school. Her life revolves around tennis, walks, trips to town and tea with friends. She is also, at the outset, blithely ignorant of Cecil`s feelings towards her: they are just chums. The letter she writes in June 1916, therefore, after he has steered her away from friends on a woodland walk and asked her to be his wife is every bit as stunning as his proposal is unexpected. She is clearly shocked, and her words as she tries to compose her thoughts are very carefully chosen, revealing her deep seriousness. "Are you quite sure?" she asks him several times, because "if you had got the wrong girl it would be tragic - nothing is so awful as domestic unhappiness and quarrelling".

We are privileged, then, to watch this courtship unfold. We see Dora`s letters waver between a jaunty optimism that everything will come right in the end and an anguished yearning for an end to danger and separation, a return to peace and intimacy. But these are not only love-letters. As the war progresses, Dora`s life becomes more busy - and her letters give a fascinating account of her daily life.

For a considerable time she is marooned in "saturatingly stodgy" Silkstone. Later she will become involved in the extensive preparations for her sister`s wedding. Early in 1917, however, she finally gets what she has been hankering after - a posting to a hospital far from home, a `live-in` job as a VAD nurse in Waltham Abbey, Essex. Here we gain a vivid impression of life in a military hospital eighty years ago: the routine, the discipline, the camaraderie amongst the nurses, the social events organised with the patients, Dora`s trips up to town on the tram and underground, her walks in Epping Forest. But all this is cut cruelly short when her mother`s health fails, and Dora is summoned home to nurse her and keep house. Almost a year passes before she can take up her work again, this time in Surrey.

During this year the Willatts return to Hull, and we are shown in some detail what war meant on the home front. The Zeppelin raids she alternately considers a mild irritant and a welcome excitement. Rationing, the servant problem, the fragmented news of the war - all are discussed in a tone that varies from the glib to the stoic to the despairing. A picture emerges too of the tightness of the social circle in which the Willatts and the Slacks moved: Newland Park at that time contained barely a score of houses, yet within them there lived most of the families closest to them. Flossie`s in-laws, the Todds, who were in the paint business, were across the road; the Mayfields, their fellow "paint fogies" as Dora called them, were a few doors down; the Farrells, who lost two sons at the front, were at "Brookside"; the Inglebys, relatives of Cecil`s closest friend and confidant, Norman Ingleby, were at "Rosslyn House". And there were the Gosschalks, the Runtons, the Tills, the Halls, the Waddingtons, the Thornton-Varleys - all business people in Hull, and all playing minor roles in the rich drama played out in these letters.

Alongside the letters Dora wrote are, of course, an almost equal number of Cecil`s. His experiences at the front, although in the broader context of Great War literature almost commonplace, are a vital part of this book: they show us firstly what Dora was learning about the war, secondly the manner in which she learned it, and finally they shed light on the way in which she responded. It is against his first-hand accounts that she weighs the snippets she has picked up from the news media, the blurred versions she hears when she bumps into East

Yorkshire men in the street, the bits and pieces gleaned from friends. And she forms her own opinions, asking occasional questions: how is it, she wonders, that some get posted to the Bahamas, or get leave after five months at the front, when able men like Cecil are called upon time after time for difficult and dangerous work? And will he please promise her that he will *not* go into the Flying Corps? She has met aviators and knows precisely how dangerous their work is.

The cost of editing this collection of letters down to manageable proportions is that at times it seems like an exclusive correspondence between sweethearts. That courtship certainly lies at the heart of the collection, but there was throughout the war a sustained dialogue between Dora, Cecil, their families and many friends which is at least suggested by a scattering of representative letters which have been included. There are, for example, one or two from Dora`s sister Flossie; a number from fellow officers written at the time of Cecil`s disappearance in 1918; and a brief selection of the many surviving letters to and from Cecil`s parents and siblings. These are included initially to introduce the several members of an extensive, close-knit and tremendously supportive family. There is his baby sister Kitty, just learning to scrawl a few letters to "my dery cessul"; young Harold breaking off from a letter to kill a moth ("BANG I have hit it it is dead"); his brother Bob, desperate to join up, yet having to suffer Latin classes - with a female teacher of all things! - and being chastised for racing his motorbike up and down Cottingham Road. Equally importantly, these letters provide a setting for the explosion of telegrams, notes and `phone calls which follows the news that Cecil has gone missing during the German Spring Offensive of 1918. This crisis activates not only Cecil`s and Dora`s parents as they seek news of their lost boy, but drags in a number of local notables, not least the M.P. Tom Ferens who, through contacts in the Red Cross in London, is in a position to catch the first scent of hope that he is actually alive.

The selection starts as Dora and Flossie, settling into their temporary home in Silkstone, send cheery greetings for a happy 1916, and continues with Cecil`s last note before he sails for France and what he hopes is a no more than a few more months at the front.

The Slack family gather around the family's first car, purchased in 1914. The house, one of a pair, is the one next door to 'Beech Croft'. The motor-bike is, in all probability, Cecil's.

PART ONE:

I WOULD BE VERY PLEASED WITH A GERMAN HELMET

Heath Cottage, Silkstone Common, Nr. Barnsley, 27.12.15

Dear Cecil,   It was a tremendous surprise for us on Christmas morning when we got your parcel. It really is awfully good of you to send us the chocolates and they are just the kind I love.

We have quite settled down in our new abode and like it much better than we thought we should, although it is awfully quiet. The country is really quite nice and very hilly and heaps of walks in all directions - much better than Newland Park and Cottingham Road for our only route march! We are only about half a mile from the camp and Pater is able to live with us. Speaking of the camp - it really is the limit. We went there on Xmas Day to see the East Riding men before they had their dinner and the mud nearly came up to our ankles - fearful splodgy mess. It may interest you to know that eight men died of pneumonia and one committed suicide there last winter so you see quite pleasant memories are attached to the place.

There is no one very exciting or interesting here except Dorothy, the landlady`s only daughter who lives with her Mother and aunt on the other side of the road - we asked her to do a route march the other day but her Ma said she couldn`t possibly manage five miles.

We had a great time in the house the first day we were here. One simply couldn`t breathe for atrocious ornaments and those paper ball fly catcher arrangements and curtains, etc. We have stored them all away and told the dear landlady we are frightened of breaking them. We are fearfully wealthy in silver candlesticks - automatic silver biscuit box affairs and uncomfortable sugar basins - some of the things are too funny for words.

On Christmas night we had the only two officers of Pater`s Co. not on leave into dinner - Stedham and Allderidge - I don`t know whether you know them. Stedham is a cousin of Col. Easton`s[1] and Allderidge is the son of the vicar of Newport - he says he remembers a Slack at Hymers[2] who used to play heaps of tricks and he was sure it was you!

I had a letter from Ma Hovey[3] this morning - she and Betty[4] are up beyond the Pwylly woods spending Christmas in their new cottage. To quote her own words she says "Hilda and Mabel Slack are very nice children and have had a very good term", so you see what good sisters you have got. I rang up Hilda one night and she seems to quite enjoy Penrhos and likes Miss Clayton very much. New girls cannot generally bear her - she is fearfully squashy with them. It was ages before Flossie and I got to like her.

Florence says in her letter that I have described our Xmas night officers minutely - Allderidge is very nice and quite jolly but Stedham looks quite like an Easton but has a very about town manner which aggravates us intensely. Florence and I are fearfully amicable considering we are together all day. It is positively miraculous. I don`t know what is coming to us.

Reggie Gaskell is having quite a lively time in France - we had a piece of shell from him the other day. If you look in the Xmas no. of the Tatler you will see towards the end a drawing which he has done called "If tomorrow come".

It was awfully lucky for you to get home for Xmas - it must be awfully jolly being such a big family - when I`ve squabbled with Florence I`ve no- one to go on and you have six[5] others!

I hope you have a bright New Year and good luck. With love from the family and many thanks, Dora.

P.S. You`ve no idea what a desolate spot this is but still it`s quite jolly. We miss the [air raid] buzzers awfully - they were exciting and relieved monotony anyway.

[1] George Easton: Colonel and County Adjutant of the East Yorks Volunteers Forces.
[2] The Hull school Cecil attended before going to Rydal Mount.
[3] Head Mistress of Penrhos College, Dora`s old school.
[4] Betty Sowerbutts, a young teacher at Penrhos.
[5] Actually there were seven: Bob, Hilda, Mabel, Norman, Harold, Ralph and Kitty.

The Family - Norman, Mother, Cecil, Mabel,
Bob, Ralph, Kitty, Father and Hilda

∂୨୪ Silkstone, 27.12.15

Dear Cecil,   Army Service Corps of Thanks for the awfully nice
chocolates. It was absolutely topping of you. I`ve spent a delightful
afternoon by the fire with my box of the dear sweet things.

We have had a very jolly visit from Emma Blamires and her family.
Willie Hallitt, Jessie`s brother, drove them over. We are going over to
Huddersfield one day this week. The Saturday before Christmas Dora
and I had a long day in Sheffield. We stayed till dark and then lost ourselves hopelessly trying to find a cake shop we`d seen earlier in the day.

This house is quite cosy, though the fires smoke terrifically and we`re
generally in a state of partial asphyxiation.

Dora and I see a fearful lot of each other, more than we have done for years! We`ve been fairly amicable so far.

With love, in which Mother joins, and many thanks, Flossie.

Flossie

ᴈᵧᵧ Wilton House, Holderness Road, Hull, 5.1.16

Dear Dora,   Just a line to say "Goodbye". I said goodbye to your Mother and Flossie yesterday in town, where we talked scandal over tea-cakes and muffins.

I am under orders for the Front again, and am now on leave, awaiting a telegram. There are four of us going, namely young Robson, the son of Pistol Peter, one of the Rollits, Jack Oughtred and myself. I am both glad and sorry to go.

Did you know that Willy Westrope had been mentioned in despatches, together with Cyril Easton and Holtby[1]. It may mean a DSO, or a Military Cross!

I had quite an exciting experience on Sunday night, when the wind was blowing at 90 miles an hour. I was going along the Cottingham-Beverley Road with the wind behind me, at about 30 mph when I went smack into a pile of telegraph wires. It took me five minutes to get off my bike, and another 10 to get the bike clear, and then about 20 to clear the road. Having done this I found more wires and a great tree. I had to go round another way, leaving my lamp shining on the tree.

Would you like a German helmet? I`ll send you one if I can manage to get hold of it.  I believe they`re rather scarce now. They make rather neat little scuttles, or plant pots.

Please come and see me again when I`m wounded.

Yours sincerely, Cecil M Slack.

[1] Cousin of the novelist Winifred Holtby

℞ Wilton House, 7.1.16.

My dear Cecil,   I am forwarding your marching order which you may require. Just at present you will probably be enjoying your dinner on the train, and we are thinking of you. I hope you all have a good journey, a good night and safe transport to your destination. May God be with you and keep you safely amidst all dangers. It is hard for Mothers to bid farewell, but we must try and be brave. It is much harder for wives to part with their husbands. I most earnestly pray that you will receive all necessary strength and wisdom, and in all things serve your God and your parents` God faithfully and well. Good night my dear boy, good luck and God bless you.

Much love from Your affec. Mother.

Cecil and his mother, Winifred

⚭ B.E.F., 15.1.16

Dear Flossie and Dora,　　　　　I arrived here safely on Thursday
evening. "Here" is 40 yds from the Huns. There are about 15 of my old
platoon left. The enemy were very quiet the first night, probably having
heard of my return and being awed thereat.

It is very muddy and wet, and very cold o`nights. Rats swarm. They
come and give one the glad eye when resting in a dug-out, and run
across one at night-time. They feed on bacon scraps and dead men.

We have spells of 4 days in the trenches, 4 days in reserve, 4 days in the
trenches again, then 4 days` rest. There is nothing to do except keep
the trenches tidy and inspect rifles and gas helmets. Every morning
everyone has to remove his gum-boots and socks and rub his feet, other-

wise `trench- foot` is contracted and the toes and feet drop off.[1]

We have roast beef for dinner. The joint is passed round and each cuts a chunk off. The same knife is used for butter, meat, jam, bread and cheese, and for stirring the tea!

Our tea is made from water pumped from the ground. You know it is tea because of the tea-leaves. Shaving water comes from the same source and you know it isn`t tea because there are no tea-leaves.

An unexploded shell has at this moment dropped outside our dug-out. We are feeling quite pleased.

Kindest regards to your Father and Mother, Yours sincerely, Cecil.

[1] If these instructions were not carried out and a soldier contracted trench foot it was classified as a self-inflicted wound.

⚶ On 13.1.16 Cecil wrote to his brother Bob, second eldest in the family and still at Hymers School:

Dear Bob,   I have had a very interesting journey up to here, about 8 miles from the firing line. The French tramway system is most amusing. At Havre we were told to go to Base Camp, by tram. It seems that as many as can hang on are allowed to do so. You can crowd round the driver until he can hardly move his arms. The conductor was unable to move, and only those near him had to pay.

This morning I went to the latrine of the farm where we are living, and on opening the door found la mere. She was not at all embarrassed; on the contrary, she begged my pardon for being there. This latrine is a deep hole, and it is necessary to take a deep breath of fresh air before going there. The family pump is a few yards away.

Your affec. brother, Cecil.

ℭℜℌ Silkstone, 27.1.16

Dear Cecil,   Thanks so much for your letter - I was sorry I missed
you before you went off to Fritz & Hans - by the way you might send
over a nice little German Hate to them when you get this letter and send
my Zeppy remembrances. You soon seem to have got in the firing line.
I`m sure a glad eye from a rat would send me flying over the parapet or
something.

I have been spending a week with Mrs Elwell in Beverley - her husband
is the artist Fred Elwell - we got to know them in the summer and they
are simply a delightful couple. They live at the Bar House. The back of
the house looks onto the Westwood and it looks awfully nice from there
down towards the Minster. I went to the Hull Art School fancy dress
ball with them last Friday. I really enjoyed it tremendously. It made me
have quite a conscience going to a dance in wartime when everybody is
fighting.

A Mr Cammidge came in one evening. He is the organist at Beverley
Minster and rather a pot in the musical world - his parents and grand-
parents etc have been organists at York Minister but he couldn`t get it
because he never bothered to take any degrees. I believe his father or
grandpa was a pupil of Mendelssohn. He carried on a very learned and
booky conversation with Freddie and Mrs Elwell - I felt an awful ignora-
mus.

We have had Col. Newell over today for lunch and tea - he has the 1st
Field Company East Riding Engineers in France and came home on leave
last Wednesday. He was telling us about the new gas methods - I think
it is simply awful but I won`t talk to you about it as I expect you get
quite enough of it.

I believe Reggie Gaskell is coming over on leave next week. He and
G.P. Huntley (another R.E. man) have managed to get into the Flying
Corps. I shall laugh if he gets sent off to the East Coast or some other
out-of-the- way place to chase Zepps about once a month.

I had a long letter from Betty Sowerbutts - she and Billy are going to get married at Easter. Billy is an O.T.C. officer at Sedbergh and the H.M. thinks he will be kept on as that instead of being called up.

Florence and I have been on a route march, but we only did ten miles. We intend doing a stunt one day and seeing how much we can do. I believe "stunt" is a bit of the latest trench slang.

Sydney Allderidge has brought his wife here and got rooms in the next village. She seems years older than he is and rather prim and proper - she gives you the feeling that you want to shock her!

Mother and I are going to Hull on Monday for a few days to air the house. I have had a delightfully swollen face so I shall have to spend a few hours in S. Storey`s torture chamber.

Father seems to have got about 15 officers now - we call them the "Fleet". The majority are fearful old buffers - they annoy Mother intensely because they can`t stand to attention decently when they play the National Anthem in church.

By the way, do they ever give you coffee instead of tea - but would you know the difference? I would be very pleased with a German helmet, but please don`t get a bullet in the effort.

Dora.

᯽ B.E.F., 9.2.16

Dear Dora, I was awfully glad to get your letter the other day. I had just come in from a long, wet, miserable route march and was feeling thoroughly fed up with life.

I am second-in-command of a company under Norman Ingleby. We are both lieutenants, but seniority does not count out here, and two captains have been passed over. This is the company that Quibell had. You will possibly have heard that he has died of his wounds.

We are living in a dug-out in a little wood about 400 yards behind the firing line. The shell-holes are full of water, and the sides are covered with young ferns, etc. There are several little streams in it, and hundreds of birds.

One of our company was killed by a stray bullet a night or two ago. I had to read the burial service. The corpse was wrapped in a blanket and lowered into the grave. An officer stands at the head and reads a short prayer and all is over.

The School for Snipers was great fun. We were taught how to disguise ourselves as a blade of grass, and how to make cunning loopholes. One of our jobs is to go out to No Man`s land at night and dig a hole in which to spend the next day, observing the Hun, and occasionally sniping. It is like a glorious game of hide-and-seek.

No, I don`t think we get coffee instead of tea sometimes. Of course, it might be. It would be quite as correct to call it coffee as tea. Sometimes it is light brown, sometimes black. Last night it was green. The taste is always the same - dead men. This is horrid, but true.

This morning two of our officers were feeling sick and fed up. Consequently I got three eggs and a double ration of bacon. We also had porridge. It is like being at home.

Best wishes to the family, Yours sincerely, Cecil.

Around this time Cecil wrote a number of letters to his siblings, including these to Harold and Bob who were at Hymers School, and Hilda who, with Mabel, was at Dora`s old school, Penrhos College:

ᘒᙌ 11.2.16

Dear Bob,   I note with interest that the Hull Police Force is on your track, and hope you will continue to evade its members. Congratulations upon becoming a prefect. Mind you keep Harold in order. I expect he`s an awful nut as he is not in the bottom form.

I am the Mess President of our company, an always thankless task. But

I am in great favour at the moment as I have arranged for us to have a small mincing machine. We are going to have rissoles etc and turn the other company messes green with envy. Tonight we are having poached eggs on toast for tea.

We have rigged up a bell from our dug-out to our servants` quarters. It is composed of a long piece of telephone wire, and a bullet hanging on a Perrier bottle.

Your affec. brother, Cecil.

♉ 13.2.16

Dear Harold,   I am very glad that you are having a good time at Hymers. I hear from Father that you scored a try the other day at football. I am delighted to hear it and hope you will get a lot more. I am going out in front of our trench tonight about 50 yards from the Germans, to put up some barbed wire so that they will tear their clothes if they try to come for us. I shall have to crawl about on my stomach and be very quiet. When it is dark the Germans send up flares like a Roman candle firework, and it makes the place as bright as daytime.

I shall be home again for a short holiday about the time that you will be having yours.

Your affec. brother, Cecil.

♉ 17.2.16

Dear Hilda,   I got three letters in one blow last night - from you, from Bob and from Norman. The post comes up at night with the rations as a rule.

I see that Rosie is in great form this term. It must be an awful tax on her brain to devise such punishments. What a terrible disgrace to attend a debating meeting in your gym costume. Is your heart broken?

Two nights ago there was a great deal of gun and rifle fire about a couple of miles from us - the Germans were attacking. We had to "stand to", namely, be ready with bayonets fixed for anything at a second`s notice. Without the slightest warning there was a huge shower of earth 100ft high. Two mines had been exploded 50 yds from where I was standing. Have you ever seen the "Fairy Fountain" at the Trades Exhibition in Hull? It was like that, only bigger. Pieces of stone and lumps of earth as big as a man were falling like hail.

In spite of all this, which is really nothing, I am very happy, and should be very annoyed indeed if I got a "blighty".

We get plenty to eat, and although the "tea" is dirty, and green and smelly, it is hot.

Much love to you, and Mabel, Your affec. brother, Cecil.

✇ 28.2.16

Dear Bob,   I went into Wipers on Friday night. I wanted to do a bit of "looting" but could not leave the party of men I was in charge of.

I ought to get my leave in about 50 days` time, all being well.

We have not had any of the new gas yet, and if we do our respirators will do their work all right.

On Saturday night I was taking a party up to the trenches. When we came to a certain spot I opened out to about 5 yds between each man. I had just got to cover when I heard a nasty whistling swish. Knowing what it was I ducked immediately behind the trench wall. Three "crumps" burst just where I had been standing. About five minutes afterwards a stray bullet passed between me and the sergeant who was walking just behind me, followed by one which just missed my face. An hour afterwards I was standing up with the same sergeant talking to him, when I heard a "plonk". He stood for about a couple of seconds and then fell dead, a bullet having gone through his mouth and out the back of his head. I felt quite sick for about half an hour, and very nervy. He was buried shortly after.

Things seem very cheery by all accounts, at present.

Your affec. brother, Cecil.

༄༅ Silkstone, 29.2.16

Dear Cecil,   I meant to write to you some time ago but never
managed it and now can`t think of anything interesting to tell you.
This place is quite one of the dullest spots on earth.

Dora and I cheered up a little on Saturday by sledging down a slope on
one of the camp fields. It was really great sport, and we wished you
could have been there. We found a slope about as steep as a house side,
with a road at the bottom of it, and then another slope. After a while
we got tired of bouncing across the road and only shot down the second
slope.

 Dora and I go to the camp YMCA on Sundays and give the men their
tea. It`s a most fearful job to get there. There is no road so we tramp
through fields and a wood, across streams and through more fields of
mud until we get to the camp where we do a balance walk on planks
floating here and there on the mud.

We were sorry to hear about Capt. Quibell. I hope you have not had
any more casualties. We`ve heard from Reggie Gaskell and he seems to
have done a good deal of flying and saw England across the water, he
was so high up.

I must stop as I have to meet Dora at the station coming from Hull.
We`re still on fairly good terms, as you will notice by my going to meet
her. D and I are going to make plum cakes next week, so prepare for
the worst.

Best wishes from, Flossie

P.S. Hope you like the lavender on the hanky. I thought it would be a
change from the smells you have there.

Flossie, Dora and Mrs Roberts, wife of the camp Adjutant. "Not quite the thing from a military point of view!"

❧ Silkstone, Sunday 5.3.16

Dear Cecil,   You seem to be having a very lively time. I saw Mrs Fred Till the other day and she said that Jack Oughtred was having a rather hot time in the trenches. You seem to be getting quite a big pot out in France - I expect you will be a pompous Brigadier General or something before the war is out!!

I believe Flossie told you about the toboggan - it was great sport. We asked the sentry on duty to push us off. Father said it wasn`t quite the thing to do from a military point of view.

Last week I went to Hull by myself as we had arranged to have some carpets taken up. Mother was not well enough. I had a great performance - there were nine workmen in the house during the morning.

We went to see "Tonight`s the Night" the other night - it was the first excitement in the theatre line we had had. It was quite good but rather silly - there were only two decent songs: "They didn`t believe me" which is awfully nice and one called "I murdered him".

We had great excitement in Silkstone on Friday night - Mrs Crooks, our landlady, gave a 6d dance for the village people and Tommies in the schoolrooms. Meat pie and teacake supper - great sport - you know the kind of do. They do all kinds of most intricate dances - one especially, called D`Alberto, makes one`s brain fairly buzz. It is a square dance for eight people - something between the lancers, quadrilles and waltz cotillion - do you feel any wiser now? Old Lines went - that is Pater`s Canadian officer who says he is 35. He puffed over a few dances but managed to pull through. The funny part about him is that he imagines himself to be rather deep and he isn`t a bit really.

Sydney Carlin went out to France last Monday to join the other E.R. Engineers. Do you know him? He had a farm at Bewholme near Hornsea in pre-war days. He is a great friend of Reggie Gaskell`s and joined Pa`s lot to be with him so now he is awfully fed up because Reggie has joined the Flying Corps.

Flossie has gone to the YMCA this afternoon to help with the teas for the soldiers. They have a kind of cafe from 4-5.30 and we have to wait on them. I went as well last week but it was a frightful swizz - Mr & Mrs Roberts came and asked us to go to a birthday party in one of the officer`s rooms. One of us had to stay and keep up the family`s reputation and Flossie likes birthday cake better than I do, so I didn`t mind so much.

The YMCA manager is half potty we think. They have a small platform and he spends his time painting black and white checks on it and told us there were 400 squares to do. He has appealed for exemption to the tribunal on the grounds that he cannot be spared from his duties!

Good-bye and good luck, Love from us all, Dora.

❧ Cecil to his parents: 9.3.16

My Dear Father & Mother,   Now that we are out of the trenches I am at last able to tell you about my doings in the last fortnight.

On Feb 24th we left the rest huts and went into support. Then the taking back of our trenches being about to come off we went up into closer support. We had a corner of a wood to live in. There was no shelter of any description. There were three officers and we had a broken-down smelly affair that had once been a dug-out. We found the remains of a dead rat and a cross from a grave, so decided to sleep in the open.

When the trenches were retaken it was a wonderful sight. You could not hear yourself speak for the artillery, and the flashes of exploding shells and the different coloured rockets were magnificent.

Two nights running I got only three hours` sleep, and no rest in the day. Snipers were very troublesome by day. One bounder put a bullet a few inches over my back just as I had bent down.

After five nights we were relieved. We left the trenches at 10.15 pm and marched here, arriving at 4.30 this morning. I had breakfast at 11.40 am and am feeling perfectly fit.

I called at the "Cloth Hall" on the way back [through Ypres] and have got a few pieces of broken glass from the windows; also a piece of a chair from the cathedral. I was in the ruins at midnight. The bricks and boulders were covered with six inches of snow. It was a sight I shall never forget.

Love to all, your affec. son, Cecil

༦༡༠ Silkstone, 17.3.16

Dear Cecil,   Florence and I have been making some very treacherous cakes and they haven`t turned out as they ought to have done - I expect it is because we are not nibs in the cake-making line, but of course we blame the beastly old oven which really is the limit. Mother has given us a few things to help the cake go down. If it really is very bad I should bomb Old Hunny Dear with it.

Last week we had another razzle in Barnsley - we went to see Vesta Tilley. Flossie and I hadn`t seen her before. She is jolly good and absolutely looks a boy. Someone told us she had £100,000 in the bank and earns £300 a week - now if you want to earn money after the war you know what to do - dress up as a girl, sing "Kitty" or something choice like that on the stage and there you are!!

I went to Hull last Wednesday for my music lesson - the Zepps seem to have done more damage than last time but Nurse Waddington said there were fewer casualties. I saw Bob on your motor-bike!

Love from us all, Dora.

ᘯᘰ B.E.F., 19.3.16

Dear Dora,   Thank you very much for the chocs, coffee and honey. They were delicious. We had the coffee one morning at 5.30, just after "stand to", and you can imagine how we enjoyed it.

I was in Poperinghe for a night several weeks ago, and went to a show called "The Fancies" run by some officers who have been at Pop. for some time. There were two French girls in it, called Lanoleen and Vaseline, but they were only in it because they were of the feminine gender. One of the songs was one of those you heard in "Tonight`s the Night"- "They`ll never believe me". I think it`s ripping.

We are living very near the International Trench, which I daresay you have read about in the papers. I have paid two visits to it and have seen some most awful sights. There are dozens of dead men, British and Hun, lying about in various stages of decomposition, and all rat-eaten. Norman Ingleby and I were creeping along up top, our knees in mud and water, when we came across a head sticking out. We found it belonged to the body of a dead Bosche, and on top of him was lying a dead Scotsman with a horribly rat-eaten face. After some hesitation we crossed over these bodies and went on a bit until we came to a worse sight, which made me feel horrible and which we did not attempt to pass. Here and there a dead hand, or foot, could be seen sticking out and we were very glad to get back to decent trenches once more. There are a lot of bodies buried in and about our trench, and just outside our dugout a pair of boots are sticking out. There are feet inside them.

I sniped three Huns yesterday, two of them being kills. In one case the observer saw the blood spread over the man`s neck. It is awful when one thinks that these men have a mother at home and a wife or sweet-heart. You must think I am awfully cold-blooded to be able to write about it. But really the only pleasure I get is the satisfaction of getting a good hit, knowing that there is always someone trying to do the same to me.

I am enclosing two pieces of glass from Wipers Cloth Hall. I haven`t been able to get any helmets yet.

Have you a good recipe for rissoles? We have got a mincing machine in our company mess but our cook is not very intelligent and our rissole dinner a couple of nights ago was rather a failure. Next time I shall make them myself or supervise the cook`s work. When he tried the other day his hands were very dirty to begin with but were quite clean, apart from little pieces of meat, when he had finished.

When we were out resting a party of us went to a village inn one night for a little dinner. We went into a room where one officer was sitting reading. He heard my name mentioned and asked if I was at Rydal. I at once recognised him as a fellow I was at school with. This is the third Rydal boy I have come across out here.

Yours sincerely, Cecil.

ᘒᘏ Silkstone, 21.3.16

Dear Cecil,   Thankyou very much for your interesting letter. We do like reading about what you`re doing, only the next time you have to cross where the parapet is blown down, go the long way round, because we want you back for a game of tennis, if the weather will ever permit, this year. Really, I think we have about as much mud as you have! And we`ve only seen the sun once these last three weeks.

We shall like to have a relic of Wipers very much. Dora has had a letter
from Emma Blamires saying she is working fearfully hard for her tripos,
which come off next term.

Dora and I feel fearfully slack here, we really hardly do anything. At
present I intend going in a hoppy again or on a farm. I think my
mighty muscle would be rather useful, don`t you?

I can`t think of anything more to say at present, my brain is getting
mouldy here, also my writing.

Love and best wishes from all, Florence.

∾ With leave in prospect, Cecil wrote to his brother: 30.3.16

Dear Bob,   Leave has started again, so you can get the bike cleaned
up, and the carburettor in order. I ought to be coming in about 36 days
time. You don`t know you`re coming home until you`re actually given
your ticket. You may be in the trenches, or you may be shivering in the
rest huts when a chit comes which states that the Orderly Room wants
to know your destination at once.

Your affec. brother, Cecil.

∾ B.E.F., 30.3.16

Dear Dora,   Thank you awfully for the cake. It was ripping. I`m
sure I don`t know why you call it a treacherous one. You can generally
tell whether a cake is good or bad out here by the length of time it stays
on the table. I have known an unpopular cakes to be with us for as long
as 6 days. This one lasted under 24 hours, without visitors.

I have just finished reading "A Knight On Wheels". I think it`s a
topping story. Thanks awfully for sending it.

It really seems as though we might get a little summer at last. This
morning I was sitting outside in the sunshine, cleaning my rifle, without

a coat. There is a slight chance of leave in three weeks` time, so don`t be surprised if you find me coming over some day to give you that promised mo-bike ride.

Yours sincerely, Cecil.

℞ Silkstone, 10.4.16

Dear Cecil, Thank you very much for the Ypres glass that you sent us - we are putting it with our collection of things that we are getting.

Florence generally does the rissoles in our house - she always manages to get that kind of job, also paring apples, picking gooseberries - horribly boring - so she says she will tell you the secret. I should give your cook seven days` C.B. if he didn`t wash his hands first.

Pater went off to the front quite suddenly last Sunday. I believe he went to gain experience for training men and to see some of the Huns` trenches and engineering work. He told us he had come across Joe Ward (a master at Hymers) and Donald Allderidge both of the R.G.A.

We have been to Hull meanwhile and had a very Zeppy time - I expect you have heard all about Wednesday night when the Zepp came and we had guns and searchlights on it. It really was a beautiful sight - we had a beautiful view from Newland. Reggie Gaskell was home on leave at the time and said that the shots at it were wretched. Reggie is having a great time flying - he dropped a bomb on one of those German observation sausages not long ago and he saw it squash out flat and the old Hun would be under it.

It was awfully jolly being in Hull again - we saw heaps of people. Kathleen Watt is working at her father`s office - heaps of girls are doing that now. Kathleen Runton[1] works at the Union of London and Smith`s Bank in fact everyone does something in Hull nowadays. Florence is very seriously thinking of going on the land. I want to get into a hoppy but the trouble is getting to know of a decent one. The people in

Silkstone and roundabout are fearfully slack - they are rolling in money
from munitions and coal.

Florence, being the eldest daughter of the house, wow-wow, has gone
with Ma to return a call on a married sister of the First Sea Lord - rather
big pots round here, but live in a comparatively small house because they
hate a big one, altho` they are millionaires or something.

We are so glad you are getting some leave - we shall be delighted to see
you anytime - just send us a wire.

By the way, I`ve learnt what a salient is, my poor old feeble mind
didn`t know before.

People here say they have tennis by the end of April so I expect they will
be starting soon. We only have a patch of lawn big enough to skip on;
the people opposite have a court but I don`t think the girl has much
vim. The vicar has lent his court to the officers so I think that will be
our only chance.

We have just heard that Lady Mabe Smith is working on the land so of
course Lady Florence Willatt must go. Sister and I are going to stay
with some cousins in Nottingham for the Easter weekend - it will be
great excitement. We are getting awfully fed up with these stolid people
round here.

Post just hopping out. Goodbye. Love from all, Dora.

[1] The Runtons lived next door to the Willats

ᘓᘉ B.E.F., 25.4.16

Dear Dora,   I am feeling awfully bucked at the moment as I have
seen the last of the trenches for about four weeks. It is moreover a perfect day and we are living at the foot of a topping little wood which has
little streams running down from the hill-top. Consequently I feel like a
young lamb.

These steel helmets are awfully good, quite comfortable when you get
used to them. During this bombardment one shell fell into a dug-out in

which were four men; three were blown to bits and the fourth only had his forehead scratched.

Hoping to see you all soon when on leave, Yours sincerely, Cecil.

ᐅᗅᗝ Cecil to Bob: 12.5.16

Dear Bob,   I should have been coming home on the 17th, but a six-day course of scouting and Intelligence has knocked me out for then and the 21st. I don`t want to miss the course.

For the last few days I have been endeavouring to make my scouts and snipers understand a map and how to find out whereabouts they are on it by means of a compass, protractor, etc.

I am going to try to work an extra couple of days when I come, by applying for a warrant to Colwyn Bay. Anywhere north of York or Crewe entitles one to this, and as I shall go to see Hilda and Mabel it will be quite fair. This will make a ten days` leave.

I was trying to get the hens tight on whisky soaked into bread last night, and although one of the cocks got outside a tablespoonful it didn`t work. One thing about being here is that one sees a real live train. Two of us went for a ride once to Hazebrouck. The ticket collector person seemed to want a ticket at the station but we just looked important and walked through. We spent our time in Hazebrouck having afternoon tea and buying pipe cleaners.

There are a lot of old Hymerians out here now, both in our battalion and other units. Helmsing came yesterday and is in our company.

Your affec. brother, Cecil.

ᐅᗅᗝ Cecil to his parents: 24.5.16

My Dear Father and Mother,   I shall not be home on the 25th, but hope to be about 10 days later. I think you will understand why I am postponing it when I explain. A little "match" will shortly take place. It has fallen to our battalion to have the honour of doing the work. The Colonel wants me to take the job on. I absolutely couldn`t come home now on any account. The affair will be one I shall revel in, and will not be dangerous. I should love to tell you what it is, but it will improve with keeping.

Must finish now to catch the post. Your affec. son, Cecil.

PART TWO:

`A FLASK OF WINE, A BOOK AND THOU BESIDE ME...`

During this period of leave, 29 May to 6 June, events of great significance took place, events which Dora discusses at great length in one of her longest letters:

ॐॐ   Silkstone, 7.6.16

My dear Cecil,   I have come into that little wood and am sitting under a tree only about ten yards from where we sat together and you asked me to marry you. I couldn`t write in the house - I felt as if I were nearer to you if I came away from everybody and am absolutely by myself. It was a very great surprise and even a shock when you told me you loved me and I had not the slightest idea you were going to tell me so then. I am going to tell you the absolute truth and just write down as I think - I mean as thoughts come into my head, and when you write back to me I want you to do exactly the same - don`t keep back anything whatever your thoughts may be about me. You must forgive me if this letter gets rather disjointed.

You may have thought I was very cheerful after I came down to dinner on Monday night but I was not - far from it - it took me all my time to try and be cheerful and jolly with the others. Cecil, I would give anything to have you here with me now so that I could talk to you - I did not get to sleep until 6 o`clock on Tuesday morning - I was thinking all the time - I felt I should like to write to you yesterday but have put it off till today so that I should feel more myself again and surer about what I am writing.

I must say that I have thought of you as my best boy friend and it is not because I have known you practically as long as I can remember - it is for yourself. Betty Sowerbutts did tell me at Penrhos - I think it was your last term there - that you were keen on me but I`m afraid at that time I didn`t think anything about you - when I left school I liked you just as I liked my other friends and it was not until after you were

wounded last year and you came to our house a good deal for tennis that
I liked you more than the others who came.

You will notice I am saying "liking" - I have never thought whether I
loved you or not - I knew you liked me, somehow, but I had not thought
you loved me - it is why I had not thought of it so much, that it has
been so hard to see if my "liking" for you had turned into love for you. I
remember dreaming, one night since we came here, that you were married to another girl and I remember waking up with a miserable, hopeless feeling. I have looked forward to getting your letters more than
anyone else`s I have ever received; on the night of Feb 9th I remember I
felt you were very close to me and I longed for a letter from you - five
days later I remember I got one from you dated the 9th and posted on
the 10th.

Before I say any more I want you to think whether you yourself are quite
sure you love me, and that when you asked me to marry you you were
not influenced by any excitement of the moment - because you had not
seen me for some time or because you were just going away. I think
sometimes I ought not to have left the other two and I must have led
you away - you would not have asked me if we had kept with the others.
If I have brought you away from the other two - Flossie and Marjorie
[Barker] - it was unintentionally. I enjoyed talking with you - I had not
the slightest intention to be forward with you or with anyone else in the
world. If it is the case, Cecil, we will not mention it ever again and we
will just be chums once more - before you read any further be quite,
quite sure - or was it because that Grindell man has been talking about
you and me and you wanted to fix things up because of that - I do not
know him, not even by sight, neither do I know any of your officer
friends except by name - except Westrope. And thinking of him, it is
not very nice for the girl he eventually becomes engaged to, to think that
he has had three or four others before her that he has had a flirt with. I
have never flirted with anyone and I don`t think you have either, have
you; I have always vowed I would never "carry on" or flirt with anyone
except the man I should marry so that I could have an absolutely clean

conscience - have you ever thought like that? I am awfully sorry the others have been teasing you.

Have you yourself quite made up your mind about me - have you thought everything over and what it all means? Think very carefully indeed - you would see me every morning first, last thing every night - same face behind the coffee-pot every breakfast - same face behind the tea-pot every tea- time - when you holiday you would holiday with me. Think of it - and then think if you had got the wrong girl how awful it would be - it would be tragic - nothing is so awful as domestic unhappiness and quarrelling. My ideal man and woman are those who give themselves whole-heartedly to each other with all their love and who help each other and go close together through life. Cecil, do think it over well - we are still very young and you seem young to want to be engaged - altho` I`m glad you`re older than I am. You know you haven`t met so many girls and I am one of the very few girls you know thoroughly.

Don`t please think it foolish of me telling you all this but you have been in my thoughts constantly since you went. I was very unhappy during the night on Monday - in fact I cried. I do not often cry Cecil - rarely - I`m afraid I was not very nice with you, when I think it over, but I felt stupefied and I think you felt I didn`t care a rap for you beyond being a bit chummy and jolly with you like I feel with everyone else.

When I went to bed I overheard Father tell Mother that your affaire you are going to do out there was jolly risky - I began to think and then realised if you never came back and I never saw you again - what I should do and what I should feel like. It is horrible of me to talk like this but I am telling you all - it made me realise that I do love you Cecil - oh, that I could see you again now - but I cannot tell if I love you as much as you love me. How much do you love me Cecil? It is awfully hard to tell when one has not been thinking about it long.

I should like to get to know you yourself better and then at the end of six months if I am quite sure of my own mind and I have that sacred love for you that only man and woman can have I would promise defi-

nitely to become your wife - until then let us have an understanding
between each other and write to each other and keep nothing back and
hide nothing. I want you to put "yourself" for "I" in the last sentence as
well. If at any time you or I meet someone that we should like better I
shall not hesitate to tell you and you must promise that you will tell me
- of course if we were to get married we should know our own minds
whoever we came in contact with, and be true - absolutely true - I swear
I would Cecil - as long as we both lived.

I promised you I would tell no-one but before I went to bed Mother
asked me if anything had happened between us as she suspected something by the look on our faces as soon as she came in. I said nothing was
the matter at first and she persisted that there was, as you were quieter
and different so I had to tell her but just told her that nothing was
decided.

I always tell Mother everything, usually, but I have never spoken of you
in any way but a friendly way until Monday night, but I only just told
her bare facts - I know I promised to tell no-one and you did too.
Mother is quite pleased if we both know our own minds but I said again
that nothing was definitely fixed. Father does not know, nor another
soul - it is a question for you and me to decide alone. Flossie and I go to
Skegness for Whitsuntide - to stay with Queenie and Frank Willatt -
Pa`s cousins. Frank is 38 and Queenie is just 30 so she is a very great
friend of mine - I should like to tell her about you very much - she and
Frank were at our play before the war - she is very genuine and possesses
a great amount of common sense - she has been married seven and a half
years and they are both very happy indeed. They live in Nottingham
but have taken a house at Skegness for June for the kiddies - the
youngest of the three is called Dora - I think I told you. Shall you mind
if I tell her? If you feel you would like to tell anyone let me know.

I do want you to be careful when your little "affaire" comes off next
week - you did not tell your Mother or she would have been anxious I
know. Will you try and remember to take care of yourself - you are very
brave Cecil to be so cheerful over it - I simply couldn`t do it or stand it

at the front - I must be a coward. Don`t do anything rash, please, and write to me before it comes off.

If you think differently from what you told me on Monday do be sure and tell me and we will carry on as before and be chums and I will be just the same to you.

Father said I looked pale today and ought not to go into a hospital - I think I shall go in the end - it would do me good to get away with fresh people - I wish I could get away to France - perhaps then I could see you occasionally - I seem to be doing nothing for the war and it worries me awfully.

Goodbye Cecil, and remember I have some love for you,

Dora.

ひつひ B.E.F., Friday 7.6.16

My Dear Dodo,   We had a nice gentle little strafe yesterday afternoon just to remind us that the Hun is still in front. We were sitting in our little canvas hut having a quiet game of bridge when we heard a whistle, and it burst right over us, so we put our little steel hats on and made to the shelter trenches just in time. We had about 20 over altogether. One officer was slightly wounded. He will be nice and comfy now, congratulating himself.

Whilst training for the raid I have been off all duties, so a bit of work now is a nice change.

How is Flossie getting on at farming? Does she shear sheep and that sort of thing, or is it cow-milking and butter-making? Does she wear a bonnet like the advertisement for Milkmaid Milk? Talking about bonnets reminds me of that photograph of you in a Dutch one. I think it`s topping.

Do you remember those photographs Harry Quant took of you, Flossie, Willie Todd, Nellie Quant, and her sister and my Aunt`s dog. You are

Probably the picture Cecil refers to in this letter

giving the dog a piece of sugar in one. They are awfully nice, but I like
the ones I have now better. I have put one of them in my cigarette case
so that I can see it every time I have a cigarette.

Last night when I was thinking of you you almost seemed to be by my
side. I don`t know whether you were thinking of me. I am a strong
believer in telepathy, and ghosts, and take a great interest in psychical
things. I don`t know whether I`ve spelt it right, but you know what I
mean.

I don`t know whether I`ve told you about a little friend I have, called
Bertha. She is a real treasure, she cooks my tea, or cocoa, at any time
and sings to me all the time. She never talks, just hums and sings. She
and my servant are great pals. I bought her for 19/6. She is my little
Primus stove.

Yours, with love, Cecil.

‿✗✗ B.E.F., Sunday 11.6.16

My Dear Dora, I got your letter this morning. It is evening now and it is the first chance I have had of writing.

I do not mind a bit if you want to talk to your friend Queenie Willatt about last Monday. I should like you to; I`m sure it will be a good thing to do. There is just one person here I would like to mention it to some-time - Norman Ingleby. For a long time he has had a suspicion about my feelings, but he does not know about whom. He and his brother [Cecil] were marching with me that day the 3/4th East Yorks marched to Hull, and back through Newland the next day to Dalton Holme. I remember how everyone was asking who were the two pretty girls in the car. I still have the ribbon that was round the box of sweets you gave me. It seems rather a foolish sort of thing for a male human being to do, but I don`t mind. Ingleby is, as you know, engaged to Kathleen Clarke. I shall say nothing if you would rather I didn`t. It is glorious to know that you are thinking and that there is a chance.

I have come out into a small wood to write this, as I can keep my thoughts collected, away from the camp. I have to parade for a rehearsal of the `affaire` at 9.30.

Love from, Cecil.

‿✗✗ B.E.F., 12.6.16

My Dear Dora, For a long time before asking you to marry me I had been thinking things over and I was and am quite certain of my own feelings. But I feel a rotter for asking you when I did. I ought to have waited, for one thing, until the war was over, and for another until I had more idea of your feelings. As it is I have given you a shock and have kindled feelings which should not have been aroused whilst I am out here. I am sorry and yet I am glad.

You ask me to be quite sure that I was not influenced by any excitement of the moment. I was not. When I came out on Monday I had not any definite intention, but I had a sort of hazy wondering as to whether I should ask you to be my wife. You think that you brought me away from the other two - I think the shoe was on the other foot. When I suggested that we should go back to look for them I had not the slightest intention of finding them. I only wanted to make our walk a little longer, and to sum up my courage.

Get rid of the idea that I acted on the impulse of the moment. I have loved you ever since I was at Rydal. A schoolboy love then - it often happens to schoolboys and then dies out. Mine did not die.

The year after I left school was the most miserable in my life. I wanted to go back to Colwyn Bay where I could see you every Sunday in chapel and sometimes if lucky during the week.

As time went on and I did not see you much the flame died down a little, with occasional flarings up, but I always intended some day to ask you to marry me.

When I was wounded and was in Hospital in London, my Mother told me that your Mother was in London with you and Flossie, and I took it as confirmation of what I already seemed to know. When you came to see me I had cancelled a drive which one of the Miss Keysers, an old friend of King Edward`s, was going to take me on.

It was after seeing you that day, I think it was a Monday, May 10th, that I knew that my schoolboy love was real true honest Love for you. You say you will let me know if you come across anyone whom you `like` better than me. You ask me to do the same. I promise - and it`s a very easy promise too, for there will be no-one. I know.

You ask me how much I love you. All I can say is that I just love you with my whole heart. I love you together with my Mother and my Father and my honour, but on a different scale altogether.

There is just one thing I want to mention before I forget it, and it is this - if I should by any chance be crippled I shall cry off everything. I would not dream of marrying if I had not a sound body. That is one reason why I`m such a rotter for having asked you in the middle of the war.

Perhaps it would be better if we put aside what has happened until after the war?

Forget what I said about that Grindell person. Neither he nor any person has had any influence on what I have done. As for "teasing", don`t worry about that, because I haven`t, a bit.

No, Dora, I haven`t flirted, for the simple reason that I`ve never wanted to. Mind you, I have always admired a pretty face and have not scorned such things as "glad eyes" etc. But these are surface things.

Dora, there is something in what you say about hoping for a letter from me on Feb 9th. I remember perfectly writing that letter, and the whole time I was thinking of you, and trying to put it into something more than words.

About this little `affaire` that will be coming off soon - it is not nearly as dangerous as one would expect. One hears every day of a successful raid. I shall do my utmost to get back whole. I am much too fond of life to run unnecessary risks.

Goodbye, Love from Cecil.

☯ Silkstone, Friday 3 pm, 16.6.16

Cecil, Cheri,   I received your two letters on Wednesday and Thursday mornings. I had not thought that your love for me is as great as it is and that you had loved me ever since you were at Rydal - it is very beautiful to me, Cecil, that you have loved me all these years. My love for you is very fresh yet - perhaps because I have only just discovered it and begun to think about it - you see I hadn`t thought about it as much as you have. I think that by the end of six months I shall know whether I can love you with my whole heart and put you first. I love you, dear, now, yes, very much - more than when I wrote you my last letter - I think I have got to know you better through that last letter of yours than I have known you all along. You will know me better by my letters and I shall know you better too.

We are both young yet. I remember Kathleen Watt and Harley Judge - they were younger still - they were engaged just before war started but Kathleen did not quite know her own mind at first but she did afterwards. Of course it is terribly sad for her now and she is very brave but I don`t think she will ever change her love.

Cecil, my dear, you must not think you are a rotter for telling me of your love - I am glad now - I think you are glad really, altho` it did upset me and prove a great shock to me at the time - I think it is because you are a rather undemonstrative sort.

No, dear, I won`t leave it over till after the war. I know that at the bottom of your heart you don`t want to. Do you remember in "The Knight On Wheels" that Philip wanted to be Peg`s knight and to do something for his lady love - won`t it help you to think you are fighting for me - I want to look upon you as my knight.

Cecil, you must remember this - that once certain of my whole Love for you - and you should by any chance be crippled in this awful war, but I pray God that you never will be, I can never give you up again - you would want someone to love you and look after you - I am made of better stuff than to give you up when I love you - my love would be too strong. It was horrible to think of and I couldn`t help thinking of it in bed last night - a woman is very handicapped and helpless at times - you see I can do nothing - we haven`t the bodily strength you men have - you don`t realise it because you are a man - it is a very helpless feeling.

I am going to keep very cheerful and chirpy - I have quite decided to go nursing after all and have sent in my papers before I came here so I shall be going to Dr Blaine next week to be thoroughly looked at and examined - horrible proceeding. I know my back is a bit twisted but I think he will pass that - I`m quite a hefty and tough old bird really - after that I have to be interviewed by the matron at Leeds, Leicester, Sheffield, or any other place. I don`t know where I shall get to eventually. It will do me good to meet fresh people. It will make me know my own mind better about my love for you.

I am staying here till next Monday and then I go to c/o F. Elwell Esq.,
The Bar House, Beverley until the Friday and then I am going to
Marjorie`s at Grimsby until the Tuesday and after that back to
Silkstone. I haven`t told you before that Flossie and I are having our
portraits painted by Fred Elwell. He began them last November. He
has had rather a tussle with my old face - such a weird concoction I
should think! I am being painted in my white tennis blouse and skirt
with a fawn silk jersey I wore last year (did you see it?) and holding my
tennis racquet and looking very sappy. Mother has wanted us painting
for years and thought they ought to be done at once before we get into
haggard old spinsters.

The Elwell portrait of Dora. Her sister's picture, entitled
"The Housekeeper" is in the Ferens Gallery in Hull.

You said you would like to tell Norman Ingleby about me - I don`t
mind in the least. Queenie is a very sympathetic soul to talk to. I think
anyone who is married understands better. It will mean such a great
change in my life. I had sometimes thought I should never marry - I
was very fond of my present life and have rather an independent soul -
there is a wee bit of the suffragette about me I sometimes think. I think
you would try and make me happy. I`m afraid I`m wandering on and
on but my outlook on life seems to have changed this last fortnight. It
was a very great disappointment that the Parents never allowed me to go
to college after Penrhos - Emma Blamires has just gone in for her tripos
exam - am enclosing her last letter - thought you would be interested -
please return it. If I had gone to college my life would probably have
been very different indeed. I don`t think I should ever have married. I
should have gone in for business of some kind.

My love to you, Dora.

☆ B.E.F., 20.6.16

My Dear Dora,   I am sitting outside in a deck chair on the
verandah of the Officers` Club here; it is a beautiful evening and not a
gun is firing. I feel just like that chap in Omar Khayam who said something like "a flask of wine, a book, and thou beside me sitting in the
Wilderness. O Wilderness were Paradise enou`". I could do without
the flask of wine and the book, and if only `thou wert beside me sitting`
I feel as if I should go mad with joy.

I have been eagerly awaiting your letter, which I got yesterday. It seems
very wonderful to me that you and I should now be as we are, you wondering whether you will ever really love me, and I wondering the same,
and knowing that I have told you at last what I have always known in a
dim way.

I know we are both very young, but not too young to know our own
minds. I shall be 23 on the 30th of next month. A palmist once told
me I should marry between 24 and 26, but that remains to be seen.

Your birthday is in May, isn`t it? I believe you`re about a year younger than I am. No, Dora, I shan`t be shy next time I see you - I wasn`t last time - only very much in earnest.

I paid a little visit to the Bosche wire a few nights ago. I went with a couple of sergeants into No Man`s Land. We got within 5 yards of a Hun sentry, and I was actually in a gap in his wire at the foot of his parapet. It had taken us over an hour to get there, but we weren`t spotted. It`s awfully exciting work, especially when you see something you think is a Hun. We stalked three lumps of mud for about 5 minutes.

The battalion had a nasty time in the recent gas attack. We had over 100 casualties with gas and shells, including several officers. I was not in the trenches at the time as I am staying behind with my merrie men training for the `affaire` which will soon be coming off. I should love to tell you all about it, but I mustn`t until it`s finished.

I am glad you are taking up nursing again. I do hope you will be able to stand it. Leave has been knocked down to 1 officer a fortnight, but it may improve later on.

Fred Elwell has certainly got two charming sitters for his portraits. You looked awfully nice in your tennis things, as you do in everything. Do you know I drew a picture of you once from photographs. It was just before you put your hair up. I have this picture at home now in my album. It took me a long time and I`m rather proud of it.

I have read Emma`s letter. I can quite appreciate your feeling about College, I had just the same myself. My Father gave me the chance of going to Cambridge and taking up a profession, or going straight into the office. It was very hard to decide. I should have had a glorious time at the University but I don`t think I should have done much work. I have often regretted my decision, but I think now that I have decided for the best.

Goodbye for the present and love from your `knight`, Cecil.

P.S. Do you think I might have a photograph of you - a small one that I could carry about.

Silkstone, 27.6.16

My dear Cecil,   I got your letter this morning. Several people
in Hull said that no-one was allowed to write from the front as the
`push` had begun. It`s all tush and nonsense, isn`t it? I had a fearfully
restless time on Sunday night - I hardly got any sleep at all and I am
sure that you were doing something very risky - it must be telepathy. In
the papers it says there were ten successful raids into German trenches
on Sunday night with very slight losses - I feel awfully pleased that you
were chosen to take charge of one.

I have been thinking, and you are the oldest friend I have of my own
age. I remember sitting in the front long desk at Miss Keen`s and sit-
ting next to you and sharing a history book with you - it was the first
thing I remember at Miss Keen`s, I was just seven I think. After that I
remember you running me round the classroom once and trying to kiss
me - I don`t think you succeeded though.

It will be lovely when you get your next leave - we must have a very
long talk.

I am sending you the snapshots we took when you were over - I think they have turned out very well. I look quite the past mistress in the art of smoking, don`t I?

I was 22 on May 21st, so you are just ten months older than I am. Sometimes I feel older than you and other times I feel a positive kid, but you don`t want me to grow old and settled in my ways, do you?

I left Freddie`s on Friday and came straight here instead of going on to Grimsby because Ma wasn`t well - I was up a good part of Friday & Sat. nights with her but she is much better and downstairs yesterday. I`m afraid I shan`t be going nursing after all - at any rate not until the end of Sept. or October because Mother really isn`t strong enough to be left. I am frightfully disappointed, Cecil - more than I can say - this place drives me potty sometimes - the people are so monotonous and uninteresting.

Do write at once and let me know how you have got on - I am longing to know. My love to you, Dora.

☿ Silkstone, 29.6.16

Cheri,   I do wish you would write to me a little more often and I will write to you too - if you would like me to - I`m sure I`m loving you more, Cecil dear, if I love getting your letters - don`t you think so? Sometimes I feel as if I want you so badly - I do now, so it must be why I am writing to you. By the way, I like your small writing heaps better than your big writing - hope you don`t mind my telling you so. You can tell me what you like, also your likes and dislikes about me - I shan`t mind. I expect I shall tell you some when I find them. I`m not a fault-finder, Cecil - don`t think that. Parents say I`m quite a comfortable little soul to live with, but I am rather particular in some things. I haven`t got a bad temper - when I do have one I keep out of other  people`s way till it`s over. I simply hate quarrelling - I only quarrel with Flossie.

A draft of 36 men of the East Riding went off this morning - Ma wasn`t
well enough to go, so I had to see them off with Pa. Ma always has to
give them chocs and cigarettes but I had to do it this time and talk to
them. I love talking to tommies - they are so natural and talkative and
jolly.

You know, if we ever got married our love would have to bring us
through all kinds of things and perhaps bad times, illness and - well, one
never knows what. Have you ever thought of that? We might get
awfully weary of each other then. It`s such a huge question. I don`t
want either of us to make a mistake.

Ma is better than she was, but I haven`t been able to go out since last
Friday except into Barnsley for shopping. I have been over to the
Marslands[1] once for tennis for an hour. It`s beastly getting no exercise.

I am still wondering how you managed your "affaire". I am awfully
anxious about you, Cecil dear.

My love for you, Dora.

[1] An eminent family in the locale. In a history of Silkstone Mr Thomas Marsland of
Silkstone Common is noted as being the first in the village to enjoy electricity in his house.

ᑕ᙭ᘔ B.E.F., Friday 30.6.16

My Dear Dora,   I was awfully glad to get your letter this
morning. I think the photographs are ripping. I have one in front of me
now. The one at Skegness where you are leaning against a gate is
simply ripping.

Our little affair was on the night of the 26th-27th. I was very restless on
Sunday night, wondering how things would come off, and whether I
should come back. I was thinking a lot of you. It turned out that our
raid and that of one of our sister battalions were both destroyed by our
artillery firing short. There were only two men out of the whole lot, one
being myself, who got into Hun territory.

I will tell you all about it, as much as I dare, in case the censor gentle-
man should open this letter. The Hun wire had been cut by our guns
and a pathway cleared by a small party of us. It was a dark night and
raining heavily. We all had our faces blackened and were armed in
various ways. I had a couple of revolvers and a bayonet, with a dagger
and a knife on my belt, and a couple of bombs in my pocket. I set off
crawling, with a revolver in one hand and the bayonet in the other.
When we were about 25 yards from the Bosche parapet our guns
started, only instead of firing onto the enemy support lines they fired
into the enemy front line and onto us. As soon as this started I got up
and ran, followed by the men, when a shell landed right in the middle of
us with the result that I was followed into the Hun trench by one man
only. I jumped in about a yard off a Hun R.E. at the mouth of a sap. I
shot him at once, having no time to take him prisoner. It was at this
moment that one of our men joined me, and on shining his lamp we saw
a Hun crawling slowly. I shot him and the man bayoneted him. I then
finished off the first one with my jack-knife. I then went to look for the
rest of my party, but it appears that our shells had spoilt everything.
The man with me was dazed with funk and I had to explore on my own.
After I had been there seven minutes overtime, that is 25 minutes

altogether, I blew my whistle in case any on our men should be there, and set off back.

I was absolutely done in and when at last I got through the Hun wire I could not walk and had to crawl, slowly. My hands and legs are covered with scratches. One pocket of my coat was torn right off, whereby I lost a good pipe and pouch of tobacco. I also left a revolver and a flash-lamp in the mud. There is going to be a frightful row about our artillery.

Love from, Cecil.

[in a letter to Bob, 2.7.16, Cecil expands on this incident:

"I was never in a bigger funk in my life than when I was in the Hun trench on my own...You know that big pocket-knife of mine - I had it buried in a Hun`s throat that night. There was no time for mercy." In a following letter to his father and mother he writes: "I know you will be disappointed about the failure of my little do, everyone is, but it was not my fault. When the General thanked me I think it was for what I had done personally. He told me that he would show his thanks in the proper way when everything had been enquired into. The Brigade have since asked for my Christian names.

I have written to Mr Saunders telling him that I have carried out the instructions he gave me regarding the jack-knife I received from him."]

ꝏꞎꝏ Silkstone, 5.7.16

My dear Cecil,   I have felt jubilant all today because I got your letter this morning. You are a brave plucky soul to go on through the German trenches by yourself. I think it`s marvellous. I feel awfully proud of you - yes, very. I don`t wonder you were absolutely done when you got back, poor old dear. Have you got some stuff on your scratches and washed them properly. Do be careful or you may get tetanus germs in. It is wicked you have to risk your life to such an extent.

I am delighted to think you will be on leave sooner, after all. I`ve been thinking things over and do you think you ought to tell your Mother and Father about it all before you come on leave? I often wonder what they will think - they may not think I am the right girl for you and they may think that in a few years you would be better with someone younger - if you were 30 someone about 21 would be a better age for you.

I have sent off a parcel for you today. The chicken affair I bought in Barnsley. The man in the shop said it was to be eaten cold. I have put in some iodine little bottle things and you must break one when you get scratched. Iodine is a very strong antiseptic - be careful, won`t you?

They have asked Mary (the maid) in Barnsley what was in the parcel and she said "Books and eatables". Don`t know whether it will get through - she was a cuckoo to say so. In haste,

Love from, Dora.

ᖇᖴ B.E.F., 3.7.16

My Dear Dodo,   Sorry I haven`t been writing often enough.  I didn`t want you to get tired of getting too many from me. You can`t write to me too often.  Your letters are practically the only thing I look forward to out here, and when I`m feeling at all fed up, or very happy, I just read them again.

I am writing this in my tent away from the crowd, one of whom is just shouting for me to play bridge. I told him ten minutes ago I was coming.

By the time you get this letter it will be just a month ago that I told you I loved you and asked you to marry me. The fifth of June was the day. I think our feelings towards one another have come to the surface a good deal in this month.

Yes, I have thought that if we got married we should have to go through everything together, perhaps bad times and illness, but I should never get weary of being with you whatever happened.

I see an old Rydal boy, F.C. Stoppold, with whom I was at school, is in the latest list of DSOs.

Yours with love, Cecil.

ᘏᘉᗢ Silkstone, 8.7.16

Cheri,   I`m glad you like writing to me because I enjoy writing to you. I often curl up on my bed or in a chair and read your letters again.

It may get harder for me loving you more - in fact it is - when you are in danger at the front, but I am glad I love you more because I know it is what you want. I am an awful little beast to say it is hard for me when it must be heaps worse out there doing what you are doing. You are a dear brave soul, Cecil, and I love you for it. You have heaps of pluck to do what you have done, but how do you stand it all? I know I should have funked straight away. `Spect when women get the vote they`ll want to make girls soldiers! I shouldn`t mind a vote, but I don`t crave for one, tho` I`m a Suffragist - it isn`t the same as a suffragette, remember.

As you say, things have altered in this last month - my feelings have altered towards you. Before, I hadn`t bothered about marriage and love for the simple reason I had never loved anyone and it was not until you aroused it in me that it made me think and realise that love is the greatest thing in the world. I sometimes wonder now why I didn`t love you before you asked me to marry you - I wonder if I did and didn`t know it was love but thought it was friendship - it was a fearful tussle for me in the few days between Mon 5th June and the first letter I wrote to you. I wouldn`t have them over again for anything. I had to keep thinking and thinking whether it was only a chumminess I had for you or whether it was love.

Mother is feeling a lot better and is coming downstairs tomorrow. I have been home a fortnight and have been nurse-cook-housekeeper all in one. I get awfully sick of perpetually grubbing round the house. Still, someone has to do it.

Pater has to go to Otley next Weds to Sat. for a bombing course and has
to stay at Wells House Hotel, Ilkley. If Ma is well enough she and I are
going with him. Have you read Prisoner of Zenda by Anthony Hope? If
you haven`t I will send you a copy.

My love to you, my cherie, Dodo.

ᏗᏯᎶ B.E.F., 9.7.16, 9.30 pip emma

My Dear Dodo,   Awfully glad to get your letter with enclosures
and your parcel today. The chicken is an awfully good idea; I`ve had
one or two from Mother and they`re ripping. Bertha will attend to the
coffee tubes in due course.

I am longing for a talk with you, and I may get one soon. You see, I
might be coming over to Blighty soon on 4 days` leave to see the King
about a little silver cross. The four days includes two days of travelling.
It`s like this - an after-order came round today and the gist of it is that
Lieutenant C M Slack has been awarded the Military Cross, followed by a
bit of rot about gallantry and coolness. So I`m in for a bashful time
tomorrow.

I don`t like the idea of telling my Father and Mother about us by letter.
About their thinking that you`re not the right girl for me, that`s all rot,
and even if they did it wouldn`t matter. They might think I`m a bit
young - I am at present - but the war isn`t over yet and when it is I
shall have to have about a year to get going at work. But for the
allowance which Father has promised me at the end of the war, it would
have been some time before I could marry.

The pipe I lost wasn`t the new one but it was a great pal and I`m sorry
about losing him. Henry was his name. The new one is called Claude.

Goodbye, Love from Cecil.

☙ B.E.F., 12.7.16, 9.00 pm

Dear Dodo,   We`re in the trenches once more, and I never have
been in a worse lot since I was a soldier - just a jumble of low parapets
and "crump" holes. I have to bend double in parts.

Yes, of course I believe you when you say you love me a little more than
you did, and it makes me very happy. Yes, Dodo, love is the greatest
thing in the world, it`s the connecting link with Heaven, I think.

Real true Love, not only of a man and a woman for each other, but being
able to love the song of a bird, or on a quiet evening being able to sit
still and love the beauty of the country and the sunset, is a part of
Heaven, and it makes one able to enjoy Life and to love It. I love the song
of a bird, and the beauty of the earth, and the Love of a man for a woman.

There are two women I love, one is my Mother - and you know who the
other one is.

The coffee you sent me came in splendidly yesterday morning. There
were three of us, tired and cold, no fire, so we just set Bertha going and
soon had some delightful hot coffee. We have got a ripping little table
in this dugout. We stole it from an RE`s dugout.

Yours with love, Cecil.

☙ B.E.F., 18.7.16

My Dear Dodo,   I am delighted you are pleased with my little
cross episode. Yes, it was for the raid "affaire". The Colonel was awfully
nice about it, and between you, me and the lamp-post he said that if the
other people had followed me into the trench I might have got something better.

About my envelopes - I like the blue ones best: they match my eyes. My
servant chooses them for me. He is quite intelligent at times for an offi-
cer`s orderly. His name is Ellis and he works in the box-shop at
Reckitt`s in time of peace.

It`s very annoying letters taking so long to get to England from here. Yours get here in four days, sometimes three.

And now about the people I play bridge with. 2Lts Furley, Rollitt, Webster, Lt Robson, 2Lt Boyle, Capts Parker, Ingleby, Barkworth and sometimes at Headquarters with the C.O. Just common or garden auction bridge, for nominal stakes, so don`t think I`m an inveterate gambler and a bad lad, because I`m not. Sometimes we play an absurd game called Vingt-et-Un, and not long ago I won over eighty francs at one swoop.

I thought Flossie wouldn`t be kept in the dark about us for very long. It can`t be expected as you keep getting envelopes from the Front in the same handwriting.

I have just received a note from the Adjutant informing me that the C.O. wants me to go out into No Man`s Land to look about for a few suspected dead Huns. It`s going to be a rotten job as there is a good moon and the Bosche line is only 60 yards away. I must go now as it`s getting dark and I want to be out before any enemy patrols.

Love from, Cecil.

🖎 B.E.F., 21.7.16

My Dear Dodo,   I had to leave off my last letter sooner than I expected as I had to go out and look for some dead Huns before the other side got them in. It was nearly my last tour in No Man`s Land. The moon was nearly full and there was scarcely a cloud about. I took one man with me and the Bosche spotted me almost at once and started firing. I got stuck in our wire and it seemed ages before I got out, and one Bosche would keep hitting the wire round about me. I got out in the end and we crawled to another spot where the Bosche again fired at us. We were out an hour altogether and found no sign of any dead Huns. It was a cold still night and one`s breath was going up in clouds.

The trenches are simply swarming with flies, great big blue bottles. In places the sand-bags are black with them. We are all covered with mosquito bites.

My latest job is to take new officers out into No Man`s Land and show them how to carry on! and I think it`s a bit thick because we get new officers every week now.

I have just been censoring my men`s letters. It`s quite good sport at times. One poor chap is awfully fed at having to have his letters to his girl read by someone else. I have taken compassion on him and told him he can stick them up and I`ll sign them if he promises to put nothing of military importance in.

Yours with love, Cecil.

ꙮ Silkstone, In dem garten, Monday 24.7.16

My dear Cecil,   I am sitting on the grass patch just about where we had those photographs taken when you were over - you remember the spot - well, the roses are out now - delightful ones - and it`s quite summerlike. Pater and I went for a new walk last night through fields and woods and things - it`s heaps nicer than keeping to the roads.

It does seems a shame that the men didn`t follow you into the trenches - but you are safe so nothing matters much, does it? I know some of your bridge pals by name but not otherwise. Of course I don`t think you`re an inveterate gambler or a bad lad - silly old thing. I know you are a true good sort, and know I could always trust and believe in you.

We have managed to get a trap for Ma at last - I went to the village last Saturday to have a look at it. It belongs to Ziah Clegg of the `Fox and Hounds` and he hasn`t had the heart to drive it since his wife died a year last December. Pater is taking it out today with an engine driver. I expect we shall look rather killing. I wish there was a horse around here that I could get to go riding with Pa - but there isn`t such a thing. When we were at Pocklington before Xmas Pa had six horses so I could easily go out with him.

Nurse Waddington and I are going to Leeds for the day tomorrow - I
haven`t been there since I left school - years ago!! I feel horribly ancient
at times and other times I feel a positive kid.

I am just going to change, to preside over the sewing meeting tea - have
asked for it to be outside - those dos get so fuggy and thick indoors.

Hope you don`t get bored with my telling you all my doings `cause
I`m afraid there`s no fearful excitement in them.

Love from, Dora.

ᢦᢦ B.E.F., 26.7.16

My Dear Dodo,　　　　　We are out of the trenches at last after 13
days. We are now living in a field, near a hedge, just like a big picnic
party. I am writing this on a log table out in the sun; I am smoking
Claude, one of my pipes, and am feeling very contented and peaceful.
There is a pile of letters of congratulations in front of me waiting to be
answered. It`s going to be an awful sweat.

Several of us went to a village last night where there is a convent which
supplies dinners for officers. Everyone got rather merry and at about
10.15 p.m. there were very few left besides our little party of 4. When
we set off on our 3 mile journey back I was the only one who could walk
straight, but I didn`t know the way home. One man who was less tight
than the others said he knew the way, but we soon got lost. We eventually got home at 12.30. My companions were covered with mud from
the various ditches they had fallen into. I have never laughed so much
since I have been out here.

Yes, Dodo, I`m sure you`ll be able to tell much better how you feel
towards me when we`ve seen each other again. Writing`s a poor substi-
tute for the real thing.

I had my first hot bath for a month yesterday, and then it was only half
a bucketful in a bath. Several of the officers and nearly all the men are
lousy. I have managed to keep clean this time.

Goodbye for today, or rather for a few minutes, for I`m always thinking about you.

Love from, Cecil.

ꝏ Silkstone, 26.7.16

My dear Cecil,   I did not think or even dream a few weeks ago that I should be writing to you in this way to wish you many happy returns of your birthday. I hope you will live till you are a nice old man.

I have sent a little parcel of to you this morning - the pocket case I got in Leeds y`day. I`m sorry it`s suede inside as it doesn`t wear as well as the smooth leather.

I hope you like the chocolate cake I have sent - it is only the second attempt at it so I am sorry it isn`t much to look at but hope it will taste better.

Pater is just here with our new trap so must go - love and a happy day, from Dodo.

ꝏ Silkstone, 27.7.16

My dear Cecil,   I am awfully sorry that you are having such a wretched time in the trenches - it is rotten for you and I do feel sorry about it - it seems a bit thick for you to have to show all the new officers round No Man`s land - why can`t someone else do the dirty work for a change?

Pa and I took the new trap out on Monday and it didn`t do half badly except that it runs all over the road, can`t keep straight - still, it manages to go so no matter. Pa went on horseback and I took Ma and Nurse in the trap - it`s rather a low affair and we sit three in a row, rather as if we were going for a joy-ride in a coster-monger`s cart. I drove Ma into Barnsley and back this morning and have bought you a fly-catcher. Have you ever tried petrol for mosquito bites? Dr Blaine says it is the best thing.

Perhaps you may get this on Sunday - so many happy returns again if you do. Do you feel 23 or older or younger?

Goodbye my dear. I do love you. Dodo.

ᘓᘐᗡ B.E.F., 30.7.16

My Dear Dodo,   It is awfully sweet of you to send me a ripping little parcel for my birthday. There is something about the pocket case that reminded me at once of you; it`s the colour.  I`m sure you wore a dress of exactly that shade. I`m not quite sure when and where, but I`m sure you did sometime, and not very long ago. I don`t think I shall use the soap you sent. I shall keep it as it is, it smells so beautifully cool and sweet.

I expect you`re thinking of me now, you said you would today.  I`m thinking of you now, hard.

What a ripping chocolate cake. But the thing I like best in your parcel is the little note inside the pocket-case which says it is sent with your love. It`s a birthday present I shall always treasure.

I didn`t get up till 11.00 this morning as I was up in the front line till dawn.  I have to set off again for the trenches in about an hour`s time.

Yours with love, Cecil.

Shortly after his 23rd birthday Cecil received this letter from his mother, along with the following note from Harold:

ᘓᘐᗡ Wilton House, 30.7.16

My dear Cecil,   Twenty-three years ago today we were rejoicing over your arrival in our little house in Sydney. What a different kind of day this Anniversary is to what we should have wished. May you have many happy returns in the years to come, filled with good works. The more I think about what you have passed through the more I feel how God has preserved you.

How you will rejoice when you are able to change your clothing and have a bath. It must be awful in this weather not to be able to change. How horrible the flies are! The wonder to me is that there is so little sickness.

Hilda, Mabel and Norman came home yesterday. They all look well and have grown. Bob goes off to Camp on Tuesday.

Colonel Easton sent you a letter of congratulation from Lord Nunburnholme yesterday.

The Annual Tea Meeting was held at Holderness House yesterday afternoon. Father went to the prize-giving at Hymers, then to tea at Holderness House.

Father is sitting in his shirt sleeves in the Conservatory. We had an Air Alarm on Friday night and were up till 4 a.m.

Very much love from, Your affec. Mother, W Slack.

ঔ৵ঔ

Dear Cecil, We are going away to Fily in two days` time. I am looking after the Hens and Chickens now but somebody els is while I`m away. Once we got an egg without any shell. The boy next door to us is going to Fily today, he is a friend of mine so we expect to meet each other at Fily. We are going spying in caves. I lost £2 4 ounces in weight last week so I have to take Malt and godliveroil and ly down for a hour and a half after dinner worse luck. We have got a Cock which has being crowing for a month now it is only 3 month old now. Mother had two teeth out with gas the other day I am going to have swote next term.

From your affectionate brother, Harold.

P.S. I hope you get Lave while we are at Fily.

A further update on Harold's livestock.

ༀ Silkstone, 31.7.16

My dear Cecil,　　　　　I expect by now that you will be in the beastly old trenches again - how long did you have out? Thirteen days in was an awfully long spell and I don`t wonder you felt fed up with life.

Your M.C. was in Hull`s Sat. paper. I should think the dinner at the convent must have been rather exciting by what you say - I really can`t wonder at some of the men drinking and making merry after the monotony of the trenches.

Mother is going to Hull on Wednes. to stay at Beechcroft and Pater goes on Thurs night for the Board Meeting on Friday, so Flossie and I will be here on our own this next weekend. We rather enjoy being on our own and we do as we like - we never squabble when we are left alone.

We had Capt. and Mrs Baumer, Stedham and Huntley into tennis the other night - borrowed the Marslands` court again. Stedham is the best player and quite good but we are not fearfully keen on him - he`s rather an about-towny sort if you know what I mean. Cephas has just gone past - he doesn`t seem to be very busy really - wanders around and talks - cuts the lawn, hoes the garden and wears a war badge for it all. Nurse Waddington went this morning - Flossie wants to have Kathleen Runton over for the weekend - she is engaged to Leslie Brown (2nd Lieut., Durham Light Infantry). She is just 20 and he is 25 but she is a head taller then he is!

Flossie came from Hull with a rumour that our company is going to be moved to the East Coast - joy if it happens. They keep appealing for more nurses in the hospitals - letters nearly every day in the paper. It is disappointing I can`t go. Dr Blaine says F must have a month`s rest and I think farming is too hard work for her. Ma wants her to go nursing but William [Todd, her fiancé] says no - so I don`t know what she will do in the end.

Goodbye, I often think of you at nights too. Love from, Dora.

☯ B.E.F., 2.8.16

My Dear Dodo,   Thanks awfully for the flysmasher. We have had great sport with it. The last two days have been the quietest I have known in trenches. It may be because the Hun has a new division in front of us, or because it is too hot for him to load his minenwerfers. Today he got fed up with the occasional shell which our gunners sent over and he got going with his trench mortars. We replied with ours and then the heavier guns of both sides joined in for about three quarters of an hour.

I lost a bet on Tuesday, 15 francs. About ten weeks ago I took on a bet of 10 to 1 that the war would be over by the end of July. I think if I had said July 1917 I should have been nearer the mark.

I feel just about 23, if anything a day or two older. I have grown a lot older since the war. I was really only about 17 when I was 20, probably through growing up with brothers and sisters so much younger.

The heat is terrific, about 250 in the shade of the dugout. Wouldn`t I just love to be bathing now, say at Colwyn Bay with some of my old school-pals. What glorious days those were. As soon as school was over we used to run down through the village to bag a van, hot and sticky, and then a long swim out beyond the jelly-fish. I could never spot you on those occasions although I always tried to. And then again there was Betty Sowerbutts teaching girls how to jump out of the boat into water at least 3ft deep. I expect she had an eye on Billy taking our names as we came in to see that we weren`t drowned. I got my bathing stopped (officially) in the end for going out too far. Of course, we got our bathing. We used to go after dinner. It was risky, as we were prefects then.

I must do some work now. Goodbye for the present. Yours with love, Cecil.

℞ Wilton House [undated]

Dear Cecil,   We have been away on holiday, at a country place, we had two pinicks while we were there. I am looking after the hens and chickens now. I got 4 eggs today from 7 fowls. We are going away in August for about 4 weeks. We have got 2 young cockerels which are just starting, they are 8 weeks old. Our hens are always fighting. I haven`t had any school since last Christmas. We have got heaps of peaches and cherries and crab apples and pears and 5 appeles. I have to drink ever so much milk a day. I am weighed every Saturday. I am now 5 stone 1 pound 0 ounces. I was at first 4 stone 12 pounds 4 ounces. Hilda and Mabel come home in 4 weeks but Norman goes farming four

2 weeks of the holidays. There is a big moth on the window I am just
going to kill it. BANG I have hit it it is dead. There is a thrushes nest
in the garden. I hope you are getting on alwright.

From your affectionate Brother Harold.

℞℞ B.E.F., 4.8.16

My Dear Dodo,   Yes we`re back in the beastly old trenches
again, only they have been much quieter this time, but I shall still be
very glad to get out and get my boots off and my pyjamas on. I haven`t
had my pyjamas on for 5 weeks.

I understand that the Kaiser is going to commit suicide this month and that the war is coming to a sudden end in September.

I suppose I ought to have kept the tunic I was wounded in as it was, but I`ve got a much better one now, the one I raided in. One pocket is torn right off and the other`s only half on, and it`s covered with other tears, and both legs of the breeches are torn too. I threw the puttees away. Some of the scratches will always be on my body.

I remember Leslie Brown coming in one evening when I was at your house, and I was rather amused at his being so much smaller than Kathleen. I`m glad I`m taller than you: I think I have it by half an inch; we tested it one evening if you remember, at the weighing machine in your hall nook. I sometimes wish I were a bit more than 5`7", but it`s very convenient out here.

We have a frightfully religious chap in one of the platoons in our company. We are not quite sure whether the texts etc which he puts in his letters are cant or not: if we find out that he`s not really serious we are going to put a naughty French postcard in one of his letters.

We are living in a pub at the moment at the foot of a beautifully wooded hill and it`s simply ripping.

Love from, Cecil.

ᘍᘘ Silkstone, Sunday 4 pm 6.8.16

My dear Cecil,   I have just discovered I haven`t written to you since last Monday. I don`t know why, but I felt awfully uncertain of my feelings for you during the week - I couldn`t tell you why and it made me feel awfully miserable. Then yesterday I felt I wanted you so much and would have given anything to have you with me - I felt as if I want-ed you and nobody else and that`s how I feel now. I think it must be because I don`t know my own mind that I feel like that sometimes, don`t you think so?

Kathleen Runton is staying the weekend with us. The skivvy is away for
the weekend and the Parents too so we are leading the simple life and
it`s gorgeous. Yesterday was simply heavenly. Capt. Baumer hired a
conveyance and took us and his family out for a day`s picnic up over the
hills to the reservoir at Langsett, about 10 miles from here. Stanley was
four so they wanted to celebrate it. We camped by a stream and made a
fire, dabbled in the water and let the infants roll in it. Ernest is only 15
months old and he simply kicked and rolled in it.

Do you know it was the 5th yesterday - just two months ago - did you
remember?

Monday morning. I got your letter from the trenches today - it must be
hot for you. When you said 250 degrees I thought poor man he must be
boiling - but I suppose you go by the Centigrade thermometer.

Do you know I dreamed about you again on Saturday. We had gone
out for the day and were lying together on the bank of a stream. It really did seem real and `twas nice being with you and then I woke up and
came back to earth and true realities with a jerk.

I thought you were very young for your age before the war. You seemed
to remain exactly the same as you were when you left Rydal. The three
weeks you had at the front a year ago made a lot of difference to you -
and then army life altogether has brought you out of your shell.

Jelly-fishes were awful at C. Bay weren`t they? It really was rather a
responsibility for Betty to have all those girls to look after. However, she
used to generally let Jennie Hallitt, one or two others and me go out a
bit with the boat and then we could swim back. I remember seeing you
once or twice after bathing just as we were getting into rank nearly
under the Pier Pavilion.

We went to Barnsley Swimming Baths the other day but the water was
most appallingly warm - like a big hot bath. I hadn`t got a bathing cap
so I couldn`t splash so very much because it`s such a nuisance to dry my
beastly old hair. It`s fearfully tempting to cut the stuff off and be like a

boy and have freedom. You don`t know what a nuisance it is some-
times. A lot of women are cutting theirs short now.

Goodbye, my cherie, and take care of yourself. Love, Dodo.

ᴗᴣᴆ B.E.F., 9.8.16

My Dear Dodo,　　　　　We are living at a real live farm, out of the
shelled area. We had a very long march the day before yesterday with
fully loaded packs and haversacks, and in the full heat of the sun. I had
been feeling a bit groggy beforehand and in the evening had a temperature of 102, so I stayed in bed yesterday.

I am celebrating my medal tonight in the company mess. A matter of 6
bottles of champagne at 18 francs apiece and a bottle of liqueur is what
it`s costing. I expect there will be a lively evening. I shan`t be able to
have more than about half a glass for fear of going groggy again, so I am
going round to another farm with some more chaps to have coffee with
some nice Belgian girls whom we made friends with last time we were
here. I hope you don`t mind. It`s rather nice talking to a young female
again after a strenuous time in the trenches. I only wish it were a certain
dear little English girl I know.

Please forgive this very short letter. I`m much too muddled to think.

Yours with love, Cecil.

ᴗᴣᴆ Silkstone, Thursday 10.8.16

My dear Cecil,　　　　　Swish! Hasn`t it been hot. We seem boiled
alive in this little rabbit hutch of ours. Mother came back from Hull
suddenly last night - had enough of it with the Zepp raid of Tuesday
night. She was in the house alone with one maid and they dropped
bombs on Westbourne Ave and Victoria Ave only half a mile away and
then went over Newland Park - so poor old Ma felt a bit scared.

Yesterday we went for a drive in our trap and took tea and Mrs Baumer with us. Fanny simply cantered practically the whole time and it really was great sport, although Flossie was horribly nervous. I`d sooner drive a car anyday - one has far more control over an engine. `Spect we shall all be too poor after the war to have cars - what do you think?

Mother is taking me to Scarboro` on Monday, till Friday. I`m not frightfully keen. It`s rather a disgrace for girls to go to the seaside now - they ought to be working, so all the articles in the papers say. Still, I can`t help my beastly fate. Gladys Runton (she went VAD nursing last year) has got a post on a hospital ship in the Mediterranean and goes at the end of this week - lucky girl. I simply longed to go on one last year but the parents put their foot on it absolutely, as they do with everything I want to do (except stay home and look after them). I shall strike out soon I think - I`m sure you would.

We are just going out to tennis at Mr Rawles`. My serves are improving just a wee bit - a little more puff behind them perhaps.

Love from, Dora.

B.E.F., 13.8.16

My Dear Dodo,   I haven`t had a letter from you, Dodo, for over a week. What`s up? I hope you haven`t got the wrong address.

We had a long train ride a few nights ago. I was orderly officer and consequently had to get out at the stops and see that no-one else did. I had several chats with the engine driver, who was a Frenchman, and I`m awfully bucked with my French. I got no sleep that night as the interpreter bagged my seat. It was a dirty trick because he would have been left behind if I hadn`t picked him and his bicycle up at the last moment. It was only the fact that he was a foreigner that stopped me turfing him out.

I`m feeling a bit like Cecil M Slack today. For the past week I`ve been feeling like nothing on earth.

I am Mess President again and enjoying the job. I am becoming quite an expert in housekeeping matters, so if you and I ever get married I

shall be able to advise as to whether it is more convenient to have
omelettes or sausage with the bacon and whether the cups which have
had beer in should be washed or merely emptied before coffee is put into
them and whether it matters very much if you don`t get the same cup
that you shaved in, and get the taste of another fellow`s shaving soap
instead. But I suppose interference in household matters is not allowed.

Yours with love, Cecil.

༒ Silkstone, 14.8.16

My dear Cecil,   I am awfully sorry you are not feeling well and
do hope you are better again. Who looked after you? Did Ellis tuck you
up etc? And who is the 4th E.Y. doctor? Is it Norman Ingleby who has
got trench fever?

I hope you enjoyed going to see the Belgian girls. Of course I don`t
mind. It would be a nice change for you. I like to meet fresh people -
I always enjoy it.

We went to see two drafts of men go off to the front on Thursday and
Friday, one of 100 and one of 40. The 100 were Durhams and were
practically all drunk. Durhams really are the limit.

We haven`t gone to Scarboro` after all as Mother isn`t very well again.
It is the parents` silver wedding on Sunday the 20th - makes them
sound rather ancient, doesn`t it, but Pater is not quite 48 yet. They
were married very young really. Still, it must be rather tame to get
married at about 35. They are getting old before they can enjoy life
together. Florence and I can`t think what to give them. It really is
frightfully brain-racking.

I don`t think I`ve told you about my cottage I`m going to have after
the war, have I? Well, I think it will be at Filey. Shall furnish it very
inexpensively. Mother has a good many necessities that she is going to
give me. I shall let it furnished during some of the summer months so
that I can just scrape enough money to pay the rent. Then the parents

can go to it if they like and I shall go to it and have friends to stay, and if I can get a nice agreeable chaperone I shall ask you too. Don`t you think it is rather a good idea? I am awfully fond of Filey. I first went there when I was six weeks old and I also learned to walk there, tusk!

When Ma and I go over to Scarboro` we are going to have a look at one of the houses I like. They have an entrance from the gate on the promenade. It would be quite at the centre of things yet quite high up and out of the way of people and we could lead a somewhat simple life there. I imagine it will be very jolly but my imagination runs away with me at times and I have to come back to earth with a thud. If I can manage to run a cottage, a motorbike and myself on my allowance after the war I think I shall do jolly well. Dot Major (of Welton) has a cottage of her own at Flamboro` and runs it by herself and finds it rather difficult to let - the station is so far away from the cliffs.

Love for yourself, Dodo.

☟☊ Silkstone, 18.8.16

Mon Cheri,   I can`t understand why you haven`t had my letter. You evidently haven`t had the one I wrote a week last Monday the 7th. Probably it has not been forwarded from the farm you left. Then I wrote again on Weds the 9th - you ought to have had that Saturday last (I have put your new address on all, ever since you told me) - I wrote last Mon the 14th, so you ought to get three letters before you get this one.

I`m awfully glad you`re better again. I wish I knew where you are now - it must be a good long way if it took you all night to travel. I wonder if you are going to another part of the line where the "push" is. I hope you are not because it`s so awfully risky there, isn`t it?

You will be getting quite a fluent French scholar if you stay abroad much longer. Six R.E. Northumberland officers went to France on Monday last. Do you remember a young Ashby - machine gun officer - who was killed a few weeks ago? Alden - one of Pa`s officers - was telling me he had a Beverley friend out in the 4th E.Y. and it was a day or two before he was killed that he told me about it. He said he was only about 18. Is Vivien Mayfield out there? I expect if he is the C.O. will think he`s rather a weird specimen of Hull!

Goodbye, Your loving Dora.

♈ B.E.F., 18.8.16

My Dear Dodo,   Your letter written on Sunday 4th did not reach me until the following Sunday, and I got another yesterday posted on the 10th. They usually only take 4 days.

I know it must be awfully rotten for you at times, Dodo, wondering about me. You can`t really tell until we have seen each other a good deal, and that won`t be till after the war, will it? I sometimes think I ought not to have told you and should have waited, but there was always the chance of someone else coming along, and if I hadn`t let you know of my love I should probably have gone mad or turned into a priest or done something silly.

I don`t see any sign of the short leave coming off. When I do get it I shall manage to see you. Your Pa would get the wind up if I came sailing down to Silkstone when I only had 2 days. But I daresay we could meet at Barnsley or somewhere.

I have started on your soap now. I think of you every time I use it. Of course I think of you at other times as well.

I can quite understand you feeling older than me a few years ago, because I was an awful kid! I feel older than you now. I know one is supposed to be several years older than the girl one loves but I don`t think it matters a bit, so long as the girl is not several years older than oneself.

Sorry you`re feeling so fed up about not being able to do Hospital work and are chafing under parental authority. I well remember the first time I defied my governor. He was awfully fed up at the time, and so was I afterwards, but nothing bad came of it, and it showed the people I had a spirit of my own. I suppose this is natural to all young animals.

In my dugout I have the bombing officer, a rather stupid person who is usually asleep.

Yours with love, Cecil.

ᘒᘓ B.E.F., 22.8.16

My Dear Dora,   I must explain why I haven`t written sooner. I have had very little time of my own, and have had horrible rheumatism in my legs, the result, I think, of last winter. I haven`t had more than 3 hours` consecutive sleep for a week owing to the pain. When I`m off parade I have a scout`s class, and then I have to understudy the Adjutant in the Orderly Room. Don`t think I`m grousing, because I`m not - just explaining why I haven`t written.

The Adjutant, by the way, is not Grindell but Holtby. He comes from somewhere near Driffield where his father farms. Bob and one of his pals are going into Holtby`s father`s farm for the holidays.

I think the idea of you getting a little house is awfully jolly. What a ripping time you`ll have!

It is Norman Ingleby who has gone home with trench fever. Our company is now in command of Capt. Parker and I am 2nd in command.

I am very glad you talk of running a motor-bike as well as a cottage. I simply love seeing a girl on a motorbike. I want to get a Sunbeam after the war.

I should love to house-keep at your cottage after the war. No, I can`t cook but I`m awfully good at washing-up.

I remember Ashby well. He was an awfully nice boy and a splendid fellow with heaps of pluck. I am very sorry indeed that he has been killed. I saw his body a few minutes after it happened. He was killed by a bomb in No Man`s Land.

I haven`t written to my people for a fortnight.

Yours with love, Cecil.

✑ Silkstone, 22.8.16

My dear Cecil,   Since I began this Cephas Marsland came in for
a minute and then I had to go and change into tennis togs - they`re all
clean today so I feel extra special now. Mr Rawles came round this
morning to see if we would go round for a game tonight, and Pater is
bringing Bertie Alexander in - he was in the R.E.T. before the war and
has been out at the front in the 1st E.R. since last September, but has
been gassed and is suffering from shell-shock. He`s awfully nice. He
lives at Hornsea on Marine Drive, one of those white houses if you
remember them. Ma had a letter from Reggie Gaskell the other day.
He`s home on leave getting his pilot`s certificate.

I had a wire from Emma Blamires at Huddersfield asking me over for
the weekend, but it`s the parents` silver wedding on Sunday. Flossie
and I went off to Leeds in the afternoon so I had to telephone through to
say I could only stay Friday night. I went, and had a very quiet time,
but enjoyed it immensely. Took a bomb to pieces that Emma`s cousin
had given her and then had a job putting it back together again. Flossie
and I burst our allowances on a pewter tea-pot, tray, sugar and cream
jug for the parents` silver wedding. They are very artistic really. Take
less cleaning than silver and are cleaned with Brasso. Pewter is very
fashionable again now.

I`m awfully sorry about your rheumatism in your poor old pegs.

Love from me, Dora.

✑ Silkstone, 25.8.16

My dear Cecil,   I thought I`d write you a note today as I don`t
think I shall find time tomorrow.

Had a wire from Reg G. to say he`s coming on the 5.18. Bertie Alexander`s coming down to dinner tonight. He says he was at Hymers with you and you were always the naughty one - can quite imagine it!

Ma has gone to Sheffield to meet Queenie Willatt and is bringing Olive (Q`s eldest) for a week. Next Friday is the Board Meeting so Pa and Ma will go for the weekend and probably after that Ma will go to Scarboro` for a few days.

Have you heard about Adrian Farrell`s death? Isn`t it awfully sad? He died on the 23rd in Hospital in London. You would probably see it in the Times of the 24th. Mrs Farrell will be fearfully upset because she made a great trouble of Bede and was simply living for Adrian to get better again.

Peggy Wellsted is married to Colin Carter last Saturday. We met him at Reighton last year. He is 22 and Peg is 21. He is awfully clever and did very well at Camb. before the war. However it has been quick work as she only met him last October. He has been at the front for some months but is home again now for a time.

Gladys Runton sailed from Liverpool on a hospital ship yesterday. Flossie answered an advert for looking after animals and helping with garden. She got a reply from a Miss Wilson, The Manse, Ackworth near Pontefract wanting someone to look after 2 goats and a kid, about 20 fowls, 24 rabbits and part charge of a few house cats! What do you think of it!!! She wrote back and said she thought animals would mean cows, pigs, etc. and was seeking necessary work.

Love for yourself, Dora.

☙ B.E.F., Sunday 27.8.16

My Dear Dodo,   Church bells ringing in the west and guns firing in the east is what I can hear at present. It seems strange to hear the bells again. The company has gone out bathing in a river so I have a few hours to spare. They needed a bath as most of them were chatty. I had a nice cross-country ride a few days ago and am awfully bucked about getting on and off, without help, on a big gee.

Yesterday we were out on a route march before breakfast and passed a prisoners` camp. The inmates have good tents to live in, good food, and nothing to grouse about. I think a Bosche prisoner is one of the luckiest people in this war. He`s done his bit and he`s absolutely safe.

Did you know that Adrian had died of wounds after 15 months? I expect the strain of numerous operations has told on him at last.

How is the little cottage affair going on? I think Filey`s a splendid place for one. One can always get fresh eggs and milk, tinned fruit, etc. That`s how we view a new billet here. Are there farms near where we can buy milk, eggs and cream? Is there a butcher`s shop and so on? We usually get milk and eggs from the farms, and tinned stuff from the nearest Expeditionary Force canteen. We always eat pork when we get the chance, whether the month has got an `r` in it or not. It`s surprising what we can buy at these canteens in tins: tinned peas, tinned beans, tinned rabbits, tinned plum puddings, tinned asparagus etc.

You asked me if there was anything you could do for me. Please send me a hot bath; I haven`t had a real one since I was on leave.

Yours with love, Cecil.

℞℞ Silkstone, 28.8.16

My dear Cecil, I am sorry about your rheumatism. If it gets any worse you ought to come home to rest and get it better. Please take care of yourself. You know how people who like sugary things always have a tendency for rheumatism, but they never get tubercular so that`s one blessing, isn`t it?

Reggie turned up on Friday evening in a very tricksome flying cap - quite chirpy and just the same as ever. Bertie came in to dinner and Mr Rawles later and we talked till 11.30. On Saturday afternoon we played tennis at Mr Rawles` and then he went back to Hornsea by train.

Pater has been inoculated today and consequently is feeling very cheap
for 48 hours. Allderidge has just come back from France where he has
taken a draft of 69 men - very fed up with life because he had to sleep on
deck and had nothing to eat but dog biscuits. I expect he would grouse
all day if he was out at the front. The vicar said he thought he was quite
33 and he`s only 23. Flossie and I get awfully sick of his talk. He talks
nothing but "shop" and Mrs Allderidge never speaks a word.

Flossie and William are going to live at Hedon when the war is over, I
think. The people there are not so fashionable and conventional.

I do love you, Cecil, and goodbye, my love, and remember to look after
yourself well for my sake because I love you.

Dora.

☯ B.E.F., 1.9.16

My Dear Dora,   It`s been raining cats and dogs for the last two
days and we`ve been having a ripping time in our cornfield. On going
to my tent I found a pair of boots and various tobacco tins floating about
the floor. Half the company was washed out of its bivouacs.

Yesterday I killed 16 lice on my shirt, and on closer inspection found
more in the seams and scores of eggs. They are awfully tough and one
can`t squash them between the fingers, it takes finger nails to out them.
I told Ellis to burn the shirt, but he boiled it all morning instead. I`ve
just had a look and the eggs are still there and look quite well.

Do you know how it feels to have a rotten headache and then to get better, how delightful and fresh one feels. That`s just how I`m feeling now
after my rheumatism. I got hold of a professional masseur and he`s
almost cured it.

Yours with love, Cecil.

ᕕᖇᕗ Silkstone, 1.9.16

My dear Cecil,   I have only time for a short note. This afternoon we are going to Barnsley to see the Battle of the Somme pictures
with Mr Rawles, Capt Baumer and Mr Bruce. People say they are very
gruesome. Still, I want to go.

I am enclosing a cutting about Adrian Farrell - thought you might be
interested. I do think it`s awfully sad, Cecil.

I have packed up a parcel for you today. I made the orange cake myself,
so say goodbye before you eat it. I have also made the marrow cream.
We really put it in tarts but I thought you might like it to eat with
bread.

No more time - just train time, so goodbye and write often to your love,

Dora.

ᕕᖇᕗ Silkstone, 2.9.16

Mon Cheri,   I only had time to write you a scratchy note yesterday. I was thinking about you a lot all last Tuesday, Wed and Thurs,
29-31st. Was anything happening?

The Somme pictures are really very sad and they do make one realise
everything. When I got into bed last night I said to myself "Thank God
I`m not a boy". I know it`s fearfully cowardly but I couldn`t help it.

How is your rheumatism? I think you need someone to look after you,
don`t you?

Goodbye, cheri. Love for yourself, Dora.

ᕕᖇᕗ B.E.F., 4.9.16

My Dear Dora,   Just 3 months ago tomorrow, isn`t it? How
ripping to read in your letters that you know now that you do love me
just a little bit more than you did.

Do you know we only just missed seeing the King when he was over here. A party of our battalion was asked to form a guard of honour for him, but the officer in charge considered they were too dirty. One can`t keep clean when making a long journey.

I expect Reggie Gaskell will be coming out here soon. I wish I had got into the Flying Corps. They have a much better time than we do, and it`s such a nice uniform, isn`t it?

That fellow Allderidge must be an awful tick. He should come out here and be dealt with by our subaltern`s picket.

I have about 15 congratulations letters to answer yet, including one from Lord Nunburnholnme and another from Reckitt`s board.

Goodbye my love, Love from Cecil.

ᘐᙎᙅ Silkstone, 7.9.16

Dear Cecil,   I`m in rather a hurry. I`ve been busy making a YMCA overall - black and white stripes - to help at the canteen here every Monday from 2 pm to 6 pm, also have to wear a black silk cap affair.

Emma is coming over this weekend. William is also coming so I shall be very busy with this blessed housekeeping and cooking and I positively loathe it. It is just sheer duty that makes me do it and when Mother is well enough to do it by herself I shall jolly well turn out and do something. I do hate being a girl at times and having to scratch around one`s hut all day instead of having one`s work outside the home and then coming back at night.

Flossie has gone to Hull and then on to Sigglesthorne today to see the Rector about a job on his little farm - milk two cows, pony and trap and feed small stock. Sounds rather decent really - she is a lucky beggar.

Ma hasn`t been well for the last two or three days and has been in bed. Olive is staying another ten days. She is quite a good little kid really, altho` rather a monkey at times. Everything is Why, What for, When and Where with her at present and it keeps one busy.

Love from your chum, Dora.

ᘔᘔ B.E.F., 14.9.16

My Dear Dora,   By the time this reaches you you will have seen from the papers why I have been unable to write before. We have all been worked until we are just ready to lie down anywhere and sleep. Today is the calm before the storm. Don`t worry if you don`t get a letter for several days now.

Round about here there are hundreds of dead men, both British and German, and helmets, rifles, rations, shells, bombs, etc. The helmets are bent and broken and no good as souvenirs. My present home is a German dugout, and a very nice one too, except for the crowding.

My next letter will probably not be for some time but I think there will be some interesting news in it. Till then goodbye, and love from, Cecil.

ᘔᘔ Red Lea, Prince of Wales Terrace, Scarboro`, 14.9.16

My dear Cecil,   Flossie forwarded your letter and I got it this morning. I hadn`t had a line from you for a whole week and was beginning to wonder what had happened to you old boy.

Ma & I came here on Tuesday. This place is a boarding house at the south end just about the spa. It`s about half full, mainly of atrocities in the female spinster line - a few old fogies and their wives and not more than two weedy unfit looking youths. I hope you won`t get fat and portly like these munition people one sees here about 45 or 50.

If Pa comes over for the weekend I shall be able to go riding with him but I doubt if he will be able to get over. The Winkleys are staying in rooms not far from here, also the Whitticks [Newland Park neighbours of the Willatts] minus dear Tommy - also the Woodhouses of the Park -

did you know that Dorothy Woodhouse was privately engaged to Hugh
Hopkinson of Sutton who was killed about a year ago? I think it was
Hugh.

I remembered the 5th and wondered if you did too. Sorry I wrote such a
fed up letter last week, but I really was fed up with life. I feel much better now. I think I wanted a change really. It gets awfully monotonous
at Silkstone. Found a grey hair the other day and spotted another today.
Isn`t it tragic?

Love from your, Dora.

ᘒᘑ **B.E.F., 18.9.16**

My Dear Dora,   We have been over the bags in this last big
push [Cecil does not mention it, but he is now on the Somme], and are a
mile further on than when I last wrote. What is left of the battalion has
been withdrawn for a few hours rest. When we went over we had one of
these new armoured motor-cars with us. They have caterpillar wheels
and go right over trenches and shell-holes. They ignore bullets and
small shells, and just wander about shooting their machine guns.

My particular job was to keep up communication between our brigade
and the battalion. This meant journeys up and down and they were
rather unpleasant because the Hun was always shelling heavily. Ellis and
I had many narrow escapes. The imitation communication trench up to
the new front lines was much too crowded with men both dead and
wounded, British and German, for us to get along it. There were some
awful sights lying about, half a body here, a head there, and so on.
Everyone keeps cheerful though, as much as possible.

Yours with love, Cecil.

∞ **B.E.F., 18.9.16**

Dear Bob,   Glad to hear you`ve had a good time farming.[1] Holtby says his father is awfully bucked with the work of you and the rest.

We have had exciting times here lately. These new "tanks" are splendid things and they give a tremendous feeling of confidence. A couple of them patrolled the streets of Martinpuich while the Bosches were actually in possession. We had one with us when we went over.

Since beginning this letter we have gone another 1000yds nearer Berlin!!

Please ask Mother to send me a tin of "Boot`s Vermin in the Trenches Killer". I am simply awful, as is everyone else including the C.O. and the doctor.

Your affec. brother, Cecil.

[1][Bob was also having a good time on Cecil`s motorbike - and getting himself into trouble, as he reports in a letter to his brother:

"I went to Hornsea yesterday with Forty, who was riding a Rudge 3.5 h.p. I shouldn`t be surprised if I got a summons this week, because a policeman told Ridgeway that another of their chaps had caught me on Friday riding in what he called a dangerous manner. I was in low gear wheeling another bike and John Taylor was on the carrier. I only went for about 400 yards and I could easily have stopped if necessary, so the chap who caught me was a blessed liar. Father said that he would stop the bike running if I got summonsed, which is a blooming swindle, as you are bound to get collared some time. Also, about two weeks ago, three old idiots complained to Father about my riding. I should think they`ll be two of those old chaps who cross the road as if they owned the place, and had to hurry a bit for me. I had a row with another chap the other day. He made some remark as I passed him and shook his fist at me, so I looked around and asked him if he wanted to say something to me. A policeman who was standing near didn`t seem to know what he wanted either."]

ᚖᚖ B.E.F., 26.9.16

My Dear Dora,   I`m awfully sorry I haven`t been able to write before but we have been away from civilisation for nearly three weeks now and are a good deal nearer Berlin. Tonight we are going a little further. I have already seen the trench we shall occupy. I went out with another chap the night before last to see how strongly a certain Bosche trench was held. There are only a few Bosche in at one point, and we got in and walked along to see if there were any more. We didn`t kill the Bosche as we could have done, easily, behind their backs because we didn`t want them to know we`d been there. It is quite exciting going slowly along a Bosche trench with one`s revolver in one`s hand wondering if you are going to surprise one or if he is going to surprise you.

It was beautiful when I woke up just now at 4.0. The sun was simply beautiful and the aeroplanes were skimming about just like yachts. I just lay on a couple of boards out in the open and thought of you.

Bob is trying to get a commission in the 4th East Yorks, and saw Col. Easton about it the other day.

Love from Cecil.

ᚖᚖ Red Lea, Prince of Wales Terrace, Scarboro`, 26.9.16

My dear Cecil,   I was awfully glad to get a letter this morning and know that you are all right. I seemed to know you were having a rotten time from about the 14th onward, especially Sunday the 17th. I was feeling awfully anxious about you.

We have been here a fortnight today. I am sitting in those gardens on the South Cliff that face the sea - the Holbeck Gardens - you would never know there was a war on at all.

We went over to Filey about a week ago and I foraged about after the cottage I told you about. The owner was fearfully crabby - abominably so. So those are off. I have decided to wait until January and put an advert in the Yorkshire Post.

Ma and I went to Hull for the day last Sat. I have chosen a green coat - long one with grey squirrel collar and cuffs - I`m not going to have it made up for a fortnight or so, so do you like the colour?

Take care of yourself my love, Dora.

෨෩ In the train from Scarboro` to Doncaster, 28.9.16

My dear Cecil, We are on our way back home at last. We only came for about five days and have stayed a fortnight and two days.

I have been reading in the paper about those caterpillary things - the Tanks they call them. They seem to be very marvellous.

Yesterday Ma and I called in at Ward Prince`s estate agents and they told me about a cottage at Filey on the beach - the Ravine end of it. It has one sitting room and kitchen, two bedrooms and large attic. I think there is a little bit of garden but no bathroom. We should have to go in the sea, that`s all. Rent 12 guineas, and rates which would come to nearly £17 altogether. I might be able to clear that amount in the letting. What do you think of it all? Ma says I oughtn`t to bother with it till the war is over, but I think that the war will be getting over by next summer.

I had to stop just then as we arrived in York. We are now in the Flying Scotsman train from Edinburgh to London. We are on what they call a slip-carriage - it is the last carriage on the train and a few 100 yards before we get into Doncaster they slip us off and we drift into the station - rather convenient really.

Love from, Dora.

෨෩ Silkstone, Saturday 8.30 p.m., 30.9.16

My dear Cecil, I had to take some flowers down to the Church this afternoon for the Harvest Festival tomorrow and when I got there the Vicaress asked me to help and decorate the Church so I couldn`t very well refuse and then I went to the Vicarage to tea and had to stay and help them after all that, so I didn`t get up here until nearly seven o`clock - after post-time.

I am glad you are getting on alright but you do get some narrow escapes. Several East Yorks officer casualties were in last night`s Hull Mail as wounded - are any of them yours?

We feel awfully sad today because Mr Rawles has left Silkstone. After the Lowmoor explosion near Bradford (you remember about some explosive works being blown up a month or two ago) the works weren`t worth repairing so they`ve sent the manager here and poor Mr Rawles has to report at the Ministry of Munitions for another job. He may have to join up with the 8th Leicesters - he`s a 2nd lieutenant in it. The Ministry have given him £500 a year and he`ll get £180 if he`s in the Leicesters.

It`s the end of the Daylight Saving Bill tonight so we have an extra hour in bed tomorrow which is rather a joy on a Sunday morning.

Goodbye for tonight my love, Dora.

ཊ B.E.F., 2.10.16

My Dear Dora,   A good deal has happened here since I last wrote. A division on our right "went over" the other afternoon to occupy a vacated German trench. It was a wonderful sight and one that made the tears come to my eyes. They had to cover about 500 yards of ground. The Bosche of course spotted them as soon as they left the trench and at once put up a barrage. The men just walked on as if nothing was happening, some with their rifles slung over their shoulders, some with their hands in their pockets, some smoking; one officer was there with a coat slung over his arm - it was glorious. They walked right on through the shells, with men dropping here and there till they got into the Bosche trench. You will probably wonder why they walked. If they had hurried they would have been tired when they got near to the

Bosche trench and would not have had the strength to charge. I shall never forget it.

I was in a barrage myself a few nights ago and had some marvellous escapes. One small "whizzbang" burst at my feet not more than three yards away, but neither I nor my orderly were touched.

How`s the cottage getting on? Have you decided on one yet? Is it that one on the hill you mentioned before? I hope it`s a cosier place than the one I am in now, a compartment of a large Bosche underground dugout.

The old rumour about our going to India has sprung up again. Wouldn`t it be fine to be in India for the rest of the war with the knowledge that your life was safe? There is always a feeling that one may die at any minute; it`s not exactly fear, but just a very strong feeling of `not wanting to`. I`m not afraid of Death, but I`m very fond of Life.

I`m afraid this is a very morbid letter, but I have seen a lot of pitiful sights lately. Somehow I think I am to come through the war. I have always thought so.

I note the pattern of the coat with much interest. It looks blue at the present because I`m writing by candlelight, but I like the material.

I expect I shall be getting another pip shortly. Goodbye for the present, my love. Love from, Cecil.

ᘓᘉᘐ Silkstone, 3.10.16

My dear Cecil,   Isn`t it getting awfully cold? You must be careful your rheumatism doesn`t come on again. Have you got your winter things yet?

Are you still having a bad time? There are going to be some more Somme moving pictures, so shall look out for you in them when they come to Barnsley.

Love for yourself, Dora.

❧ B.E.F., 5.10.16

My Dear Dora,   Just four months ago today, isn`t it?

The Colonel`s just sent to see if I will play bridge so I`m afraid I`ll have
to go. The colonel`s wish is the same as the King`s in the Empire,
namely a command. 8.1.16 Lost 5 francs to the Colonel, no time to
write on the 6th, went to Amiens on the 7th. We did all sorts of things
in Amiens, chiefly eating. I had my second hot bath since leave. It was
glorious - a great big bath nearly full - the water came up to my neck
when I sat down. We had a tip-top lunch, and dinner, with real plates,
knives and forks, etc.

Yours with love, Cecil.

❧ Silkstone, 6.10.16

My dear Cecil,   I know what a sight it must have been to see
those men go over to the German trench. I think really only British
men could do it, and I don`t wonder tears came into your eyes, Cecil my
love.

I should be awfully glad for your sake if you were sent off to India. I
don`t think your letter was a bit morbid. I have heaps more to say
really but haven`t any more time today.

Love from, Dora.

To Cecil from Bob

❧ 8.10.16

Dear Cecil,   Thanks very much for your letter. You must be
getting it jolly hot.

I have been passed as fit for general service, at the City Hall, so all I have
to do now is to get a copy of my birth certificate and give the lot in to
Colonel Easton.

There have been four more killed added to the school list. One of them, E. W. England, was only out three weeks. Another, Crabtree, has been missing for some time but is now reported killed. I think they both came to the school after you left, but Helmsing and some of the other officers would know them well.

The bike is running very well at present. I took it down and decarbonised it during the week and it has made a lot of difference.

I have skilfully avoided nearly all homework this term so far and am going to see how long I can go on doing so. I have chucked Latin now and do Science instead, so the female no longer takes me, which is rather a good thing as she was beginning to find out that I didn`t strain myself.

Harold is fed up with Cobby as a form master as he makes him work and shouts at him.

Your affec. brother, Bob.

⚯ Silkstone, Monday 9.10.16

My dear Cecil,   I`m feeling awfully tired today, the result of having all these kiddies here I should think. They`re awfully good on the whole. The baby is a positive gem as babies go. Stanley is getting to be rather a rip and wears one out with "Why" and "What for" from morning till night.

Love from, Dora.

⚯ Silkstone, 12.10.16

My dear Cecil,   It will be a week tomorrow since I heard from you. The Baumer family went off at 11 a.m. and it is blissful to be quiet once more. Flossie is staying at the Todds until Monday next while try-ing to get a job thro` the Labour Exchange in Hull.

I don`t think I told you about the Filey cottage. I wrote to Mrs Martin but it`s not what I want - I mean as regards situation, `cause there are respectable cottages opposite and it would be far more conventional up there than on the beach and not so free and easy.

Mother has heard from Nellie (Quant) Hemmons the other day - John Hemmons has finished the OTC and has 14 days holiday before his commission. Probably Harry Quant will be coming over here soon for a weekend. He`s bought a new camera to keep in his pocket so that the authorities won`t see it.

Love from, Dodo.

✺ B.E.F., 14.10.16

My Dear Dora,   It`s quite strenuous being a company comman-
der. I have six officers now. Their names are Monge, Brown, Waite, Van Oppen, Speight and Evans. It`s the same old company, `C`. Norman Ingleby had it before he went to England with trench fever.

Having had no fighting for several days we had a water battle this evening. I received a direct hit on the back of the head with a full buck-et; dirty water too.

Sorry the kids are such a bother. I used to get awfully fed with my younger brothers and sisters when they were that age. I didn`t look after them but I used to smack their heads, especially Bob`s and then get dry bread for tea.

This writing is pretty rotten because I`m sitting on my bed and have no table and only one candle.

Yours with love, Cecil.

ᚹ Silkstone, 14.10.16

My dear Cecil,   It was awfully kind of you to think of me when you had your day`s holiday to Amiens and send me those two lovely bottles of scent. I use ever such a wee bit of scent so you have given me enough for years. I`m glad you had a good scrape and meal while you were there. It`s one of the things we look forward to when we go away from this hutch to have a real hot bath with a real hot water tap etc - it`s awful messing about with this flat round bath.

I wrote a long letter to Miss Hovey y`day for her birthday (how old, I wonder?). I had to tell her I couldn`t get off nursing just yet for a few months as she had given me a reference - so I expect it will be recorded in next term`s magazine. She always puts in all the tosh she can scrape up about Old Girls. So-and-so is busy washing up in a Hospital. Somebody else taking a Sunday School class once a week and so on.

Dorothy Crooks wanted me to go across this afternoon but I said she must come here as I had the YMCA overall to finish and she just turned up - rather a nuisance really: she never has anything to say.

I think Ma and I will be going to Hull on Tuesday for a day or two - shall get my green coat.

Bertie in Reggie`s letter is Alexander - he has got into the Fortress R.Es now and is on the Humber Batteries somewhere. His heart isn`t strong after the gassing and he isn`t a scrap keen on going back again. I wonder if you would be keen to go back if you came back for a few months again.

Sydney Carlin of the REs has got the MC as well as the DCM - he had a leg amputated just below the knee.

I must stop and talk to dear Dorothy the nuisance - very naughty of me to say that.

Take care of yourself my love. Love from, Dora.

ᗅᗅ B.E.F., 17.10.16

My Dear Dodo,   Your letter of the 12th came in a few hours
ago. You`ll be glad of a rest now the Baumers have gone.

I`m sorry about the Filey cottage. No, it`s not the right kind. What
you want is a place where you can have a glorified picnic, isn`t it?

It`s raining fast and it`s very cold, but we`re very happy because we`re
not in the trenches. I understand *John Bull* says there`s a treat in store
for the 50th Division. But the same paper has already told too many lies
for its information to buck us up much. The only way to get a soft job
out here is to be a wash-out at one`s proper job.

There`s a frightful row going on in the tent - six people discussing the
best way to disguise ration meat. My little mincing machine comes in
very handy. Fortunately we are all very fond of rissoles. There`s a treat
for us for tomorrow`s breakfast - mushrooms. As they have been picked
by some of the men and examined by us it`s quite likely we shall soon
all be in Blighty on sick leave.

I`m glad you think about me at night when you`re in bed. I always do
as I go to sleep. I try to imagine that we`re talking to each other by
telepathy. I used to before I told you I loved you. I seem to feel as
though I`m talking to you now, and you`re listening. Are you? It`s
just after 9.30 pm Wednesday. I`m going to get undressed and to bed
now, to think of you my love. I shall be able to gaze into the brazier
which we have in the tent. It`s rather nice lying in bed looking into a
glowing fire, isn`t it?

Yours with love, Cecil.

ᗅᗅ Silkstone, Sat morning 21.10.16

My dear Cecil,   It`s just a whole week since I wrote to you, but
I`ve been doing tons of things and haven`t had a minute to spare. On
Tuesday I went to Hull and came back Friday. I stayed with my grand-
father who lives past the tram terminus on Holderness Road. Harry

Quant is coming over for the weekend on the 12.32.

We saw Kathleen Watt in Hull and she is awfully excited - she is going off to the Bermuda Islands in about a fortnight. The Reserve 4th E Yorks are going out - Jack Ferens and that lot; K. Watts`s sister married Major Ted Collingwood and she is going with her and taking 4 children - youngest 1 yr - they are going on the troopship, passage paid by Government, and will be there two years or until the end of the war. Jolly nice soft job and quite safe until the end of the war. I wish you could get a job like that. Marion Ferens isn`t going out with Jack. I think she`s missing a good chance and it would be good for her chest.

Isn`t it awfully cold nowadays? I`m nipped to the marrow. Have you got a rubber hot water bottle to take to bed? Would you like one? Or do you scorn one?

Love from, Dora.

ᛞ B.E.F., 22.10.16

My Dear Dora,   I had another trip to Amiens on Friday. We spent most of the time eating. Lunch cost us 22 francs each, and dinner 38, so you can see we did ourselves well. I was with Capt. Seed - you may know him, he lives in Hessle - and 2Lt Boyle.

I have stopped cold baths now. They`re a bit thick in weather like this, and one`s toes take such a long time to get warm.

I have read Reggie Gaskell`s letter with interest. I wish I could get a home job like Bertie Alexander, but I daresay I should want to get back here after a few months, more from a sense of duty than anything else. Yesterday one of the men broke his collar-bone at football. He got no sympathy, he was just told he was a lucky devil, as it meant a trip to Blighty. I should love to be nicely wounded, and yet I don`t want to be - you understand the feeling, don`t you?

I`m going to bed now, and think of you. Yours, with love, Cecil.

ᘉ⅄ᘎ Silkstone, 24.10.16

My dear Cecil,   Flossie didn`t take that job at the vicar of
Sigglesthorne`s: he wanted a rough farm girl. She has been at the
Labour Exchange at Hull for a fortnight and still got nothing at all.

Leslie Brown (Kathleen Runton`s fiance) has got night blindness - what-
ever it may be - and has got a job down at the base camp.

On Saturday morning we had a wire from Reggie Gaskell asking if he
could come over, so he arrived by the 11.8 train and Mr Quant came at
12.32. Flossie arrived back last night. On Saturday afternoon Mr Q and
I went for a long walk and then we asked Dorothy Crooks in last night.
On Sunday we all trotted down to church and then Emma arrived for
dinner. Did another long walk in the afternoon and then two of Pa`s
sub[altern]s were in for supper. Mr Q went yesterday, and one of Pa`s
subs on the way to France called for lunch. I had to go to the YMCA at
5 to 7 and then another of Pa`s subs was in for supper also on the way
to the front and who was the limit - then Flossie came in at 8.35. So
you see we have been very busy altogether. Reggie is very nice altho` a
little quieter than he used to be. He is friendly with the Todd boys and
we have known him about four years. He says he`s quite sick of the
army and wants to get back to his architect`s business.

We did enjoy having Mr Quant - he is awfully nice and genuine in
everything. He says he`s sick of the works - sticking in an office all day
- and wants to travel again. He told Mother he wanted to find a wife
and get married and take her to S America.[1]

Flossie is talking to Reggie at present so I thought I would hop off and
write to my love.

Marjorie Barker has asked me to go over and stay with her at Grimsby
on Monday for a few days, so I might. I am going over to Huddersfield
to Emma`s for the night on Thursday to see "Peg o` My Heart" again.

I don`t know whether I was thinking of you last Wednesday at 9.30 or
not. I know I was late in bed that night so it would be late before I had

my little thought of you. I often lie awake and long for you - sometimes
so badly, Cecil, my love, that I wonder when I shall see you.

Goodbye my love, from your Dora.

[1] [H.E.H. Quant, a head office manager, had travelled extensively for
Reckitts: in 1914 he was stranded in Russia when war broke out. As to further
adventures, he got his wish: in 1919 he was in S America for the firm - with a new
wife, having recently married a Miss Carruthers.]

⚭ B.E.F., 27.10.16

My Dear Dora,   Just a few lines to let you know I am all right
after a rather strenuous time.

When I last wrote we had just received orders to go up to the line next
day. We had to get up early and pack in a hurry. While we were
parading before getting into the buses I was told that I should have to
take 400 men to the front line for a working party. The first trouble was
dinner, which we did not get till 3.30 pm. We set off, with our packs
on our backs and each man with a spade, just before dark. The ground
was wet and it soon came on very dark. It took us four and a half hours
to go a mile and a half. After a short rest the men went up to the front
line to dig, returning at daybreak. It rained all night and up till midday.
After the men had dumped their packs and gone up to the line I went
back with 3 orderlies to try to find the cookers which had got stuck fast
in the mud. I could not find them and had to put it off till dawn. So we
lay down in the rain and tried to sleep. Daylight came: the cookers had
arrived but no rations. I managed to get some warm tea up to the men,
however. Most of them got no sleep owing to the rain and the cold and
lack of shelter. Then we heard we should have to man the front line that
night. I did not tell the men this. Later on the order was cancelled.
The men got a hot dinner at about 3 pm. Then when it was dark I
received orders as to where I was to take the 400 men. I found the spot
all right, but none of us had ever been there before. It was raining and
pitch black. The only thing to do was to turn in anywhere for the night.

I turned into a dugout and slept in the cold for nearly 10 hours. The next day but one we were shelled out. Two officers were blown to bits five yards from where I was. The CO, Adjutant and Doctor had a miraculous escape. The officer who was in my dugout has gone down with shellshock. I don`t think I`ve had such a rotten time. But it`s over now. We came off in such a hurry that I had no time to get washing and shaving tackle.

Yours with love, Cecil.

ꙮ Silkstone, Sat 28.10.16

My dear Cecil,   I came home from Huddersfield yesterday and got in at 1.20 and then had to pay a call with Ma on the village schoolmistress. This morning I had breakfast in bed - I have got a dawful gold in my dose.

Ma, Pa and I went to a military wedding in the village church this afternoon. One of the Northumbrian officers got married to a Llandudno girl. The story goes that the girl`s former fiance told the present bridegroom to look after his girl while he went to the front - which he did, only too much so. I haven`t been to a wedding for years and years - 1906 when Auntie Alice Batty was married. The bride looked a bit dithery and pale and didn`t smile much but Whalley looked decidedly cheerful.

On Monday I am going to Marjorie Barker`s, The Mount, Bargate, Grimsby.

Love from, Dora.

ꙮ B.E.F., 3.11.16

My Dear Dora,   You say in your last letter that I won`t like sticking in an office year after year, but I don`t think I shall mind it as I once used to. Of course, I simply couldn`t be a common or garden clerk for long, but I have to start there. I shall take a real interest in business after the war. I didn`t care a damn before.

Poor old Mr Quant, he must feel a bit lonely at times, especially after the travelling life he has led. I am awfully fond of him. Of course you know he`s an old pal of my governor`s. They used to camp out together in the Australian bush. What a glorious life it must have been.

We have had a hard time since I last wrote to you. We have been up in the front "ditch" - it is not a trench. It is everywhere knee-deep in mud, from the consistency of water to that of treacle. I have not had more than six hours` sleep out of the last sixty. We came back this morning and are now in comfort. Men have stuck fast in the mud and have been too weak to get out. One of my officers go stuck and it took three men to get him out. I seem to have lived through months these last ten days. I am due for another pip now, having been in charge of a company for a month.

Yours with love, Cecil.

ԃ՜ The Mount, Grimsby, 3.11.16

My dear Cecil,   I didn`t come here until Wednesday after all - my cold got worse on Saturday so I stayed in bed Sunday.

I don`t think I have told you about Marjorie`s engagement, have I? It really is very romantic and was only fixed up about three weeks ago. She came up from Jersey in August and travelled up from London in the same carriage as a naval lieutenant. Neither spoke but I suppose he noticed Marjorie and also her name on her suitcase. He sought out someone he knew in Grimsby to introduce them, played tennis etc, called on Mrs Barker, and three weeks ago they were engaged. He is 25 and Marjorie nearly 24. His name is William Rayburn Richardson and is a full lieutenant in the regular navy, also senior submarine officer at Immingham. He is very broad, fair, blue eyes, nearly 6 ft and doesn`t part his hair but brushes it straight back, so now you have a full description. Marjorie quite knows her own mind and is very happy.

He came in on Weds night and brought his sub and we all went to the pictures. This morning we worked in Marjorie`s kitchen garden. She sells the vegetables for the war supply depot.

Richardson is out on his submarine today until Sunday and then he has invited us to Immingham to tea on HMS Vulcan - their depot ship.

Goodbye, my love, it must be awfully cold for you now. I often wish you could get a wound - but only a little one that wouldn`t hurt you but bring you home. Then I could love you more and know you more.

Love from, Dora.

   ᴔᎶᎶ **Beech Croft, Newland Park, Hull, Thursday 9.11.16**

My dear Cecil,   I got a letter from you yesterday, written on the 27th when you had taken those 400 men and had such a rotten time. Fancy it taking eleven days to come!

I left Grimsby on Tuesday and have been staying at Grandpa`s since then and go back to Silkstone tomorrow. I thought I would be going straight back to Silkstone but Mother wrote and said the car was getting mouldy inside so I have had to clean it also vaseline silver work and see that the maid put on fires, etc. I did all that on Tuesday and today I have come down and put three fires on downstairs all by myself and they are blazing merrily now but it still seems chilly and now I am sitting in the dining room writing to you. It does seem ages since we have lived here and ages since you used to come from Dalton.

By the way, I saw Bob on your motorbike yesterday but he didn`t see me.[1] Marjorie came over to Hull yesterday. William asked us out to lunch and we went to Polly`s - do you remember those glass coffee-making affairs they have there and you can make it on the table yourself, `cause Ma has bought Pa one for his birthday. Marjorie is an awfully nice girl all through - so awfully genuine and unselfish. She was 24 on Monday. I think Billy Richardson is a jolly lucky man. I stayed until

Tuesday because they got a wire to say that Richardson`s brother had come on leave from the Somme and would come up on Monday. He is a Capt. in the D.L.I. - 33 but looks 40 and frightfully haggard and ill. An attack of trench fever came on while he was at the house - fearfully cold and shivery with a bad headache; and then he went awfully hot and says the temperature can go up to 102. Poor man, we did feel sorry for him. He took 3 aspirin and that seemed to pull him round and then we went to "The Marriage Market" at night, quite good on the whole but we couldn`t stay to the end as they had to get back to Immingham.

On Sunday I enjoyed going to Immingham immensely. Mr Richardson took us on his submarine - had to walk along a plank 1 foot wide to get to it! It was awfully interesting but there isn`t much room, and two officers go out on them. Looked through the periscope too. Then we had tea on HMS Vulcan which is the depot ship for the submarines - they had borrowed the captain`s cabin for the occasion & I thought it was rather poky but they said as cabins go it was immense!

I really have had quite a gay time last week. Last night I took Nurse Waddington to see "A Little Bit of Fluff" at the Grand. It`s a bit "high" in parts and one has to put moral sentiments aside and enter into the fun of it!

I met Miss Takhurst yesterday (Adrian Farrell`s aunt) and she stood talking and told me all about Adrian etc, and also she wanted to congratulate me as she had heard about a year ago that I was engaged! I said no - no - and wished afterwards I had asked who the unfortunate gent was! Goodness knows who creates these rumours.

You have had a simply wretched time, Cecil - you must have a lot of vim to stick it. I think they ought to send your lot home for a rest, it is five whole months since you had leave. You do have marvellous escapes, I think, but I feel sure you are being taken care of in some way that we don`t see, my love. Goodbye, dear one, I have been thinking about you such a lot today and wanting to see you so badly.

Love from, Dora.

[1] Bob had a lot on his mind, as he wrote to Cecil about this time:

> "I went to York last Wednesday to see the General, or whatever he was. He was quite a decent chap and didn`t ask me much, only my position at school, what sports I went in for and a few other things. I told him I motor-biked in my spare time.
>
> The Head kicked up a row again about motorbikes yesterday because some silly old fool had written to say that a boy had nearly knocked him down and had then sworn at him.
>
> Later on he interviewed the motorcyclists alone and generally ran us down, saying that if he were the Chief Constable he wouldn`t allow a motorbike to go more than 4 mph (poor chap). However, he asked us what was the slowest speed our bikes would do. I said mine wouldn`t do less than ten, so he kindly consented to allow me to ride to school so long as I didn`t exceed 10 mph. Of course I shan`t, I don`t think.
>
> Five of us went over on motorbikes to Pocklington to watch the first play. We won 15-5 although the refereeing was all for them. We were fairly lucky on our bikes, nothing going really wrong. I had three nuts missing which hold the engine to the frame. The mudguard also had about three inches play.
>
> Colonel Easton now says it is no use sending my papers up till the end of January as they will be sent back if they are sent too long before I am 18$^{1/2}$, and he says it is no good going into the Inns of Court at 18$^{1/4}$ as I should only learn what I can learn in the school OTC.
>
> I am fed up as it means waiting till about the end of February, staying on at school, with which I am fed up. I cut about six periods a week, 2 of them the Head`s, as they are so feeding."

♊ Silkstone, Saturday 9.45 p.m., 11.11.16

My dear Cecil,   I got another letter from you yesterday, written on 3rd inst. It was lovely getting one only two days after the other one. It is a comforting feeling to think there is somebody who wants me and

loves me - but you are such a long way off sometimes, and other times
you seem quite near. Tonight you do. I would love to have a nice comfy
talk with you now and sit over a nice fire all by ourselves. I think I
should have that lovely feeling of understanding you told me about. It is
quite different from any other kind of love - I remember you told me in
one of your first letters that you loved me in quite a different way from
anyone else but you couldn`t describe it. I think I am loving you a little
more in the way you want me to, don`t you?

The mud in the trenches must be simply awful. A company must be a
very big responsibility out at the front. I am afraid all this will have
made you a lot older - has it?

*Semaphore practice, probably at the Hull Naval Hospital. Dora is the second
nurse from the right.*

Emma and I are going off to Penrhos for the weekend next Friday the
17th. Miss Hovey has always given an open invitation, and says she will
be very pleased indeed to see us again. I haven`t been since a year last
February when I went and taught some of the girls semaphoring and
morse with flags. I don`t know any of the present girls, except Hilda

and Mabel of course. I shall also have a talk with your dear little friend
Miss Clayton - you don`t like her, do you? She really is very nice and
broad-minded in most things - but she has a kink somewhere. I think
the sordid existence at P.C. year after year is enough to make anyone
have a kink somewhere. I really must remember to curb my language
for Ma Hovey next week and drop all colloquialisms and slang by then!

I must go to bed now. I dreamed of you last night - I was sitting in a
train - but only for a moment. Then I woke up - disappointing, wasn`t
it?

Love from, Dora.

ᘏᘏᘏ B.E.F., 12.11.16

My Dear Dora,   I have not been able to write to you before as I
have been in Hell for the last few days. I have had the means of writing
but both they and I have been too wet and muddy.

Two days after my last letter we were again called up to the line. My company were led by a guide who lost his way. I found our trench eventually, and it was watery and muddy. Next morning we sorted ourselves out a little and in the evening set off to relieve another company further up the line. The communication trench was knee-deep in mud and water, and in other places up to the thighs. Our new trench was worse than the last - in no place could one stand on anything solid. There were a few holes in the side where one could shelter one's head and back from the wind and rain but these were continually falling in.

We spent 24 hours in this and then relieved a company in the front line. The Bosche were about 200 yds in front of us. There was a wounded English officer out in front. He had been there three days and nights. The company I was relieving had made several attempts to get him, but the Bosche snipers were too keen and several men were hit.

I had orders to put out 4 strong-posts 70 yds in front of our line, each party to consist of 12 men and a commander. The moon was bright enough to read by - you can imagine my feelings. Orders have to be obeyed, however. I set off with the first party, all of us crawling as near to the ground as possible. We were spotted at once and fired at, but only one man was killed. I found some suitable shell-holes and the party started digging themselves in. I then had to get back, which I did with luck. Then I set off with the second party. We were furiously sniped at but nobody was hit. Having fixed this party I returned and took out a third lot. A man was killed a few yards from the trench. I got the fourth party out safely. Then when rations came up we had to get them out at great risk. The following day we were shelled by our own guns. One shell dropped at my feet. My feet were on a ration box when a dud went through it. If it had gone off you would never have received this letter. By this time the water in the trenches was up to our waist in places. There were about a dozen men who had to be left until next day when parties were sent up with spades to dig them out. We were being shelled continuously.

When we at last got clear it was only to find that our new home was a sticky trench with a few holes in the sides. Fortunately the cooks, who had been sent on in advance, had some hot tea, and after a drink we lay down and dozed, absolutely done. I took my boots off and had the greatest difficulty getting them back on later in the day, owing to swollen feet. Many men could not get theirs on, and had to go to hospital. However, we are out of it now. Do you know, when I took my clothes off the night before last they were stuck to my skin with mud, and it hurt to get undressed.

Please give my congratulations to Marjorie Barker. It really is quite a romantic engagement. There are rumours of leave, so maybe we shall see each other soon.

Yours, with love, Cecil.

☙ B.E.F., 19.11.16

My Dear Dodo,   I expect very soon to be home on leave. Our colonel is going tomorrow if the ports are open - they have been closed for a few days. I don`t think I shall let my people know. I shall just roll up at the front door as I did last time.

Since writing last we have been in the front line and had a rough time. Norman Ingleby has come back and has been given his old company, `C`, thereby giving me the push. I have now got `D` company, not nearly such a nice lot. There will be a rough sea for a week or two, for the last company commander was rather lax, with the result that the company is rather sloppy. It`s going to be my job to turn them into soldiers. I rather enjoy a strafing job like this.

This last tour in we had an encounter with the Bosche and I am sorry to say we came off second best. Another company commander and myself went down to Headquarters and whilst we were gone the Bosche took our trenches. Some greasy Hun now has my trench kit, including my British warm, field-glasses, etc. There are some wounded men up there from recent fighting who have been left there for three or four days. We got as many of them down as we could but there are a lot who will die there. It`s terribly hard to see men dying and not be able to help them. Some of the wounded would be left in freezing mud.

I expect you would rather enjoy being home again at Newland for a few hours. I wonder where Adrian Farrell`s aunt got her rumour from.

Yours with love, Cecil.

৩৫৩ Silkstone, Tuesday 21.11.16

My dear Cecil, What an awful time you have been having. I can hardly realise that anyone can go through what you are - and the escapes you have seem simply miraculous. But I think the conditions you have to live in are simply awful. I wish they would send the whole battalion home for a rest and send another one out - I`m sure it`s jolly well time you came home.

I really was beginning to wonder when I should hear from you - it`s a fortnight all but two days. I`ve been awfully anxious about you for a whole week. I thought you were wounded and I thought I wouldn`t write as I didn`t know what would happen to my letter.

This war seems loathsome and vile from end to end. It wouldn`t be so bad if we had some idea when it would be over. Sometimes I feel as if I hadn`t an ounce of patriotism left in me where you are concerned - I don`t care a hang for the nation so long as you come through all right. I think I shall go down plop in your estimation for that - so I will change the subject.

Cheerioh about leavo! Don`t forget to send me a wire from Folkestone - but you must consider your Father and Mother first - I really have no right to take you away from them.

I never went to Penrhos this weekend after all as Emma contracted influenza. I am going to Wolverhampton tomorrow to stay with Doris Cullwick - I slept with her at Penrhos for two terms after Flossie left;

after that I had a room to myself. Her fiance was killed in March and she has been feeling rotten with life in general so I hope I shall cheer her up a bit.

I sometimes think it`s rather disgraceful of me trotting about when you are having such a rotten time, but I am going to have a jolly good burst at working after Xmas. Ma and I went to Manchester for the day yesterday and I interviewed the Matron of the Royal Infirmary and she filled in my paper for service in Military Hospitals. I wrote to HQ yesterday and asked them if I could be sent abroad when I am 23 - they won`t allow them out of England under 23. I should love a hospital ship (as long as one wasn`t drowned) and go cruising in the Mediterranean. Gladys Runton is on one and has been to Cairo - seen the Pyramids and been about a good deal.

I`ve been awfully naughty since I came from Grimsby - the first two days I burnt some jam that Ma had been saving up sugar for, I forgot to post an important letter with cheques in and Pa had to run all the way to Barnsley to catch the post, and I`ve broken the glass in our lantern we take out with us when it`s very dark. So you see if you married me what you would have to stand at times.

I have had to leave off as Pa came in for me to go and look at a mine that was going to explode - 80 lbs of powder I think. I saw it go off which was very interesting and then the vicar and vicaress of Thurgoland came for tea - they are awfully nice people, quite different from the coal magnate specimens. Unfortunately they are leaving their parish. They can`t stand the people round here and I don`t wonder.

I am spending two or three hours in Nottingham with Queenie Willatt on my way to Wolverhampton tomorrow.

Bye-bye once more, my love. Dora.

☙ B.E.F., 22.11.16

My Dear Dora, I am sitting on a camp bed in a wooden hut with nine officers at present. The colonel has said he wants every officer to get himself a bed and a stove and to pay more attention to his personal comfort. I have a Primus with a sheet of tin, and yesterday Norman Ingleby and I bought a bed each in Amiens. Four of us, the doctor, Ingleby, Boyle and myself, spent a ripping time eating, shopping and taking a scented bath.

No, I haven`t answered all the congratulations letters yet, but I am going to.

Yours with love, Cecil.

⚭ B.E.F., 25.11.16

My Dear Dora,   Only a few more days & I shall be back in Blighty, with any luck.

Ellis, my servant, was wounded in our last tour and I have got a new man now. He surprised the hut the other morning by asking whether I would have hot or cold water to wash in. He got me hot water, too, and gets it every morning.

Yours with love, Cecil.

⚭ B.E.F., 26.11.16

My Dear Dodo,   Delighted to get your long letter today. Leave has been put off another two days. I don`t expect to get mine before next Sunday at the earliest.

I`m glad you`re going into a hospital after Xmas. I expect you`d have an awfully decent time on a hospital ship, but it`s a bit risky now that the Bosche torpedo them so shamelessly.

I`m afraid this paper`s rather oily in places, but I`ve had a bit of trouble with Araminta (nee Bertha). Araminta has a pal now in Ethel, our new table-lamp, who burns without a glass chimney.

Yours with love, Cecil.

ᘯᘯ Douro House, Wolverhampton, 27.11.16

My dear Cecil,   It was jolly to get your letter of the 19th about leave coming off soon. I hope you won`t find it deadly in Silkstone - walks are the only excitement.

We went to "The Happy Day" on Sat. night. It was quite good but nothing extra special. I am awfully keen on some of the "Bing Boy" songs at present - "If you were the only girl in the world" - it`s in my head a.m. to p.m.

I am enjoying being here very much - going to Birmingham for the day tomorrow and Wed.

Cheerioh old sport, Love from, Dora.

ᘯᘯ B.E.F., 1.12.16

My Dear Dora,   I forgot to say "Rabbits" this morning and am wondering if it will mean my leave being stopped. I think I shall leave here on Monday next, that is if today`s Friday: I think it is, but I`m not sure.

The Adjutant told me a few days ago that I might as well put my third pip up, as the General had sanctioned the promotion, but I think I`ll wait till it comes out in the Gazette.

I`m in a most untidy state to come home - both tunics are torn and dirty and my best breeches are gone at the knees and elsewhere. I am, moreover, disgustingly "chatty".

I`m just longing to see you again, so I`m going to turn in and think of you.

Yours with love, Cecil.

PART THREE:

THERE ARE NO ZEPPS TO RELIEVE THE MONOTONY.

ᙁᙏ   Cecil and Dora became engaged on 11.12.16 during his ten days leave; on 13.12.16 Cecil`s father wrote to him as follows:

"Your letter received this morning gave me great pleasure. You are a lucky fellow and I am only too pleased that Dora has said "yes" and that Captain Willatt and Mrs Willatt have approved.

I know that you are not demonstrative, but that is a Slack failing for several generations, but I know you have "character" and that is far more important.

Nothing can give me pleasure equal to that caused by you and your brothers and sisters leading useful and worthy lives. You have proved yourself during this wretched war to have the manly qualities which are worth more than anything else, and I have the fullest confidence in you.

Give my love to Dora and say she will receive a hearty welcome for her own as well as for your sake. May God bless you both and preserve you to one another until the day of peace is declared.

With love, your affectionate Father."

ᙁᙏ   Evidently Cecil`s parents, realising that the newly-engaged couple wanted to spend as much time as possible together, invited Dora to accompany him when he came to their house. Here she writes to thank them:

Wed 13.12.16

Dear Mr and Mrs Slack,   Cecil and I have come over here
[to Hull] for the day to see some cousins of Father`s, and Mother has just telephoned Mr Slack`s wire through to us.

It is most kind of you to ask me to come back with Cecil especially as his

leave is getting so short now, but I shall be delighted to come and see
you. We could have come along to Hull tonight, but our train does not
get into Silkstone until 8.30 pm. There is a train at 11 a.m. tomorrow
and arrives at Paragon at 2.29 and we hope to come by that one.

With love, yours very sincerely, Dora.

ᗯᗷ A few days later, with Cecil on his way back to France, Dora wrote to his
parents again:

Silkstone, Sunday 17.12.16

My dear Mrs Slack,   The train was an hour late getting into
Silkstone last night - stopping several times because of the fog, I think.
Cecil and I left here just after seven o`clock this morning and caught the
8.30 to Sheffield at Penistone, and then I saw him off by the 10.22 from
the Midland. He got into a luncheon car so he would be quite alright as
regards his dinner, and the train was an express from Leeds to London -
so I`m sure he would get there in ample time to catch the three o`clock
from Waterloo.

Mother thanks you for your kind invitation for Wednesday dinner but
we are sorry we shall not be able to come as Mother has already arranged
with Young and Pecks to come and do some repairing to the hot water
system.

I should like to thank you again for your great kindness to me during
the past week. It has been the happiest week in my life and I shall never
forget your welcome to me.

With love to you and Mr Slack and the family, Yours affectionately,
Dora.

ᗯᗷ Cecil, meanwhile, sent this note to Dora from Waterloo Station and
another from Le Havre as he made his way back to his battalion:

17.12.16

My Darling,   I am at Waterloo now and shall be off very soon. I do hope you got home all right - it was frightfully rotten for you. I know you felt just like I did. I had a good old splash in the train - a thing I`ve not done for years.

Train`s in now. Goodbye. Love from, Cecil.

☯ Le Havre, 18.12.16

My Darling Dora,   My last note was a very scraggy one, as I was standing up and waiting for the train. You must have felt awful after I had gone - I did. But although I shall feel the being away from you very badly I am going to be outwardly cheerful and you`ll be the same, won`t you? I shall live for that glorious day when we meet again. Every night I will remember 10.30-11.00. I went to sleep last night on the floor of the steamer thinking of you; I woke up thinking of you. I am thinking of you, and loving you, and longing for you all the time, and always shall do.

We spent the night on the boat and arrived here about dawn. Our train goes about 7.0 am tomorrow (Tuesday). I and another fellow have got a bed each at an hotel near the station. Do go to Hull this week and see Mother. It will be good for both of you.

Goodbye my love. Love from, Cecil.

☯ B.E.F., 21.12.16

My Darling Dora,   Just a few lines to let you know I`m still alive and kicking. I am giving a little dinner on Saturday night, the 23rd, in honour of something very special which happened when I was on leave. The Colonel is coming, Norman Ingleby and a few others. There will be ten or twelve altogether.

Yours, with love, Cecil.

("Yours with love" seems a very tame and mild ending to a letter, till one thinks about it for half a minute.)

⬥ B.E.F., 26.12.16

My Darling,   Your letter came on Christmas Eve - I had been
waiting for it, for I knew you`d write soon. Yes, the parting was very
hard, but perhaps it will help us to realise what a great and wonderful
thing this love of ours is, more so, perhaps, than if things had been very
smooth.

Perhaps it will not be very long before I have you in my arms again - oh!
how I long for that moment.

Poor old Reggie [Gaskell]. I feel as though I have lost a friend in him,
although I did not know him as well as you did. I am returning the
newspaper cutting about his funeral.

We have had quite a merry time this Christmas. On Saturday we had
our little dinner. On Sunday I had dinner with another company, and
then on Monday we had a very jolly time with all the officers together.
It was a ripping do, and no-one became vulgarly drunk except one silly
young idiot in my company, and he has been very subdued since.

It is 10.45 now, part of the precious half-hour. I shall go to sleep thinking of my love who is loving me just as I love her.

Yours with love, Cecil.

⬥ B.E.F., 28.12.16

My Darling Dora,   Do you remember when we were in
Sheffield I found a penny on the road and you said it was lucky? Well
yesterday I found a purse with an English and French halfpenny and a
five-franc piece in it. And the luck is this - when the battalion goes
forward again I am going to stay behind as a Musketry instructor. I do
hope it is for a long time, or will lead to a job that will keep me out of
danger. I don`t want to go back this time. I have never been very keen
on the trenches and am far less keen now than ever. Of course, if I have
to go I shall do my job properly, but shall always be on the look-out for
a `soft` job. I don`t feel ashamed of myself for feeling like this for I`m

the only officer in the battalion who went through 1916 without being off trench work for a day either through sickness or on a course.

Thank you awfully for the parcel. The cakes are just right, and the tie is ripping. The pillow I shall use to sleep on, and dream of you.

Germaine, the stove, has gone out and it is very cold. I am alone in the mess, thinking. I am going across to my bed now, as my little watch tells me it will soon be half past ten.

Yours with love, Cecil.

ꙮ **B.E.F., 30.12.16**

My Darling Dora,   The battalion has gone up and I haven`t. I am a sort of Musketry Instructor at a reinforcement camp and have about 200 men to look after.

I too have felt awfully tired since I came back, and I simply hate my servant in the mornings when he brings my water.

Notes, etc, keep coming in to me and there are all sorts of things to fix up as this is our first day here, so I must obey the call of duty.

Yours with love, Cecil.

ꙮ **B.E.F., 3.1.17**

My Darling Dora,   I am writing this in bed, with Bertha burning merrily by my side. I live in a tent with a fellow called Green. There are about a dozen fellows in the mess, but as they are mostly Durham Light Infantry it is not up to much.

The pillow is very comfortable. I use it every night.

Yours with love, Cecil.

ᴥᴥ Shortly after Christmas Dora took a posting as a V.A.D. nurse in the converted Town Hall in Waltham Abbey, Essex.

Dora in her new V.A.D. uniform

Town Hall Hospital, Waltham Abbey, Essex, Wednesday 3.1.17

My darling Cecil,   Joy!!! I got a letter from you this morning
- the first since the Le Havre one.

I am getting into the work more now, and finding the places for all the
things - I felt an awfully foolish kid at first not knowing where things
were kept, and then they have three shifts a day for the nurses - 7.30 to

2 p.m., 2 p.m. to 5, and 5 to 9 p.m.. (we are off during the middle shift now everyday), but two different lots of nurses a day rather bewildered me. The nurses aren`t very particular about cleanliness and tidiness so Hartley (she is the other V.A.D. who sleeps in my room and is awfully good and a good sort) and I are working harder this week to bring the ward up to a better pitch. Yesterday we both felt quite done as we had to stay on an extra hour because of the Dr - making 12 and a half hours - swish! I was done when I rolled into bed last night. However, I shall get used to it in about a week: it`s my feet that feel so done.

I am writing this in the tram going to Enfield. They say it is rather nice there - the reason we are going is that Hartley has contracted five blisters on her feet so she is going to get a new pair of shoes. The majority of nurses and helpers are a bit mincing and fussy in their ways. Several of them have a fearfully cockney accent and I am developing one at breakneck speed. Shall be quite an "`Arriet on `Ampstead `Eath" next time you see me, old chap!

Waltham Abbey Town Hall, converted to a military hospital

We have half a day off a week and a day a month. Hartley and I are
going to London for our half-day this week. I don`t know whether we
shall be wanted here more than a month.

Goodbye my love. Yours, with love, Dora.

ᘯᘉ Waltham Abbey, Sat 4.30 pm, 6.1.17

My Love,   I have only time to scratch a little note to you as the
Q.M. has just been in our room and stayed gassing for ages - and now
we have to get some tea and be in the ward at 5 pm.

I am getting into the work better now and not so tired - excuse scribble,
my hands are frightfully cold.

Goodbye my dearest, take care of yourself. Your Dora.

ᘯᘉ B.E.F., 7.1.17

My Darling,   Your two letters of the 28th and 31st arrived yesterday.

I note your Mother says that you won`t be getting married for years yet,
but I agree with you that one of the joys of married life is to enjoy it
together, young. We had a wonderful week together, a week I shall
never forget, and as you say, when we are married we shall have a
wonderful week together all the time. Yes, Dodo, we shall be lovers all
our lives. I simply can`t bear to think of us a stodgy old couple. I`m
sure we won`t be.

You have gone to the Hospital in rather a rush in the end. I`m sorry
the hours are so long, but in spite of that the work will help you pass the
time till we see each other again.

It`s going to be 9.45 each evening then, right oh. To make quite sure
shall we say 9.30 to 10.0

Bob started work on munitions on January 1st, and starts work at 6.0
am and knocks off at 5.30 pm.[1]

I have had letters of congratulation from Arnold Cleminson and Mr Cousins, Reckitts` Liverpool representative. Do you know him?

Yours with love, Cecil.

[1] **About this time Cecil wrote to his brother as follows:**

"I suppose you`re a frightful nut now that you are earning a bit of money and are allowed to walk about the streets by yourself. Harold must be frightfully awed. Do you take your meals in one of those square tin things like money boxes, and do you carry cold tea in a tin bottle, and do you wear a dirty scarf round your neck, and a bird-nester two sizes too large?

It is very amusing to read some of the letters the men here write. They think they are wonderful bugs because they have heard the big guns roar, and have seen several aeroplanes in the air together. I felt very sorry for them a few days ago when I had to send a certain number up the line. Poor devils, they had not the slightest idea what they were going to. I felt a frightful louse staying behind in comfort and security."

Waltham Abbey, Sunday 4 pm, 7.1.17

My Love,   I had two letters from you today. It is heavenly - they came at 8 am but I never had time to read them until eleven and I was simply aching to. I`m glad you`ve had a nice Christmas and the concert and dinner was a success.

I`ve been here a week now - it really seems ages since I came but I expect the time will fly now. I think it is really good to go through what we are - we shall be more fit in every way when we start life together.

I am awfully glad you have got a musketry job; do try and stick to it or anything else, rather than go into the line again. I don`t want you to get wounded either - not when I see what some of the men are going through - it is quite bad enough to see the men suffer. I am sorry if I

am a wee bit doleful but we have rather a bad patient in the ward at
present. Do try and stick to a safe job.

It is 4.40 now and we have to have tea and be in the ward at 5. We
have only been out for about half an hour today - we came in and lit our
fire it is so cold; Hartley has been asleep and I had begun this letter and
then looked into the fire a long time in between writing to you on my
knee. I was thinking of you and how we looked into the fire together at
Heath Cottage.

Yours with love, Dodo.

Waltham Abbey, Tuesday, 9.1.17

My Darling,   I am writing this in the train - hence the wobbliness.
It is our half-day and Hartley and I have caught the 1.17 to London.
It`s gorgeous being off - I have never wanted half a day off so much
before. We are coming back by a 6 pm train and then will light a fire in
our bedroom, get our stiff collars, cuffs and aprons and caps off and sit in
the firelight and talk or write letters or something and then roll into bed
- that`s what we do every night after we come off duty.

Do you know the last two nights I haven`t been able to wear my dear
little ring. I can get it on, but by next morning my hands get so swollen
- the other day I thought I should never get it off. It`s with the hard
work and putting one`s hands in water and not being able to dry them.
I can`t bear not wearing it - I love to wake up and feel the two little
stones and think who gave it to me.

Hartley is engaged - at least privately - to an Australian and she says she
is going to Melbourne after the war, with him, but the parents and
relations are against it. She feels awfully down about it sometimes: I
think we have been awfully lucky.

I am finishing this letter in Harrods` waiting room. It is about 5.20 and
we are going back by the 6 pm. We really feel as if we want to get a
little extra sleep tonight: we haven`t been getting off until about 11.30

- just sat over the fire, and then getting up at 6.30. There is a rumour that we may go on night duty from the end of this week - 9 pm to 8 am - think I shall like that again. I have only done a week of it in the Naval Hospital.

We must now get to Liverpool Street station - we can get a tube from here. Goodbye and cheerioh - Hartley and I are very chirpy.

Yours with love, Dora.

ツ⅛ **B.E.F., 11.1.17**

My Darling Dora,   Yesterday I made a tremendous effort and wrote three letters in succession, two being letters of thanks for congratulations on my engagement to my love. Have you told Ma Hovey yet? I should like to hear what she has to say.

In the New Year`s Honours my late company sergeant major has been awarded the DCM. He is a splendid fellow and thoroughly deserves what he got. He is the man who called in to see Father when he was on leave, and told Mother to call him Percy.

Yours with love, Cecil.

ツ⅛ **Waltham Abbey, Thursday night 10.30, 11.1.17**

My Dearest,   I thought I would just scratch a line to you before I hop into my bed and say goodnight. It is just the beginning of our half-hour too - it is lovely to think there is one half-hour when we think of each other when the day`s work is done.

After I finished that letter to you in Harrods Hartley and I took a tube from Knightsbridge for L`pool Street but were told to change at Holborn. We did so but couldn`t find the other tube we had to go from and that made us miss the 6.5 train. It was pitch dark and I simply couldn`t find the place and we wandered about for 20 mins. There wasn`t a policeman to ask either - I was very thankful I wasn`t alone: I

should have been a bit scared. Neither Hartley nor I know London at all
well and this was the sickening part of it. Still, we managed to pull
through all right.

I am so tired - I will finish this tomorrow.

Friday afternoon, 12.1.17. Got a letter from you this morning, written
on the 3rd and 4th. I often think of the little home we shall have someday when I sit over the fire at nights after work. Hartley generally gets
in first, then I turn the gas out. One of the two sisters has got her fiance
over and is having him for tea in her room - Hartley and I feel awfully
lonely and wish we had our own ones here. Still, s`never mind - some
day, old chap.

Yours with love, Dora.

B.E.F., 13.1.17

My Darling Dora,   I had two letters yesterday and two letters
and a parcel the day before from you! The cakes were ripping, although
the icing had slipped off one of them.

I`m awfully glad that your room-mate is a decent sort - it would have
been rather rotten if you had had to carry on with someone stupid.

You ask who was at the little dinner I gave in honour of our engagement. I will go round the table. There was the Colonel on my right,
then Capt. Jackson, 2Lt Oakden (who was in our company mess and
whom we couldn`t very well get rid of) 2Lt Boyle, 2Lt Waite (Mess
President) 2Lt Green, 2Lt Revell (vide remarks re Oakden) 2Lt Young
(Transport Officer, mentioned in despatches) and Capt. Quigley on my
left.

Waite and I arranged the dinner, but it was chiefly done by Waite, and I
am most frightfully obliged to him for it, and told him so. He is an
awfully nice chap. His father is the managing director of Marris,
Willows and Smith.

We rather got the wind up at one time as the people from whom we had ordered the turkey, champagne, etc let us down by saying the stuff would not turn up till 8.0 pm on the night. Waite and another fellow

Captain, later Major, Jackson.

and a few orderlies set off to buy chickens but only managed a couple of cock birds! But Madame of our billet, who is an Englishwoman, said it would be all right, and when those birds were eaten they were like spring chickens. One of the things she did was to cook them in white wine.

We prevailed on the Headquarters Mess President to lend us half a dozen bottles of champagne. Waite got quite a lot of dainties in the village, and concocted a ripping hors d`oeuvres; there was also soup, fish-cakes, almonds and raisins, coffee and liqueurs, and a milk pudding especially for the colonel, and then port and cigars.

Right oh about 10.30. If you hop into bed about then we shall both go to sleep thinking specially about each other.

The Jackson person referred to is a chap I once dropped into the sea at Colwyn Bay. We were rather pals.

Yours with love, Cecil.

ᔥᔥ Despite his preoccupation with Dora, Cecil continued to write to his parents. Here is a sample letter dated 14.1.17:

My Dear Father and Mother,   I`m sorry Father has been down with influenza. I hope he is all right now. Mother says she doubts whether I will appreciate the job I`ve got as being too tame. Anyone would appreciate any job that kept one out of the mud and cold of the front line. This is certainly a most monotonous job but it is Heaven to what it might have been.

Dora is in a hospital at Waltham Abbey, Essex. She is there for a month, filling a vacancy.

I and many others are very disgusted with some of the New Years Honours amongst officers. In our Brigade there are 3 hopeless cases. One man gets an MC because he commands the Brigade Trench Mortar section, whilst other men junior to him who have done far more get nothing at all. Another is the award of the DSO to a colonel in our Brigade. His only qualification is that he has been out nearly two years. And then our own colonel who has done splendid work the whole time is passed by. I am not by any means alone in thinking like this. Everyone feels it.

Your affec. son, Cecil.

ॐ **Waltham Abbey, Monday 15.1.17**

My Love,   We have just come back from a long walk, Hartley and I
- we have been as far as the outskirts of Epping Forest. It is lovely -
little cottages dotted here and there. I go on duty in a minute or two.

It is awfully cold and frosty - I have got beastly chilblains on all my
fingers and on my feet and ears.

Have been here a fortnight last Saturday and don`t know where I shall
go to at the month`s end. Must go now - this is just a little note to my
love to let you know how things are.

Yours with love, Dora.

ॐ **B.E.F., 16.1.17**

My Darling,   The gramophone is playing and making me awfully
goosey. There are some really ripping records, and it does make me
want the war to end and to be with you. I think of the little home we
are going to have together. Not that I don`t think like this when the
gramophone is not playing, but it accentuates my feelings. "Tales of
Hoffman" has just been played - I first heard it at the Grand Theatre,
Hull. You and Flossie were there, a few rows in front of me.

I have given myself a holiday today, having all my men under another
officer for bombing. I have been in Amiens with a Capt. Michael of the
4th Yorks, an awfully nice fellow, and Adjutant of this camp.

I was wondering whether the putting on and taking off of your ring
when you go off and on duty would be hurting your finger. You tell me
that you have a lot of trouble owing to the finger swelling. Perhaps you
would be better to leave it off and wear it, say, on your half days and
days off. Que pensez-vous?

The watch is going splendidly. It stopped once, about 10 days ago but
it`s quite all right now. I take it off in the mornings for a few minutes
whilst I wash. I love to see the C and D joined together.

There`s no work doing today as we are covered in snow.

Yours with love, Cecil.

ᘓᘯ Waltham Abbey, Wed. 17.1.17

My Darling,   It`s just a month ago today - 17th - since I saw you last. I wrote to Ma Hovey on Sunday - I wanted her to get the news before Hilda and Mabel arrived on Tuesday.

Your photographs came on Monday. I have got two of them on my dressing- table and a little one I took of you at Silkstone tucked into my little looking-glass.

Hartley is a real sport - rather on the plump side, but a jolly sort. She packed me off to bed at 9.30 last night and I feel tons better for it today.

Mother hasn`t been very well - thought they would have to wire for me, so Pa said, but I had a letter from her this morning saying she is much better so I feel relieved.

What do you think? The Matron has asked us to stay on another month and said we had done very well - and were very pleased with us!! We have said we will stay a fortnight but are not sure about a month.

Goodbye my love. I do love you. Your love, Dora.

ᘓᘯ Waltham Abbey, Friday 19.1.17, 10.10 pm

My Love,   I am sitting by the fire "en deshabille" and the fountain pen seems a little too eager to begin. I was going to write this afternoon but we heard of a lady who used to be a lady`s maid and did shampoos so I had mine done this afternoon.

Keep all your letters, won`t you, then I can see them sometime, and you can see mine too.

Did I tell you I was doing massage - I have been on it for about a fortnight now - I mean as well as the other work. The sister has taught me.
I shall massage you when you get your little Blighty.

I expect you are wondering when you are going to get your fawn socks -
I finished one before I left Silkstone and started another but I never had
time to knit a stitch since I came here.

Hartley and I are going to have a half day off on Sunday and it is jolly
well time - have been here three weeks tomorrow and had one half day
only off. Hartley is going to a friend`s for tea and I am going to Flossie
who is staying at St John`s Wood and learning motor driving at a school
of motoring somewhere in London.

I must go to bed now - it is 10.45 and I am so sleepy. I`m just going to
roll in and fall asleep thinking of you, my own love.

Yours, with love, Dodo.

☿ Waltham Abbey, Tuesday 23.1.17

My Love,   Hartley and I are sitting over the fire having a cup of coffee we have just made - munching a biscuit. She is reading and I am
writing to my love. I have either been out or been too sleepy to write
since Friday. On Sunday we set off by tram to Finsbury Park from
Waltham Cross (a mile from here) and then tubed to Oxford Circus
where I met Flossie and Hartley met a friend of hers. I went with F. to
St John`s Wood (near the Zoo) where she is in a boarding house. I
think I told you that she is doing a six weeks` course of motor driving
and mechanism at a school of motoring in Piccadilly, and then she says
she is going to take a post somewhere. A Miss Varley - friend of ours -
her fiance (a great friend of Pa`s) died 14 years ago and she has never
got over it yet - is staying in the same boarding house so Flossie is more
or less under her care. I stayed there until about 6.15 and then Flossie
saw me to the Metropolitan Railway and I went back that way to
L`pool St. Station changing at Baker St - hadn`t been in an

Underground by myself before so I felt awfully frightened I should go wrong or do something silly.

We got back about 8 pm. One of the patients had made a topping fire in our room for us and then at 9 pm Fitzroy, one of the other VADS, came up for coffee. She left Monday morning - couldn`t stand the work or something.

H and I settled up with Matron that we would stay as long as she wanted us to stay. We have to put up with a good bit and we get fed up at times. As it is a VAD place everyone is voluntary except an orderly and a couple of charwomen and the voluntaries come to look after the soldiers not the nurses, and Hartley and I are the only two sleeping-in and on-all-day nurses so we have to get up and get our own breakfast and cook it etc, cart all our own meals into a room etc, and generally pig it all throughout. Still, it will do us good, and we have a decent bedroom and fire - so long as we light it, so it isn`t at all bad, really.

Talking about my ring, do you know I couldn`t get it near any of my fingers on Sunday when I went to London - not even my little fingers, my hands are so swollen with chilblains - like an old ruffian`s!!

I`m glad you think of the little home we are going to have - but I don`t know when the war will be over. I get horribly down about it sometimes. Oh Cecil, I do want you so much in the evenings after I come off duty. Goodnight, my darling - it will be a beastly tussle to get up in the morning. I have been looking in the fire and thinking about you.

Yours with love, Dora.

Did you hear about the big explosion near London? We heard it - this is a very Zeppy spot so might be quite thrilling before we leave.

◦ B.E.F., 22.1.17

My Darling Dodo,   I got a parcel from Silkstone a few days ago, sent off on Jan 2nd. It was the two chocolate cakes that hadn`t set when you left. They were quite all right though, and ripping eating.

Flossie says she`s going to a driving school in London. I wonder what she`ll be driving, a taxi or a bus, or a goods van.

Has that letter of mine of Dec 20th turned up yet?

It`s been freezing here now continuously for a week and it`s impossible to keep warm. Sorry you got lost in the dark. It`s a rotten feeling, isn`t it? I`ve done it several times, and amongst shell-holes and dead bodies.

Yours with love, Cecil.

ꙮ B.E.F., 25.1.17

My Darling,   It`s most wickedly cold here. People who have lived in these parts for forty years say it is the harshest frost they have known. The other night we had a kind of rice pudding with custard on it, and it came in frozen hard. In the morning my shaving brush and sponge are absolutely stiff. I don`t get undressed at night, but just take off my coat and boots and put on my dressing gown and crawl into my flea-bag. I have three blankets and a raincoat on top and a mackintosh sheet and a lot of brown paper underneath and I still don`t get really warm. It must be Hell in the line.

I wish you were here to see the country. It`s all hills and valleys and woods and looks beautiful in the frost and snow.

Yours with love, Cecil.

ꙮ Waltham Abbey, Thurs. 25.1.17, 10 pm

My darling Cecil,   I had a letter from Aunt Alice Batty y`day and she told me how ill Ralph is (she said Harold, but I think it must be Ralph as he is the one who has had chicken-pox). I am so sorry about it. I wrote to your Mother and a little note to Ralph. It really is awfully sad for them to see one of their own children like that and Ralph really is a rather sweet little kiddy and I`m awfully fond of him.

I seem to have heard of so much sadness lately - old Pa Todd has had a
stroke on top of his illness and is quite helpless now and not expected to
live more than a week or two. Then the Sister in my part of the ward
has just had a sister die in Guy`s hospital - only 21 and her fiance out in
France, so it has made us rather subdued this last day or two.

However, this afternoon we have had a half-day, Hartley and I, and been
to London - saw Dennis Eadie and Marie Lohr in "Home On Leave" at
the Royalty, a matinee, and really forgot everything and enjoyed
ourselves, although the play was a wee bit sad in parts and made me feel
a bit throaty; but it does one good to think a bit at times.

I really feel too sleepy to write a long letter. Yours with love, Dora.

ᘉᘉᘉ Waltham Abbey, Monday 28.1.17

My Darling,   I had a letter from you today, but before that
hadn`t had one for nearly a week.  Isn`t the cold awful? Freezing here
all the time - never stopped for about a week. I wish we were all at
Silkstone and could skate. I haven`t skated since that time at
Stoneferry: you were a shy little nipper then and I was a gawky
schoolkid. I have got a wicked cerise chilblain on the end of my nose.
You wouldn`t know your own old girl!

We divide our bedroom into two cubicles - Hartley`s we call the "house"
and mine the "Chat" and we have two big black boxes one on top of the
other with doors that open, with "Capt. Fisher, Royal Artillery" printed.
We call them the upper and lower house and keep our pots, cake, etc
and hats in one and boots etc in the other.

I had a letter from your Mother on Sat. afternoon and she says Harold is
a little better. I quite thought it was Ralph that was ill. Had a letter
from Hilda this m`g - she said that some of the mistresses were very
surprised about me! Didn`t think I would go astray, I should think!

Going to have a half-day tomorrow, I think - Drury Lane panto, Puss In

Boots. Cheerioh old sport and take a run round your tent or your flea-bag to get warm.

Yours with love, Dora.

ᐁᐯ෮ **B.E.F., 30.1.17**

My Darling,   Our camp is breaking up tomorrow when we all go back to our battalions. I am very fed with the postal people. This is my sixth day without a letter.

Later. Since starting this five letters have come for me, three from Father and two from you. I have got very rotten news from home. Harold has got tubercular meningitis and the doctors have very little hope, although Father adds a postscript that they have been greatly surprised at a slight improvement. I do hope the little kid pulls through. Do you remember the night he came in with his hair nicely brushed and his face washed the night I brought you to our house from Silkstone?

Yours with love, Cecil.

ᐁᐯ෮ **B.E.F., 2.2.17**

My Darling,   I am back with the battalion again, resting. I got my company back for about ten minutes, then the Colonel told me he wanted me to take on the Adjutant`s job. By the time you get this letter it will be nearly 2 months since we were in the train together just leaving Barnsley and you promised to be my wife.

No, I didn`t know you were doing massage. I shall ask to go to your hospital when my Blighty comes.

I`m sorry the hospital is in the Zepp. area. It might be exciting, but excitement of that sort is a bit thick for girls, I think. What a terrible explosion. I`d no idea you were so near it. I expect you feel awfully bucked with yourself for being asked to stay on at the hospital.

I`ve got much better news about Harold today: there seems to be hope that he`ll pull through.

Yours with love, Cecil.

ᐁᐅᐊ Waltham Abbey, Friday 2.2.17

My Darling,   Just after I had finished my letter to you on Monday at 5 pm the Sister came in and said a convoy of 37 coming in at 9 pm, so H and I had to buckle to and help with things - beds ready, etc. - and they began to arrive at 9.30 and we didn`t get to bed until 1245 - in the wards at 7 a.m. and only had one hour off duty all Tuesday, 1¹/₂ hours off Weds, and y`day we went out to get a little air, so you see I`ve been awfully busy - no very bad cases. Two of my twenty patients had operations Weds and one needs continual attention so I never have a moment to spare from a.m. to p.m. Still, it is awfully interesting and I`m glad we have got some fresh ones. One kid - he is up and about now - was here before I came, a L/Cpl Rule of the 1st Herts - is awfully decent: helps me with beds and runs round with things for the dressings and helps me a lot. He`s 21 but like a kid of 18 - got a girl called Rose who comes and sees him occasionally.

Hartley and I are going on night duty on Sunday. We shall like it, I`m sure, as we shall have all the day to ourselves so I think we shall be able to go to London in the morning and sleep in the afternoon, or vice versa, and do a matinee.

Old Pa Todd died on Monday. I haven`t written to Mrs Todd yet - I know I ought to but we have felt too tired to do anything but roll into bed. I am awfully glad Harold is so much better. I had a nice letter from your Mother yesterday but hadn`t time to reply yet. I believe I`ve got a blinking cold coming. Hartley fell down in the ward the other day with a bowl of water on top of her! - poor old bird - rather an awkward moment for her.

Tootle-pip, old sport, and write soon. Yours with love, Dora.

ꩺ Dora`s stay at Waltham Abbey was now abruptly curtailed, as she relates in this letter written as she made her way back to Silkstone:

In the train, King`s Cross to Doncaster, 4.45 pm Tuesday 6.2.17

My Darling, I expect you will be surprised to see where I am writing this letter, but I am on my way back to Silkstone. I heard from Ma last week to say she was not up to the mark and this mg I had a long letter from Pater saying that mother was not so well and if she got any worse he would wire for me to come back and must come at once if I did get one. At 12.15 a wire did come and I left by the 1.39. I do hope Ma isn`t very bad - shan`t get in until 9.30 tonight.

Do you know, I haven`t heard from you since a week yesterday and I am really awfully anxious to know what has happened to my love - it is almost a whole fortnight since I heard from you. I do hope you are not ill.

Hartley and changed onto night duty on Sunday, so we came off duty at 9 pm Saturday and had all Sunday off. Had a really topping day: we slept on in bed until 9 am, got up and lit our fire and had coffee and toast, and then turned into the Abbey for service at 11 - the first time we had had the chance. We went for a walk after lunch and then rolled into bed again at 4 pm and got up in time for duty at 9 pm. There is heaps to do on nights, altho` you wouldn`t think so. Breakfast has to be prepared, bread and butter for 50 cut, our own cooking to do, and I had three dressings to do at 10pm, 2am and 6am and get odd drinks for my 20 patients, then at 5 am I begin to wash the beggars and make all their beds and help with breakfast and all to be finished by 7.30. Hartley of course has the same number of patients on her side - just the two of us on all night and a trained sister. All dressings have to be cut and the drums containing them sterilised and sterile water to be done and lotions to be made up so it all keeps you busy.

Hartley and I had got into bed by 9.30 this mg and they brought the wire up at 12.15 so it took me all my time to get dressed and pack a handbag and come away. The Q.M. or acting matron who was so

crabby to begin with was awfully sweet and said I was to try and go
back if I possibly could in ten days or two weeks. Father in the wire told
me to bring my baggage but I hadn`t time. The Q.M. over the men -
he is the acting matron`s husband - was awfully nice and said I had done
excellently for them and quite exceeded their expectations. You will
think I am an awfully conceited little pig telling you this but I am so
glad I have been some good to them.

You`ve no idea, Cecil, how sorry I am to leave the work now - especially
Hartley. I feel fearfully miserable about it all `cause it really is too satu-
ratingly stodgy for words in Silkstone and absolutely no work going on.
It really seems as if every blinking thing I start in the world has been cut
short - it gives me absolutely no chance to get on in life with anything -
it really is feeding - it is always I who have to go and look after them at
home. I don`t know why they couldn`t wire for Flossie instead. You
see, just when the Waltham people are giving me more responsibility
and I`m getting on I have to leave and shall have to start again in
another hospital and shan`t have Hartley either and we wanted to stick
together if we could. Father said in the end of his letter that once he got
me home he would want to keep me always, so I don`t know what I`m
in for. It is rotten and I do feel fed about it all. I know I`m a beastly
pig to talk like this and you`ll think I am one too, but I can`t help it -
and it`s rotten of me to talk like this when Ma is ill and wants me to
look after her. I really feel awfully tired now - I`ve only had $1^{1}/2$ hours`
sleep since 3 pm yesterday.

It really is awfully cold here - the coldest winter since 1881 so they say.
Hartley and I went for a walk yesterday evening and the frost and the
snow were lovely and the moonlight on it too - just like the old-
fashioned pictures. We had a jolly good slide along the road to get
warm. It was horribly cold in the ward kitchen last night - there is no
fire, only gas cooking ovens and rings, so no heating and the kitchen
itself is a separate building built over a running stream, so you can
imagine how starved we were - then at 2 a.m. the gas failed and we had
a fearful performance getting the breakfast ready - porridge cooked,
water boiled, etc.

Goodbye, my love - I feel horribly fed and I know it`s selfish of me to feel like that.

Yours with love, Dora.

ᎧᎧᎧ Silkstone, Friday 9.2.17

My Darling,   I feel so happy today because I have had three letters from you. Hartley forwarded them to me here. I really did feel so anxious about you, and last night absolutely miserable, but today I feel every so chirpy.

I am glad for some things that you have gone back to the battalion - you will like being with your friends again, but there`s the huge danger of it all and besides that the wretched discomfort of it all. I do hope the war will be over soon. Do you think it will be very long or will it hang on for years? I sometimes think it will - I should be quite an experienced nurse by then, shouldn`t I?

I have been busy looking after Ma and doing special cooking for her too. She was not so well y`day, but a little better today. The Dr says she must keep quite flat on her back in bed for another two or three days. We have got another doctor - not the old village beast who was so surly and rotten, but the Camp Dr, a man about 45 and jolly good and awfully nice too which means a great deal.

I`m awfully sorry I wrote you such a grousy letter in the train on Tuesday, but I felt and still feel so disappointed at having to leave my work when I had got so interested in it all. I do try not to be selfish but it is the naughty spirit in me that keeps spurting out. The Matron is expecting me back in a week or ten days but I don`t know whether I shall manage to get off by then. I know Ma and Pa want me to give it up altogether and stodge along here but I should be driven potty, I am sure.

The latest news for you - Emma [Blamires] is engaged!!!! I got a letter y`day and was fearfully astounded - Jimmy Raffan, a physician and surgeon. I really am awfully glad because the last time I was round

there she was getting quite sniffy about such things, so evidently Jimmy
has brought her round to her senses.

Goodbye, my sweetheart. Your love, Dora.

P.S. Waltham Abbey is only for tommies so I couldn`t smuggle you in
with your blighty. Try for any hospital in London. Get a nice bronchitis
or something - that is easy and comfy.

ঝ৫৫ B.E.F., 10.2.17

My Darling Dora,   I`m sorry this letter is such a long time
after the last one but I`ve been moving about a lot and have finally
settled down with the French. They are awfully polite, and very
generous. They do themselves very well in the matter of food and drink.
The dishes are beautifully cooked and the wine is very rich. The entente
cordiale is very high after dinner. One is always shaking hands and
saying au revoir. My servant, one Bush, is having a wonderful time. He
shakes hands with colonels and has coffee brought to him in the
morning.

I`ve had a frightful lot of work and have only had three hours` sleep in
the last 48.

I`m glad you`re on night work now; I expect it`s easier, and besides
it`s rather decent having the whole day to oneself.

Yours with love, Cecil.

ঝ৫৫ Silkstone, Sunday 11.2.17, 11 pm

My Love,   It is two months since I promised to be your wife - someday. I wonder how long that "someday" is off. It will be such a huge
change in our lives; I only hope neither of us will live to regret it. I have
been thinking about the week we had such a lot today and I can picture
you so plainly and I do long to be with you so much.

I must go to bed now - I believe you are thinking of me as I am thinking
of you.

Monday 6.15 pm I had a letter from your Ma today and she said Dr Eve
is not quite so pleased with some of Harold`s symptoms - I`m afraid it
is going to be a very slow job for all of them. Mother is getting better
but very slowly, sitting up in bed today. She often says she would like to
have a talk with you. Mother and Father are awfully fond of you - it
makes me gurgle with joy sometimes to think things have run so
smoothly for us: some people have such rotten times.

I haven`t been out at all since I came here except to go to the post. I
haven`t been able to leave Ma at all. Have got a cold in my throat, nose
and neck swollen a bit with leaving my blinking stiff collar off - they
really are appalling inventions.

Do look after yourself and take care. Yours with love, Dora.

ᛞᚷᛟ Silkstone, 15.2.17

My Darling Cecil,   Mother is still just about the same. Dr
Kemp comes down every day but Ma has got awfully nervy and
depressed and wants Dr Baine to come over, but Dr Baine`s time is so
precious nowadays that I don`t know whether he could.  It`s frightfully
disheartening at times because Ma worries so that it tends to make her
worse. It makes me awfully miserable at times. I believe I could have a
big howl sometimes. I expect I am rather tired really, but Ma doesn`t
like me to leave her. I really am trying awfully hard with her to get her
better.

Father`s orderly comes in every morning to get coal in, clean lamps etc -
so it is a great help and he is an awfully decent kid too.

Have had another letter from Matron at Waltham Abbey asking me to
go back indefinitely. Don`t know whether I shall be going - not for
another week at least.

All my love to you, from your Dodo.

∞ B.E.F., 16.2.17

My Darling,   I am very sorry your Mother has not been well and
that you have had to come back in such a hurry. I hope it`s not serious.
I`m sorry you`re feeling so fed up about having to go back to Silkstone.

You say you haven`t had a letter from me for a week, and my folks
haven`t had one for a fortnight, so I`m afraid another post has gone
west.

It`s been a lot warmer lately, and the rising of the sun has been glorious.
The Bosche is about 100 yards in front of us, on a hill, and as the sun
comes up slowly behind his lines I have been watching and waiting for a
shot. It`s pretty awful, isn`t it, waiting to kill a fellow man on a beautiful
clear pure morning when there`s not a cloud in the sky and everything is
still?[1]

I shaved off my little moustache today and my face looks just the same.
Shall I grow another?

Yours with love, Cecil.

[1] **The next day Cecil wrote to his parents:**

   "...Fancy 3 years ago waiting like this to kill a man just for the sake of it,
   and for the delightful thrill of having got a good shot home. The man who
   told Mrs Ferens that I was always killing Germans is rather romantic. I
   only know for certain of 4 whom I have killed, and 2 wounded. There are
   two or three other doubtful cases. I am delighted to hear of Harold`s
   improvement. I did not expect at one time that I should see him again."

∞ Silkstone, Sat. 17.2.17

My Love,   I hope the cakes won`t be biffed at all - have packed
them carefully round with straw so they ought not to be. The orange
cake and the chocolate-all-over one sat down in the oven but the other
choc one is fairly respec. I think.

Mother was a little better y`day and a little better again today so I hope

things will go on improving. I went to Barnsley yesterday for shopping -
quite an excitement for me.

Heaps of love from your Dora.

🜨🜨 **B.E.F., 20.2.17**

My Love, This is a very wobbly train and the light is one candle
power. I am going on a short musketry course with about 100 of our
men. I`ve been on the move for quite a time now - left the line at about
8.0 last night, getting through the mud to billets at about 10.0.pm, up
again at 4.30 for a cup of tea and then a weary march with weary
spiritless men through the rain to the station. It`s 8.30 pm now, and I
expect we shall reach our destination about midnight. But there is a
good billet in a real house to look forward to at the other end, so I`m
not grousing.

I`m very glad to hear that your Mother is a little better and is able to sit
up in bed.

Yours with love, Cecil.

🜨🜨 **Silkstone, Wed. 21.2.17**

My darling Cecil, I am so glad you are enjoying being with
the French. You will be parleying hard by the time I see you. I expect
you will be an endless source of knowledge on rifles after your course.

Yes, I do know what you mean when you say longing isn`t the word - to
see you again. I feel much more chirpy today - `spect it`s because I
have just been out for trot. Housekeeping does feed me to the marrow,
absolutely - it really is a rottenly monotonous existence; would sooner
scratch for my living outside anyday. But will housekeep when I get
married because I love you.

Mother can sit up now. The Dr thought I should be able to get back to
Waltham Abbey next Tuesday but I don`t think it will be as soon as

that. I really can`t think of any news to tell you as nothing happens in this woebegone spot.

Goodbye my love. I want to see your nice cheery face. Yours, with love, Dora.

⤪ **B.E.F., 23.2.17**

My Darling,   This billet is the best I have had. I have a ripping four poster bed in a bedroom all to myself in an old chateau belonging to a count person. One of your photographs is on the mantlepiece and the other on the wall. I love the sepia one, and I want to kiss it every time I

look at it. The one of me reminds me of a little baby rabbit just peeping out of its hole.

Everyone seems to be getting engaged nowadays, don`t they? I remember being at Beech Croft when Emma and Jessie Hallitt were there, and I think Marjorie Barker. They`re all engaged now, or married.

Yours with love, Cecil.

ᘺ᚛ Silkstone, Friday 23.2.17

My Darling,   I think from your last letter that you are still with
the French. It must be a beastly job, sniping, when one thinks of the
sentimental side - but it is as well one doesn`t at the time.

I am awfully sorry I told you I was fed up when the rotten time you are
having is not to be compared with the little bit of scratching I do here.
I`m not going to grouse anymore henceforward and I`m going to
squash my beastly little spirit.

Pa is going to lift Ma to the sofa in her bedroom tonight - so she is
getting on, only very slowly. Flossie will be finishing her course next
Wed. so will be coming back here then I suppose unless she gets a job
straight away.

Please do let your little moustache grow at once - I love you very much
more with it on.

Had a letter from Matron at Waltham Abbey today: scarlet fever has
broken out and they are in quarantine for 10 days. I am glad I haven`t
caught the beastly thing - it is such a spotty do.

Tootle-pip old chap and do take care of yourself and don`t take any risks
with the beastly sniping. I don`t care a hang about it. I don`t mean
I`m not proud of you, because you know I am, but do look after yourself.

Goodbye my love, Dora.

ᘺ᚛ B.E.F., 26.2.17

My Love,   We have news of fresh victories for the British, big
victories that look like being the beginning of the end. How I long for
the end and what it will mean for you and me.

You seemed to be very near me last night. I don`t know whether you
were dreaming of me. It was about midnight, I had stayed up late
playing bridge.

It`s only 9.30 but I`m off to bed to read and smoke until 10.30. I hope
to be dreaming of my love in an hour or two.

Yours with love, Cecil.

☿☿ Sister Chapman`s Home, 64 Clarke Grove Road, Sheffield, Weds 28.2.17, 3 pm

My Love,   I am sure you will be surprised to see where I am. Since
Friday Mother has seemed much weaker and worse. Dr Kemp came as
usual Monday mg but she seemed very bad indeed in the early afternoon,
then Dr Phillips came over from Sheffield at 6 pm and said Ma must
come here for an operation, so Pater, Dr Kemp and I came along with
Mother in a taxi yesterday morning. She is absolutely white as a sheet
and frightfully weak. She had her operation at nine this a.m. and the Dr
said she is doing very well indeed. She can only talk in a whisper. Poor
Pater seems fearfully worried about her.

It was arranged before we came that I was to have a bed in the same
room as Mother and help to look after her too. All the nurses and Sister
Chapman are exceedingly nice. It is really a relief in one sense to know
that Mother is here under far better conveniences than at Silkstone - and
trained nurses too. Cecil, I really had felt the responsibility of it all since
Saturday. Mary the maid has left to make munitions and be nearer her
mother, and the other maid we had got couldn`t come until the 28th -
today - so we have been without a week or two: have had an orderly in
the mg and a charwoman in the afternoon. To add to everything a fresh
orderly came on Monday mg and the charwoman couldn`t come, and
then having to prepare for the Sheffield Dr coming at night and after
that collecting things for us to bring here it was 2 a.m. before I got onto
the couch (had been sleeping there the last four or five nights) and then
had to get up in the night for Mother so after all that I felt quite done

last night - must have been a reaction as I hadn't felt tired at all the last few days. I did want you so badly, Cecil - I simply couldn't help crying and shoved my head under the bedclothes. I hope you won't think I'm a baby but if I could only have held your hand it would have been a comfort.

Yes, my love, I am going to continue making you happy when we are married for always. Now do be quick and scratch up a little bit of leave somehow - anyhow - and I shan't sleep for a week beforehand with excitement.

Had a letter from Kathleen Watt in Bermuda today: she likes being there very much - dancing, tennis, concerts and all sorts. Why don't you get into the 2/4th E.Y. and go out there and have a good time.

Father wired for Flossie on Monday night and she arrived y'day. She is now at Silkstone keeping house for Pater. Ma seems to be getting on very nicely I am glad to say - it does take it out of one to see one's own loved ones very ill.

Yours with love, Dora.

∞ B.E.F., 3.3.17

My Love,   I hope the field postcard which you would get a few posts before this did not put the wind up. I sent it as I hadn't written for two or three days and had broken my glasses.

I got back to soldiering again the day before yesterday. I am in the trenches on a carrying party. I am in a nice safe dugout in a battered village. The machine gun bullets are a bit annoying at nights, but haven't done us any harm yet.

I don't think you'll mind housekeeping as much when we're married, you know as you do now. It'll be different when it's your own house and your own hubby you're looking after. And besides, I can always help. I'm awfully good at boiling water. And then there will be the diversion of keeping hens. We're going to keep hens, aren't we?

Mother tells me in her last letter that they`re going to grow vegetables and hens in the garden now.

If leave goes on regularly I am due in about 7 weeks` time. I expect all sorts of things will crop up to delay it.

Yours with love, Cecil.

ᖆᕤᖆ Sheffield, Sunday 4.3.17

My darling Cecil,   Mother is getting on very nicely indeed - still very weak of course, but the Dr and nurses are quite satisfied with her. Being so weak makes her frightfully nervy and worried - still, I am thankful she is on the right road. I had a letter from your Mother y`day - she seemed very anxious about Ma. Am glad Harold is nearly better and will soon be going away.

I am really having a jolly good rest now as I have very little to do. Yesterday Father came over from Silkstone at noon; we had lunch together and spent the afternoon with Ma. I don`t think Flossie is going back to London - she has had enough of it and Pater said she was quite glad to be back home again. Full of houses and furniture now - I almost think they are getting married this year but nothing is settled yet.

When do you think you will come again, Cecil? I`ve lived on the memories of the one week for years, it seems, and I do want another week.

Goodbye, my sweetheart, take care of yourself. I do love you, Dora.

ᖆᕤᖆ Sheffield, Tues 6.3.17

My darling Cecil,   Flossie brought me a letter from Silkstone yesterday, written just a day or two before you went back to the battalion. I`m sorry my phizz got cracked in the post and I was so careful how I packed them. I will send you another as soon as I get some cardboard to pack it in - there is a shortage of everything in the nursing home.

I shall soon be able to put your ring on again: my chilblains are nearly better now altho' my left hand's a bit beefsteaky. Still, it's all for King and Country so why worry! I have a peep at it in the box sometimes.

Mother is doing very nicely altho' still fearfully weak. It will be quite June before I can go nursing again. I am awfully sorry about Hartley - not to be with her - she is such a sport and so decent. It isn't often one comes across a girl who is an all-round sport and decent sort, is it?

Awful slush and snow here today. Goodbye my love, your Dora.

QJ⌀ B.E.F., 7.3.17

> My Love,   I am awfully sorry to hear about your Mother, and am extremely thankful that she is now going on well after the operation. It is very nice that you can live in the same room as your Mother: it will make a lot of difference to her. I quite understand how fed up you feel, old girl.

> This morning I sent in an application for transfer to the Royal Flying Corps. They have been asking for officers as observers.

> Yours with love, Cecil.

QJ⌀ Sheffield, Friday 9.3.17

My darling Cecil,   I got your field postcard today - I expect you had just arrived back with the battalion. I do hope you are not going to have a very rotten time.

I had a letter from your Ma. Harold seems to be ready for going away now but your father has got the flu very badly and Bronchial Catarrh.

Joy! I can get my ring on again now - the first time for ages, it seems. I had a long letter from Hartley y'day - she is awfully fed because I am not going back yet and she has got another vile VAD, she says, and it will take her all her time to keep on peace terms with her. She is

probably going home for the summer to be with her Mother so that her
sister can go off and work for a while and she wants me to go and stay
with her in Lancs and then take up nursing or some work again in the
autumn.

We think Ma and I might go down to Brighton for a month - perhaps
April.

Heaps of love for yourself, Your Dora.

ᏭᎶᏬ Sheffield, Mon. 12.3.17 4 pm

My Love,   I was so glad to get your letter on Sat. - only two days
after the Field P.C. No, I didn`t get the wind up about the p.c. because
I knew you wouldn`t have it sent if you hadn`t been in a hurry or
something, and besides, I was glad to know you were alright, which is
the main thing.

I remembered yesterday - the 11th. I seem to have been engaged ages.
It seems such a long time since the times when I hadn`t you to think
about. I`m glad you liked the chocolate cakes.  I`ll make them for you
when we`re married - of course if you`re very good!! I`d quite
forgotten about the hens we are going to keep - we shall have to read up
about the little blinkers beforehand though.

Father and Flossie came over on Saturday and Flossie stayed with Ma
while Pater took me out to lunch and tea and we went to the pictures in
between but they were horribly feeble. Still, I enjoyed the change.
Mother seems ever so much better today and is sitting up in bed. I go
out for nearly two hours every morning now. I went to the service at the
cathedral yesterday morning - the first time I have been to church since
Mother was ill.

Goodbye my dearest, Yours with love, Dora.

ༀ B.E.F., 14.3.17

My Love,   I am very glad indeed that your Mother is getting on well. I hope you`re soon able to get her away for a holiday.

I am living at present in a little compartment of a shed and am quite comfortable. I have rigged up a brick stove which smokes abominably but causes quite a lot of entertainment and profane language.

I`m so glad you have been able to get your ring again and the fingers are better.

I got a letter from Hilda the other day. She`s a full prefect now and a frightful nib. Bob has gone to some OTC in Devon to learn how to be a soldier.

Yours with love, Cecil.

ༀ Sheffield, Friday mg 16.3.17

My Love,   I would have written yesterday but we had Queenie over from Nottingham for the day. It was a delight to see her again. She sends her love to you.

It was a surprise that you had sent in your name for the RFC as an observer but I hardly think the O.C. will accept it as you are jolly useful to him. I know the infantry work is a thankless job but I wonder which will be the safer for you. I know the RFC would be a change and you would learn a lot - apart from the mechanical side even - and also you would live in a comfortable billet, which is another great thing after the loathsome trenches. Still, Reggie`s affair has made the RFC seem pretty wretched to me. All the same, do whichever you know to be best for yourself - this is only foolish anxiety on my part, I know, but you know how I feel, don`t you?

Mother is getting on splendidly and has been out of bed for two nights now to have her bed made and is going to walk round the bedroom tonight. Dr Philips has said that unless she has another operation she will keep having a return of these illnesses. It will be in three or four days` time. It will be an anxious time until two or three days afterwards.

We all seem to be under a cloud at present, don`t we, but I am sure there is a brighter time before very long...I don`t think it will be so very long really and then I will try and make you ever so happy in a nice little house and a nice garden and love you all the time for always. So cheerioh, my darling, I`m sure all these rotten times will be over soon.

Your own love, Dora.

℘℘ Sheffield, Sunday 18.3.17

My darling Cecil,   Isn`t it simply lovely weather - I`m sure the spring is coming at last. Mother has her bed right in the bay window and the window open all day so she really gets heaps of fresh air. It seems an awful pity she has to have this other operation when she seems almost better.

I feel so fed up about my finger, Cecil. It isn`t small enough every day to wear my ring and yesterday I went with Pater to the shop you got it from and he said it would have to be cut to be made larger. However, I`m not having it done as Pater seems sure that in a little time my hands will be the same size again, and if it had to be done I should go to Barnby & Rust`s in Hull.

It was out last night that Bapaume as taken - was that the good news that you said you couldn`t tell me. Wilfrid Todd left London y`day for France with the RFC. William is down there seeing him off.

Here are your little sockies at last. There`s my photograph too: I`ve put it up with wood this time so that it doesn`t break. Tell me if you hear any more about the RFC or what is happening.

Heaps of love, Dora.

ରୟ B.E.F., 19.3.17

My Darling,   By the time this reaches you I shall with any luck
be in Paris on 48 hours` leave.

Owing to recent developments on the Western front, and the certainty
of open warfare instead of trench warfare, I am reconsidering my transfer
to the RFC. I know the Colonel doesn`t want me to go, and the
fighting will be very exciting.

Yours with love, Cecil.

ରୟ Sheffield, Thurs. 22.3.17

My darling Cecil,   Mother hasn`t had the operation yet. Dr.
Philips is waiting until she is a little stronger so I think it will be
Saturday - she really is looking much better than she was. It is an
awfully anxious time for us at present - the waiting is wretched.

I am wondering what is happening about the RFC, but I expect I shall
be hearing again soon - the British advance seems to be going on but
I`m glad your lot are resting and out of it. The last letter I had from
you was dated 14th March and the one previous the 7th so I am
wondering if one has been torpedoed or something.

Keeps snowing here all the time - not a bit like spring, is it? Fearfully
cold and nippy. What do you think - I found a real live grey hair right
in a conspicuous place in my parting yesterday.

Yours with love, Dora.

ରୟ B.E.F., 24.3.17

My Darling,   I am so sorry your Mother has to have another
operation.

Norman Ingleby and I got back from Paris last night. We had a ripping
time. We got into Paris at 3.0 a.m. on Wednesday. We got a topping

suite at the Hotel de Castiglione. We were in bed by 4.0 and up again by 9.0. We had a slap-up breakfast and then set off for the city. We were beset by touts wanting to guide us. We know the sort of thing they would guide us to, but as we were out to see everything we took one, and saw some very dubious things.

After lunch we had a lightning tour of Paris. We visited Notre Dame, the Jardin des Plantes, the Invalides place where Napoleon is buried, and several other places. The Louvre was closed, owing to shortage of men and coal. In the evening we went to the Folies Bergeres which is rather warm. During the interval we were accosted no less than fifteen times. On Thursday we went out by the Champs Elysees and Longchamps to Versailles where we had lunch. In the evening we went to the Opera where we saw La Tosca. It was ripping. On Friday morning we did some shopping when I bought you the little vanity bag. It might come in handy for carrying a handkerchief or a box of matches. I got one for Mother too. Yours is the greyish one with a "D" on the flap thing.

Our time alters tonight, and at 11.0 it becomes midnight. Has the time altered in England? I hope so because of 10.30.

I am Adjutant again for a few minutes, because Holtby is on leave in Paris.

Yours with love, Cecil.

ᲝᎶ **Sheffield, Sat. 24.3.17**

My Darling,   I`m so glad about your little holiday in Paris - it will cheer you up, and I do hope you have had a good time and enjoyed yourself. It would be awfully nice for you going with Norman Ingleby. Do tell me what you did and all about it. Father and Mother took us to Paris on our way there and back from Italy. The Parisian life seems alright for a day or two but I shouldn`t like to live it for very long.

I`m glad you haven`t decided about the RFC yet - please don`t go, Cecil. I feel sure you are heaps safer where you are and now the summer

is coming things won`t be so bad in the trenches. William and Flossie
came over yesterday after spending a few days in London with Wilfrid
and some of his RFC friends who are flying to France any day now. The
casualties in France are terrific just now, they say, and they are going to
do some great stunts a little later on so that is why they are wanting as
many pilots and observers as they can get, I should think.

Mother`s operation is postponed until the middle of next week. Father
is coming to spend the afternoon with her today. Goodbye, my love.
Yours with love, Dora.

⚭ B.E.F., 28.3.17

My Love,   I`m so sorry you`ve been without a letter from me for a
whole week. It must have been a torpedo or something, because I`ve
never missed more than 4 days at the most.

I like the crepe de chine very much. I`m sure you`ll look ripping in it.
I`m awfully sorry about the ring. I do hope the finger gets better and
the ring hasn`t to be cut. If it has, it would be better to let Barnby &
Rust do it as we know them, and they won`t swop the diamonds for bits
of glass.

I don`t think I shall transfer to the Flying Corps after all. You aren`t
very keen on it, and Father & Mother aren`t either. I had a joy-ride in
an aeroplane yesterday for about ten minutes. I had several `bumps`.
One feels one`s guts coming up, and gets the wind up horribly, especial-
ly when the pilot "banks". I enjoyed the trip immensely.

I am glad your Mother is getting on so nicely. Yours with love, Cecil.

⚭ Sheffield, 29.3.17

My Darling,   I got your letter all about Paris an hour or two ago.
I have read it two or three times. It would be awfully jolly for you
having Ingleby. I can remember nearly all the places you went to -

wasn`t the "Rose" window lovely in Notre Dame - but I thought it was
a bit dark inside and I was a bit disappointed with it after seeing all the
gorgeous cathedrals in Italy. I remember Napoleon`s tomb very well.
We had a day at Versailles too. Isn`t the Grand Opera a huge place?
We went there to the Meister Singers but Pa didn`t take us to any
Folies Bergeres or anything - probably thought they were a bit "high" for
us! What an interval!

Flossie telephoned from Silkstone and said a parcel had come from you.
I am awfully excited about it and I know I shall like it because you have
chosen it.

Have got a bath-chair and a man and took Mother out on Tuesday,
yesterday and today. I managed to get a Victoria and we went for a
drive. It really is very pretty around Sheffield.

Our clocks do not go on until April 8th so I will think of you at 9.30
until then.

Friday morning. Flossie has arrived and brought the parcel. I am so
awfully pleased with the bag, Cecil, and thank you ever so much for it. I
will give you a kiss for it when I see you. The colour is awfully nice: it
will go with all the things I have.

Flossie and I are just going out to town. We are trying to get Nurse
Waddington over for the first day or two after Mother`s operation.

I am so glad you are not going to the RFC after all. The RFC is rotten
in France just now. Everyone says so - and look at the results in the
papers too, always some machine lost every day.

Goodbye old boy, thankyou ever so much, Dora.

ᘐᘐ **Sheffield, Monday 2.4.17**

My Love,   Mother had her operation yesterday morning and has
gone on very well so far. We have had Nurse Waddington over and she
has been with her over the worst part.

It really was an awful day yesterday and I shall never forget it. It is a different thing altogether being with one`s own people if they are ill. The operation took nearly two hours and it was an awfully big one. I shan`t be able to leave her for a year, I think.

It is just eight weeks today since I came home from Waltham Abbey - I`ve really done nothing but look after poorly folk since I last saw you, have I? I feel at present as if I don`t want to see any more at all. The Sister of this hospital says it is a very great mistake if I don`t go in for training and be a trained nurse - what do you say? It takes three years of scratting and slaving before one is considered anything.

Yours with love, Dora.

P.S. I am awfully glad about the RFC - it has taken quite a weight off my mind to think you are not going there.

✵ B.E.F., 12.35 am, 5.4.17

My Darling,   Just a line to let you know I am alive and kicking. I have taken over the Adjutant`s job at a most awkward time - the censor won`t let me explain - and I have not had a minute to spare the last four days. One thing to be thankful for though is that I get a very decent billet, and also five bob a day and groom`s allowance extra.

I simply must turn in now, my love. I can hardly keep my eyes open.

Yours with love, Cecil.

✵ B.E.F., 11.4.17

My Darling,   You may have received a letter from one Major Jackson telling you I`ve got measles. They`re only German measles and are practically better now, but I`ve got to spend three or four more days here[1] to stop being infectious. I`m awfully annoyed about it because I was most awfully busy, but it`s a nice rest. Breakfast in bed, get up when I like, nice fellows in the other beds, nice nurses and plenty of books and papers.

The weather`s simply awful here, six inches of snow, and cold winds.
It`s rather bad luck just at the beginning of the Push. I wonder if the
Push will finish the war in a few months. I hope so.

Yours with love, Cecil.

[1] at a hospital in St Pol.

🜨🜨🜨 **Sheffield, Friday 13.4.17**

My Darling,   I am wondering whether you have gone up to the
line yet - there has been a pretty stiff do on by the papers this morning
and things seem to be going very well. Pa was over yesterday and thinks
the war will be decided by the autumn and peace declared by the spring
- so I think the worst will be over by Sept.

Mother is getting out of bed tonight for five minutes and I expect we
shall be going back to Silkstone about the 23rd. I have made a
delightfully chic little hat out of the dark green silk that was on top of
that grey fur hat I wore when you were over - have put little flowers
round it and it really is a little duck. I am sure you would like me in it.

We still keep having snow here - I don`t know when the trees are going
to bud. We had your aunt from Rotherham - Mrs Percy Slack - over on
Wednesday. It was so nice to see someone fresh.

I notice that Vimy Ridge is taken by the Canadians. I remember you
telling us about it last June, I think - but I`m not sure.

We shall really be awfully glad to get out of this nursing home. They
are not particularly clean, and when there are people ill in a place and
one or two with some kind of germ I think they ought to be most
particular - but they don`t seem to bother.

Goodbye my love. Yours with love, Dora.

☿ Sheffield, Friday 6.30 pm, 13.4.17

My Darling,   Flossie brought a letter this noon from Major
Harold Jackson which had been sent to Silkstone and said you had gone
to an isolation hospital with a mild attack of measles on April 8th. I do
hope you are better now - you ought to be over the worst. I only hope
they are looking after you properly. Don`t begin to read until your eyes
feel strong enough, will you, because it affects the eyes if you are not
careful. Shall you be able to work a bit of sick leave for Blighty? I
daren`t think about it too much because it seems too good to be true. I
had measles at Penrhos once - German measles. It was about Nov. 1908
and there were about 20 of us and we had a lovely time except for the
first few days.

Goodbye, my love, and don`t catch cold - `cause one is very liable to it
after measles (see what a learned bird I am!) and tell those VADs off if
they don`t look after you properly.

Your love, Dora.

☿ Sheffield, Sat. 14.4.17

My Darling,   I have just been writing to Major Jackson thanking
him for letting me know about you and have told him where you are so
probably he will forward some letters to you.

Pater was at the [Reckitts] board meeting y`day and came as far as
Doncaster with Neville Joy [employed in Reckitts` laboratories]. He
has got a gorgeous job - inspector of gas something for the Humber and
Lincolnshire Garrisons.

Marjorie Barker was to be married yesterday (I think I told you) and we
were going for the wedding but Billie Richardson had to go to sea at a
few hours` notice so it is postponed until his next leave. I may be going
to Huddersfield for a night next week to see Dr. Jim Raffan - Emma`s
young man. She says they are contemplating getting married in
November before he goes to the front again - everyone seems to have got
it very badly just now!

Goodbye, my love, and get better soon and get a wee bit of leave, do.
Yours with love, Dora.

↻ B.E.F., 15.4.17

My Darling,   I`m leaving here tomorrow, but I shall be glad to
get back to the battalion - there will be some letters waiting for me.
The Brigade have had heavy casualties, so I am told, during the last few
days. I saw Sir Douglas Haig yesterday. I was awfully bucked when he
acknowledged my salute.

I`ve got absolutely no news, having been shut up here for a week.

Yours with love, Cecil.

↻ Sheffield, Tuesday 17.4.17

My Darling,   I was so glad to get your letter yesterday and know
you were alright. I got it when I was just going to bed and was simply
frightfully disappointed about no hopes of any leave - I really had been
absolutely living on it since I got Major Jackson`s letter on Friday so I
felt simply horribly miserable last night. It`s only now and again I get
these wretched miserable lonely turns and can`t help it altho` you know
I try to keep cheerful, don`t you? I know I shouldn`t get them if I were
VADing or with other girls but when I`m alone in a room all day with
Mother I can`t help it - I expect Mother thinks I`ve got a monkey on
my back or something today!

What I was thinking about being a trained nurse was that when I go
back VADing I might just as well go and train at a proper hospital and
have lectures etc and then by the time I had finished the war would be
properly over and you would have got through your exam and would be
ready for having me. I should be much more experienced by then and
would feel as if I had accomplished one thing in life anyway. Then if we
did happen to get very poor I would always have something to do so that
I could help.

I looked up St Pol on the map and it isn't very far from Arras, is it? Do be careful when you go up and have your turn - still, as you will be adj. and with the C.O. you will be safer, won't you?

Goodbye, my love. I can wear my ring always now. I often think of the little home we are going to have someday and picture you in it - we will keep the garden nice, won't we?

Yours with love, Dora.

⳥⳥ B.E.F., 19.4.17

My Darling,   I am back with the battalion now, in the trenches, as Adjutant. It was rather a sweat getting here from hospital as the RTOs were very antagonistic (RTO means railway transport officer. They're a sort of station master and are usually duds.)

In great haste. Yours with love, Cecil.

⳥⳥ Sheffield, Sat. 21.4.17

My Love,   I am wondering how you have got on now you are back with the battalion - things seem to be humming a good deal by the papers at any rate.

Mother is doing splendidly and we go back to Silkstone on Tuesday afternoon - we are taxi-ing as Ma can't manage a train yet. She will be upstairs a week and then come down an hour a day at first.

Wilfrid Todd is out in France flying - has been over the lines once. The R.F.C. have a very bad time, I think. I am more than thankful that you haven't joined them.

William says it is rumoured that Arnold Cleminson is engaged to Mrs Theilman (the Major's widow). I believe she is about ten years his senior and two small kiddies too - so he is taking a handful. We used to call him the "Mother`s Hope" in Hull because everyone said he was such an eligible bachelor!

Goodbye my darling, Dora.

ᏊᏊ Silkstone, Wed. 25.4.17

My Darling,   I got your letter about the R.T.O. this morning. I did know what it meant so I know a little more than you think! I feel sure you are having a stiff time in the trenches, but you don`t say anything.

We arrived back in lousy old Silkstone y`day afternoon - it really is lovely to be in the country again after the town. I don`t want to live in town any more. Pa is awfully fed up with his job here - he is frightened they will eventually send German prisoners here to guard!

I have been weighing out my bread today and I`ve only had 6 oz., so I`m two oz. under the ration. It`s rather interesting all this food economy - I made a maize flake pudding today and Ma & Pater liked it very much, and I`ve made some very nice oat scones too - all war economy things.

Ma hasn`t been so cheerful for ages. It`s nice to be in one`s own nest again, but I wish it was Beech Croft.

Post just going so will write more next time - have been `orribly busy today.

Yours with love, Dora.

ᏊᏊ B.E.F., 29.4.17

My Darling,   It`s weeks since I last wrote & I expect you`re feeling horribly fed up with me. I simply have not had the time: I`ve done nothing but work, eat and have short sleeps since I left St Pol.

As you may know by now we have been over the bags again, and the battalion has been absolutely ripping. The Division is awfully bucked and has every reason to be. Perhaps you will have seen from the casualty lists that the battalion paid very dearly for the glory it has won. Cyril Easton, Harold Oughtred and Boyle were killed, and two others are believed killed. Norman Ingleby is among the wounded. A machine gun got him across the chest and arm.

I could not go over with the rest as I had to be with the Colonel. We were about 400 yards behind the front line. We were round the line just before zero, seeing that all was in good order and wishing good luck. We were spotted going back, and about half a dozen Bosche started sniping at us, and we had to run, doubled up, below the ridge. It was a glorious morning, clear and nipping, just after dawn. At zero the terrific barrage began, creeping slowly on, and followed by the infantry.

Prisoners very soon began to pour in. Wounded men coming past HQ reported that all was going well, but after a while serious reports came down, and later none at all. The Bosche had counter-attacked and had got back his front line and was expected to come further. We all stood to at HQ, and reinforcements, tardily arrived, lined the bank. But the Bosche came no further.

Soon we received a message from a lance-corporal that he was back in our original front line with seven men of the battalion. I set off to the line with a couple of orderlies to see what was doing.

There was no communication trench, so it was quite a lively little journey. The Bosche was shelling pretty heavily too, and there were some horrid sights about. When I got to the line I found two companies of a reinforcing battalion and only ten of our own men with no officers and only one NCO.

On our right were some more English but we were not in communication with them. The Bosche was about 200 yards in front. The people on our right were not in a trench but out in No Man`s Land, 50 yds away, in shell-holes.

I left my two orderlies in our trench, jumped out and ran like hell across the open, and got to the shell-holes safely. There I found out what I could about the situation, and gave them what information I had. Then I set off back hell for leather but I was spotted this time and when I was about halfway - crack! went a bullet. I thought I could just manage the remaining 25 yds before another came and just as I reached our trench I took a low dive and fell in just as another shot cracked over me. I expect the Bosche put it down as a bull`s eye.

The news is very bad - 17 officers killed, wounded and missing, and all but 10 of the battalion. Later in the night and the next day a few men rolled up in small parties and these, together with those who had to remain back in billets, make things look a bit more cheery now.

This is what happened: The Division on our flanks failed to keep up. Our battalion and another pushed on towards their first objective, nearly a mile ahead. They did not all get there, only about a company of our people. We had a lot of casualties and this, together with the fact that reinforcements did not come up to time, leaving our flanks unprotected, made things moderately easy for the enemy to counter-attack, which he did on our right and left. He was held up on the right, but broke through on the left and cut off the whole battalion. It is a most awful pity, because the battalion did most splendidly, and took over 400 prisoners and a battery of guns before it was cut off.

We who are left are most awfully proud of what the battalion has done.

We are in a village now. I am billeted in a house with a ripping garden, and am very comfortable.

I am delighted that your Mother is getting on so nicely. This delightful weather ought to buck her up.

Remember this, my sweetheart, risks in plenty I have taken, but they have all been necessary to my duty, and because of you and my people at home I will be as careful as honour and duty permit.

Yours with love, Cecil.

⚕ Silkstone, Monday 30.4.17

My Darling,   I have not had a line since last Wednesday. We
saw in the Hull Times that Capt. Cyril Easton was killed and that was a
week ago yesterday so you must have gone into action just after you
wrote or rather finished the letter to me on the Sat., so I am wanting to
hear again very badly. It is awfully sad about Capt. Easton - I thought
he was still at Catterick.

I do wish you would write to me more often, Cecil - I feel very much on
the strafe about it, in fact. I only get a letter from you three times a
fortnight and sometimes only once a week. I know you will think I
haven`t written to you so often lately but it isn`t half so nice to write
more letters than one gets, and it`s rotten having to live on one letter
every five, six or seven days. Perhaps you don`t know how I look
forward to getting your letters. I look forward to them more than
anything else - except the next time I shall see you - but I don`t want
you to write if you don`t like writing very much. You know the week
you were over in December made a very big impression on me and you
have seemed very different to me ever since, and during that time - tho`
it seems strange that just a week changed things so for me.

William has been over for the weekend. Pater and I went to Penistone
by train, met him by the 10.10 and walked back. Yesterday we had
Major & Mrs Terry and two daughters for tea. He`s the O.C.. The girls
seem awfully nice, but the Ma is quite impossible - absolute gasbag.
Still, we enjoyed seeing someone fresh.

Ma wants me to do my blinking accounts - haven`t had my quarter`s
money yet, and it`s a month overtime too, but I don`t think I shall
have more than a cent or two as I have got into debt with Mother
somehow or other. Do you know, I`ve just discovered you`ll be awfully
rich with your 5/- a day extra allowance - it`s nearly £100 a year.
You`ll be an awfully wealthy little sub. - is it because you are the
adjutant?

Have you heard about the little Leech kiddie pegging out? It`s awfully sad, and Mr Leech away too, but the kiddie never looked really healthy.

Later. Have done my blinking accounts and after all my debts are paid I`m on £5 till the 1st of October - it`s a beastly blow. Flossie is determined to be patriotic and has bought a 15/6 War Loan card and sticks 6d stamps on when she manages to save 6d! Money is a frightful worry, really - it`s heaps easier to be frightfully poor.

I`m off to bed now. We have breakfast at 7.30 now. Love from, Dora.

☿ Silkstone, Thurs 6.15 pm, 3.5.17

My Love,   I am so glad to know you are quite safe. You must have had a fearful time and it must have been dreadful to see your pals wounded. Your Mother said that Norman Ingleby was wounded and the eldest Oughtred boy killed. Their names are in the officially casualty list today, also Waite wounded and seven E. Yks missing, among them Cowl - is that Cowl`s of Reckitts son. There`s a Lt Jackson wounded too - is it the old rheumaticky one you told me of?

There has been a good deal of excitement here - at 7.5 a.m. a huge explosion went off and simply shook our house. It was a boiler at those sniffy picric works just by the station. Pa said it was just like being alongside a 6" gun when it goes off. We thought at first the whole picric works would be blown up and we should go to smithereens but they said it was alright and Pater and Flossie and I hurried up and were at the works at 7.20 and helped to bandage up a few of the wounded. The worst was a girl with a broken leg and a man with a bit in his tummy. It was rather funny afterwards, I suppose, because the alarm had been sounded in Barnsley and a perfect stream of motors, ambulances etc kept coming past here till 10 o`clock - and they had to go back again.

I sent you a parcel y`day. I`m sorry I couldn`t put chocolate icing on top of the cake but I simply can`t get the right kind of sugar - it is illegal to sell it now.

Goodbye, my darling. I am so thankful you have come through all this safely - it is such a dreadful time.

Yours with love, Dora.

✿ Silkstone, Sat. 5.5.17

My Darling,   What a terrible time the battalion has had - it has done gloriously, but what a price to pay. It is such a great pity that the flanks didn`t follow up or you might have followed up still further. You explained it all so clearly that I understand exactly what happened and I have read it over heaps of times. I suppose they would never mention in the papers that nearly a whole battalion was gone.

You`ve no idea how thankful I am that you are adjutant, altho` you have had a very rough time and some lucky escapes - but I know for one thing that you are awfully quick and agile and "got your buttons on", sort of thing and that all helps I`m sure - or else you would never come through things in the miraculous way you do. Yes, Cecil, my love, I will always remember what you say about taking risks - please don`t think I ever dreamt of you neglecting your duty or your honour when I asked you to be careful: I never thought of it in that way and never should.

Sunday afternoon. Father was at the Board Meeting on Friday when they got your letter at home and your Father had had the part about the fighting typed out and gave it to Father to read. You know, I`m awfully proud of my soldier-boy.

A draft of 300 R.Es went out to France last night - Durhams mainly - Father has got the 530th coy Durham R.Es now - reserves. They went at 10.35 pm last night and Father wanted the canteen closing - you know what Durhams are - but the silly O.C. wouldn`t bother. The result was that 80% were drunk and they couldn`t even take a roll-call. Pater was absolutely disgusted with the whole thing - he had warned the O.C. about it beforehand. It looks so rotten for the officers who`ve been training them. There are hardly any men left in the camp now. I went up with Pater and some of the other ossifers to the camp this morning - there were not enough for a proper church parade. Only about ninety men in camp but literally dozens of officers. Pa wonders what will happen next. He thinks the Americans ought to come over and get their training in these camps. I expect it might be German prisoners and then I can tell you we shall be fed to the core.

Mother is going to Brighton on Friday and Father is trying to get leave to take her down and Flossie will follow on during the week. Mother wants me to go for a fortnight after Flossie but I don`t feel a bit in a holiday mood - would much rather wait up here till Ma comes back and then go nursing as soon as I can leave Ma.

Flossie and William have been looking at houses in Beverley and want to get married in September, but Mother doesn`t want her to till next spring. Flossie isn`t a bit keen on housekeeping, etc.

I have made a green silk collar for my green coat and taken off the fur and it looks ever so nice and Mother has made some cuffs. Goodbye, I hope you will get a long rest after the strenuous time.

Yours with love, Dora.

ᗿᗷ B.E.F., 6.5.17 1035 pm

My Darling,   I got your letter of 30th this afternoon. I really am most awfully sorry about not sending more letters, but the very day after my last one we got sudden orders to move from our cosy little village and go up the line again. This took five days, and when we got there we stayed one day and were ordered back; now we`re in the same village after five days of travelling.

I have a lot of work to do on these occasions, making all the arrangements for Transport, cookers, rations, water, etc., and I get very tired. I haven`t been quite fit either and have just got over a dose of boils. Please, Dora, don`t think I haven`t written because I don`t like writing to you. I do. Of course I do; I love it.

It`s awfully rotten about Captain Easton. He`d only been out a month, the second time.

About your training for a nurse. Three years is a frightful long time, you know, and then the war`s going to be over in about four months, if not less, and I should think the Territorials would be sent home first, especially our Division, because we`ve done such good fighting. The clearing up should be left to the Divisions who can`t fight and don`t come up on flanks and let other people down. And then, after a holiday, I shall set to work to pass my exams and then, I think, will be about the time for us to get married, don`t you?

Yes, I still remember 10.30. I always have done. I`ve felt you very near to me at times.

Yours with love, Cecil.

∞ B.E.F., 10.5.17

My Darling, I am lying in a beautiful little wood just outside our village. It`s the end of another perfect day as far as weather goes. I`ve just come in from a ride round the rifle ranges. The country`s simply lovely with just enough unsown fields for a gallop now and again.

Bush, my old servant, has made me a ripping bath in a copse in the grounds of the chateau where I am billeted, and I have a cold bath every morning amongst the wild flowers.

Yes, the Cowl from our battalion, who is missing, is a son of the Cowl at Reckitt`s. We know nothing about him nor about any of the others. A lot of them must be prisoners - they were seen to be marched off after they had fired the last round in their Lewis guns.

We`ve got a ripping Mess President now. He lays out the table himself with violets etc; and the billets, and the band which is very good, is making this little holiday one of our best in France.

Your with love, Cecil.

♈ Silkstone, Sat. 12.5.17

My Love,   I`m quite happy now that I have heard from you again.
I got your letter this mg and it has taken nearly a week - and you are
going to try and squeeze in a few more letters to me. I am awfully sorry
you have had boils - it must be because you are run down and want a
tonic or a change of air or something. Have you seen the M.O., because
I think you ought to. Tell him you want a smell of Blighty to put you
right.

Father took Mother down to Brighton yesterday and comes back
Tuesday night - it`s the first leave he has had since last May. Flossie goes
on Tuesday for a fortnight and then I am going down, about the 28th.
Your leave may come on about then, so I won`t bother about nursing
until I have seen you. Hartley has left Waltham Abbey - she got quite
fed up with all the disadvantages of the place. She is at home now and
expecting her brothers on leave from France and then wants to go nursing again in July or August and wants me to go with her.   That would
mean nursing soldiers again. You don`t mean you don`t want me to
nurse again at all do you? I think I would rather go with Hartley really
than amongst total strangers into a general training hospital. They are
appealing for 15,000 more nurses at home and abroad.

Flossie and I are by ourselves this weekend. Since Mary left we have had
an awful maid - aged 50, a positive divil, so we made her leave y`day
when the parents went away so Flossie and I are nicpicing and quite
enjoying it. Jane - the awful woman - was a fearful misery and never did
her work properly. I seemed to spend half my time running round after
her. I have foraged out another maid to come next week, so with the
orderly for coal and boots, etc we shall get on quite well. Our orderly is
just waiting to be gazetted for the R.F.C. - Flossie made an awful faux
pas one day when she asked him if he was going to be a mechanic!

Bye-bye, old boy. I feel much more cheery and shall be happier still
when I see you and have another talk with you.

Love from, Your Dora.

🕉 **B.E.F., 14.5.17**

My Darling,   I got your letters of 5th and 6th today, telling me you`d got mine about the fight.

The battalion is growing up again. We get men back from hospitals who were sick and slightly wounded, and then drafts from the Base come. You wouldn`t know we`d been wiped out only a week or so ago.

Norman Ingleby is in England now. He got some bits of trinkets in his chest & expects to be about another month. Waite wasn`t badly hit at all. He got a bit of shell in the fleshy bit of his arm and shoulder. He`s in a hospital near Birmingham and is very bucked with life, and with the nurses.

Boyle was one of the fellows I had at the dinner in honour of my engagement. The fellow I was with at the theatre that night when I came in from Dalton is a man called Hildyard. He is missing, and may be a prisoner.

Goodnight my sweetheart. Yours with love, Cecil.

🕉 **Silkstone, Tues. 15.5.17**

My Darling,   I`m glad you have such a good billet - you seem to have every comfort, from a delightfully situated bath to violets on the table!

The country is heavenly just now. I was in the woods last week. I took the Major`s two girls through them and followed up the stream on the stones. Flossie and I used to do that for hours when we were on our holidays in the country. Our peas are coming up - they are one or two inches high. We dug a potato up on Sunday and found it was sprouting so put it back again. Flossie is growing the sweet peas this year - I could never get them to be really successful at Beech Croft because the trees round the garden caused so much shade. Flossie says there are tons of things coming up in the garden in Hull but the whole place wants attention badly. I wonder what`s happening to my little rock garden with the moss between the stones - do you remember it? It was just getting to look respectable when we left.

I hope you are quite better now. If your blood isn`t quite up to concert pitch you ought to drink plenty of water and eat plenty of vegetables and lettuce etc., but not mustard and cress because one never knows in what dirty surroundings it had been grown. I`m a positive Minerva telling you all this! By the way, you aren`t getting any fatter, are you?

I`m expecting Father back from Brighton tonight. Mother says that they can sometimes hear the guns firing in France and she says it seems so near that you ought to pop over and see us while we are there - so take the hint to your little blinking heart and sleep on it.

I have been oh! so busy today - Flossie intended getting off on the 8.38 but missed that and had to go by the 11 a.m. via Doncaster to King`s Cross. It was a fearful rush to help her off and then I had to tidy up after her - she is an awfully untidy little beggar. I do like things kept tidy - altho` not painfully tidy. Are you an untidy little mortal, Cecil?

Had a note from Emma today - she hopes to be married on the 2nd June!!! Never heard of such quick work! They must both have got it very badly to do things so quickly, I think.

I`ve got a new maid coming tomorrow - quite young: no more old beggars - and she seems quite a nice kid too.

Your Mother doesn`t seem to know what to do about Harold because the Dr says he must go into the country and your Mother doesn`t want to leave your father to take him. She says she has been house-hunting in Kirkella and North Cave. I`m sure if they once lived out of Hull they wouldn`t feel like going back to Holderness Road again - do you think so?

Goodbye - and write to them more often. Yours with love, Dora.

ꙮꙮ B.E.F., 18.5.17

My Darling,   We have moved again and are just outside one of the villages recently evacuated by the Bosche. It hasn`t been shelled at all, but there`s hardly a house standing: the Bosche knocked absolutely everything down before he went, and cut all the fruit trees down. There`s a ripping cherry tree just outside the mess, about 2ft in diameter, sawn right through.

I`m glad you`re going to Brighton after all with your Mother.

No, I don`t mean nursing soldiers that I`m not keen on. Do, by all means. It was the general hospital work that I wasn`t so awfully bucked about.

It`s 11.25 now, so I`m afraid you may be asleep when I get to bed and think of you.

Yours with love, Cecil.

♊ Silkstone, Sat. 6.15 pm, 19.5.17

My Darling,   I got your letter of the 14th just before I went off to Emma`s at H`field for the night. I enjoyed the change and met Dr Raffan - he is very nice indeed and very jolly. Looks his age and is a widower! Emma is to be married on 2nd June and wants me to go over on the Thurs. till Mon.

Of course I think of you at 10.30 every night, my sweetheart, unless something extraordinary happens - but always last thing at night and first thing in the morning.

Goodbye for today. Yours with love, Dora.

♊ Silkstone, Sunday 20.5.17

My Love,   Major Terry has sent Pater`s name in to take charge of a Field Coy at Welbeck near Worksop. We don`t know yet whether he`ll get it. It is awfully exciting. If he goes this week I am going over for the day on Sat. to get another house or cottage or something. The Major there has just been sent to Egypt. It`s the Dukeries round there and real country - no blinking mines.

Went to church this morning - a Rev. Parker from Hull preached on
behalf of the curates` fund and he was a misery - like a moulting hen.
At the Blamires they have a distant cousin staying with them, a
chaplain, Captain Blamires, Wesleyan, from New Zealand. Originally
came from Australia and knew your Mother`s people. He certainly was
what one would call a social bore. His one topic was the front, what
he`d done, etc, and he possessed a most monotonous voice and always
talked as if he were holding a prayer meeting.

We hear from Mother every day. She seems to be getting on nicely,
although slowly.

Willie Hallitt was at the Blamires - he is going to be best man. He`s
been in St Thomas`, London, with a partial breakdown, high
temperature etc due to nervous strain, I think. He has been an observer
since the end of July. He`s an awfully nice boy of 19 - gone frightfully
thin. He was in the same squadron as Capt. Ball. I should love to have
seen him bring down an aeroplane. He does it all in a scouting machine
and takes no observer as a rule. It seems a wicked shame he is a prisoner.
They say he was sent up in a rather dud machine.

I made some rather nice salad dressing the other night. Do you ever get
bunny food, `cause if you`d like some I`ll send you some.

Bye bye my sweetheart. I do love you.

Yours with love, Dora.

ᴔ B.E.F., 22.5.17

My Darling,   We are still in our little broken-down village having
a fairly easy time. There are just a few thing the Germans couldn`t
destroy when they left, namely fresh young rhubarb and carrots. It is
rather marvellous how they have destroyed everything, including the
water. It seems funny to see all the roofs lying on the ground, the walls
having been pulled away.

I`ve been playing football the last few evenings, and am a bit stiff. No,

I don`t think I`m getting any fatter. I don`t know whether I`m tidy
or not. I seem to collect a frightful lot of rubbish in my pockets, etc.

Yours with love, Cecil.

⚥ Silkstone, Weds 23.5.17

My Darling,   Welbeck Abbey is off now - but something else is
on instead. Sir John Maxwell of the Northern Command buzzed round
the camp on Sat and said that two officers would be wanted for duty on
coast defence, to teach the infantry to dig trenches, I suppose. Yesterday
the order came through for Pater and Capt. Hall (rather a silly bloke) to
go on coast defence shortly. We might find ourselves landed at Beech
Croft again. Pa hopes it isn`t Aldbrough or any spot like that.

I got your letter of the 18th this morning. It was Friday night that you
wrote it, when I was at the Blamires. I got into bed about 11.
I remember I couldn`t get to sleep till a long time after twelve and you
seemed quite near to me. I think the following night I dreamt about
you and it was beautifully real. I could even feel you, but I didn`t like
the waking up part.

I have had another letter returned to me today, written April 4th -
that`s the second this week. They were those that arrived when you
were in hoppy. I am going to Emma`s wedding after all - it`s on June
2nd. She is the first of our school gang to get married. Flossie says I am
to keep my eyes open and get hints and tips on the wedding - I`m not a
bit well up in them - so that I can give her and William a little
information on the subject. The bridegroom ought to be well up in it if
he`s a widower.  I simply couldn`t marry a widower for anything -
could you?

What friends have you got left now that so many are wounded? It does
seem wicked that the Huns cut all the trees down and the houses.

Yours with love, Dora.

ᲐᲧᲝ Silkstone, 26.5.17, Sat.

My Darling,   I am wondering if you are anywhere near the German attacks that are in the papers just now - round about Arras.

We have not heard any more about Pater moving but I expect it will most probably be next week.

The new maid is a great success so far - quite clean and cheery and polishes things up beautifully: different from the old misery we had. We`re awfully early birds nowadays - I get up at 6.45 and have breakfast at 7.30 to the tick so that Pater can be at the camp by 8 a.m. It`s lovely in the garden so early.

I had a letter from the Matron at Waltham Abbey y`day - a most pressing invitation to go back and scratch for them as they are so busy. It seems funny when she nearly snapped Hartley`s and my heads right off the first few days we were there.

There absolutely isn`t one atom of news in this lousie spot - altho` it`s lovely just now - the trees and the woods and bluebells in them. I had a letter from your Mother just after my birthday - she sent me a tray cloth for my "bottom drawer". I never dreamed of a bottom drawer till she mentioned it!

Bye bye my sweetheart. Yours with love, Dora.

ᲐᲧᲝ B.E.F., 27.5.17

My Darling,   Please do send me some of your salad dressing. We get plenty of green stuff whilst we are behind the line.

We put up an aeroplane man the other night who`d had a forced landing just outside our village. He`d been on a raiding expedition and something had gone wrong with his engines. We couldn`t get a joy-ride because it was only a single-seater.

We`ve got a tremendous lot of officers lately. One of them is from

Reckitt`s and another is a fellow called Anderson who used to live in Westcott Street.

I note that Emma is marrying a widower. I suppose it`s all right, but I don`t think I should want it if I were a girl.

Yours with love, Cecil.

♋♉ Silkstone, Wed. 30.5.17, 6 pm

My Darling, Yesterday Pater came in and said that moving was a wash-out and only little subs were required for the coast defence - consequently we both felt rotten wash-outs and fed up with life in general. However, we made up our minds to it and this morning I staked up peas and planted out about fifty little blinking lettuces. This afternoon Pater came in and said he has to report at the C.R.E. offices in Hull tomorrow,* so we are frightfully busy packing up - we have accumulated a tremendous lot of things. Pater is getting packing cases to get them off by "Goods"- we want to get as much done as possible tonight because I shall have to do all the rest by myself with no help except this domestic. I am going to Emma`s on Friday, Saturday the wedding - 12 noon - and will return Sunday or Monday, then leave here Tuesday for Beech Croft. Hope to take this new maid with me then with a charwoman etc I want to get the house ready for Mother to come the following Friday - `twill be rather a sweat to get it all straight after being shut up for 18 months.

I`m not a bit excited about your leave - not a bit! - swish!!!

Had another letter from the Matron at Waltham Abbey asking me to go back - she says she`s got an X-ray apparatus and hopes that will attract me! Pater says I shall be a conscript if I don`t go nursing again soon - there seems to be talk about calling up VADs in the papers. Am awfully busy - up to my blinking nose in it in fact - so too-to-loo old boy.

Yours with love, Dora.

*[a fuller explanation of this move is made in a newspaper announcement about this time: EAST YORKS VOLUNTEER FORCES; GENERAL ORDERS by the County Commandant Col and Hon Col W LAMBERT WHITE No 12 - 14th June 1917 FORMATION OF NEW R.E. UNIT By kind permission of Major-General Sir S.B. von Donop, G.O.C. Humber Garrison, Captain W.H. Willatt, Royal Engineers, has been attached for raising and organising the East Yorkshire Volunteer Signal Company, R.E., which the Lord Lieutenant has been asked by the War Office to raise in Hull and the East Riding. The headquarters of this company will be at the R.E. Barracks, Colonial Street, Hull. (Sd) G. Easton Colonel, County Adjutant.]

ᘜᘜ B.E.F., 2.6.17

My Darling,   By the time this reaches you it will be a year since I told you I loved you, in the woods behind your house. I was in a frightful funk, but I`m awfully glad I did it, old girl.

I had a ripping dream about you a few nights ago. I was just getting out of the train at Paragon Station, on leave, and you were there to meet me, and I kissed you and it seemed absolutely real. I was awfully fed about waking up.

We got news the other day that three of our officers, missing on April 23rd, are prisoners in Germany. One of them is Hildyard.

We had some transport sports the other day. We came out top again.

Yours with love, Cecil.

ᘜᘜ Bradley Lodge, Huddersfield, Sunday 3.6.17

My Darling,   Am just writing a little note to you now - the wedding is over and went off splendidly and they left for their honeymoon at 1.45 and motored to Sheffield where they caught the train. Emma looked awfully sweet in her bridal things and awfully happy and so did the groom too. I felt very envious when I saw them drive away together.

I`m going to Beech Croft on Tuesday and will be fearfully busy getting things in order. The Blamires are motoring back to Silkstone this evening, taking Jessie and Willie Hallitt to Wakefield.

Goodbye my darling. Yours with love, Dora.

☯ B.E.F., 6.6.17

My Darling,   I had a joy ride last Monday. A large party of us went back to the Somme battlefield to see the ground over which we had fought. It was most awfully interesting, but very disappointing from a sight-seers` point of view as the trenches are crumbling in and the whole place is covered with mustard plant and long grass. I visited the remains of the trench from where the Bosche pinched my British warm and field-glasses, and went down the dug-out I had there. There is a lot of battle rubbish lying about still, and a dead body or two that have been missed by the burial parties. We had our lunch sitting down in a place where a shell burst every five minutes the last time we were there. We had a look at the country from the top of the Butte de Warlincourt and paid a short visit to Bapaume. Bapaume Town Hall was blown up by a time-mine after the Bosche retirement. There`s just a hole there now, full of bricks and stones.

I feel rather bucked with myself today because I`ve got a new pair of boots and a pair of saucy leggings from blighty. I`m brushing my hair a new way. I`ve been going about without a moustache lately. I shaved it off when I had a boil on my lip. When I started to let it grow again I got the wind up horribly because it wouldn`t grow where the boil had been, but I think it will be quite a nice moustache soon.

Yours with love, Cecil.

ౘౘ Beech Croft, Newland Park, Hull, 7.6.17

My Darling,   I arrived here on Tuesday afternoon with dozens of
packages.

Tuesday was the 5th and I thought about you and last year at this time.
I felt awfully sorry for you, you know, but I couldn`t truthfully say "yes"
then by any means.

Beech Croft is in a fearful mess, everything mouldy, down to hide gloves
even. It is simply awful - have got a charwoman in and I hope to get it
fairly presentable for Mother coming home.

Pater is in Grimsby for a month on Coast Defence but will be in Hull
after that, I think.

Bye bye. I must seal this blinking note up for William to take.

Yours with love, Dora.

ౘౘ B.E.F., 10.6.17

My Darling,   I`m awfully glad Emma`s wedding went off so
well. You must have felt a bit envious: weddings are such ripping things
and everyone seems so happy that one always feels a bit lonesome after
it. I remember feeling like that at Colwyn Bay once after a big wedding
there, when all the cars and carriages were going away.

I expect we shall be going back to the line soon. We can`t grouse
though, can we? We`ve had the greater part of this year in rest.

Isn`t this new advance ripping? We used to live near Wytschaete. It
was not far from there that I had my little raid and stuck a Bosche in the
neck with my pocket-knife. I should like to have seen the mines [at
Messines] go up. Acres and acres and acres of earth have been blown up,
and hundreds of Germans and guns have been buried.

I am writing this in my bedroom. Your photograph is on the mantlepiece.

Yours with love, Cecil.

℞ Beech Croft, Sunday 10.6.17

My Darling, I`m sure you will be tired of having scratchy notes from me, and getting fed up too - I expect I shall be getting a strafing letter from you in a day or two. You must grow that little moustache of yours before you come on leave - you know you never mention when you are coming on leave. Is it because if it were stopped I would be disappointed?

Emma and Jim Raffan come back from their honeymoon today. I had a letter from Marjorie on Friday - written from Co. Donegal - she is there with her Ma & Pa waiting to be married on Wednesday 13th. Killybegs is the place and they are going to Donegal for their honeymoon for 48 hrs - so it will be very short and sweet.

I should like to see you in your new boots an saucy little leggings - you will look a dapper little officer. On Friday your Mother asked me to go down to tennis, but I couldn`t as I was entertaining paperhangers and plumbers, etc. Father wired to say he has orders "to be in Hull for an indefinite period" so it looks like a job here.
A biplane came over Newland Park this morning and twisted and twirled about overhead and came quite low once. William thinks it`s Wilfrid [Todd], as he is now near Lincoln with absolutely nothing to do, and he doesn`t think any other RFC would come and twirl over Newland Park for the fun of it.

How awfully interesting, going back to the Somme. I suppose you didn`t find your British warm, etc.

It is lovely being at home again, although the house was dirty and still is - but it will be in order again by next Sunday

Goodbye. Yours with love, Dora.

℞ B.E.F., 14.6.17

My Darling, Today is our last day of comfort. We move very early tomorrow morning. It will be quite a change to go into trenches again.

I expect you rather like being back at Beech Croft, and having a bit
more room. It`s rather like going home on leave.

I`m afraid I`m going to have to stop. Breakfast is going on and I can`t
think properly. I`ll write a decent letter from the trenches.

Yours with love, Cecil.

꠸ꠗꠖ Newland Park, Thurs. 14.6.17

My Love,   It`s ages since I`ve written to you in the morning, but I
have just a little time to spare - all the people are working on different
things. I have two charwomen and a kitchen-maid, two plasterers today
and two paperhangers later on tomorrow. I have a man to put down
carpets and hang curtains, another to hang pictures, and a piano tuner
coming, so I shall be busy. The man is coming from Beverley with our
two portraits and we are putting them on the dining-room wall, so you`ll
be able to pass your opinion when you see them.

I am sending you some photos of Emma`s wedding.

It`s rotten to think of you going back to the line again, old chap.
You`ve had quite enough of it.

It says in the paper this morning that they heard the mine explosion in
Dublin. I wish I`d known about it and I would have listened for it.

I`ve been awfully lazy since Sunday and haven`t got up until 8 o`clock.
It`s lovely having my own room again and my bed right under the win-
dow so I get a cool breeze all night long.

Mother comes home next Wednesday I think, and the house will be
quite straight and clean by then. I`ve been awfully busy turning out
drawers etc. We did the box-room and today the dark-room, which was
in a frantic state of untidiness. I came across a lot of my old drawings
and designs there. It was quite interesting looking through them but it
made me feel as if I wanted to do some more.

The air-raid on London seems to have been pretty bad, doesn`t it? I expect there will be far more casualties than it says in the paper.

Heaps of love my Darling, Dora.

ᐇ Beech Croft, Sunday 6.30 pm, 17.6.17

My Darling,   I`ve been frightfully lazy today: it`s been too hot to do anything. Pater was a gem: he brought my breakfast up about 9.30 and I didn`t get up until eleven. I read "Getting Together", a pro-American little book by Ian Hay - he has been out to America for the Government to establish a feeling of goodwill and the book is what he has discovered about the Yankees. Have been reading Bulmer Lytton`s "Last Days of Pompeii" this afternoon. It is awfully interesting, especially as I have seen Pompeii.

All the room are cleaned now except the billiard room, so we shall not be long. Mother and Flossie are coming on Thursday, I think - not staying in London `cause of the air raids, etc. I think I told you they left Brighton for Rottingdean about a fortnight ago. Brighton is too trippy and noisy for a long stay. Rottingdean is a most delightful little village about five miles away. Burne-Jones lived there.

The kitchen-maid I have now called Eva is a very good sort but unfortunately stutters - still, that`s nothing in wartime. Her brother (Howlett) went out with Col. Shaw - been wounded twice, I think, and out again now. I`ve got a housemaid coming on the 29th so we should be alright then.

The King and Queen are coming tomorrow. He is coming to this new hospital on the Cottingham Road behind the students` college ["Brooklands", now the University`s Dennison Centre]. Pa and I are going to stand on a plank with the Todds at the end of their garden (it stretches to Cottingham Road). Poor old William has to special constable himself at the hospital entrance. Pater`s unit isn`t formed yet so he hasn`t anything to do. The King will be going to the Naval

Hospital too. It`s rather a pity I haven`t been going for a year and a half now, so I shall miss all the fun.

I`m awfully sorry I haven`t made that mayonnaise for you yet but I`ve only had time to do the absolutely necessary cooking. It`s heavenly to be in a civilised sort of house again.

It`s just six months today I said goodbye to you on Sheffield Station. The War Office are stingy old blighters about leave.

Yours with love, Dora.

ᎧᎩᎧ B.E.F., 19.6.17

My Darling,   Am writing this about 30 ft below ground in a little trench off the Hindenburg line. We came here two or three days ago and have been very busy.

Your letter with the photos of Emma has just come in with the rations. Jimmy and Emma look awfully bucked with things, but not any more than you and I will be. I am just longing and aching to see you again.

You`ve had a frightfully busy time cleaning up your house. Do have a good long rest now, old girl, and don`t bother about VADing just yet.

The heat here is terrific. The sweat simply pours off me.

Yours with love, Cecil.

ᎧᎩᎧ Beech Croft, Friday 22.6.17, 7 pm

My Darling,   Mother & Flossie came home last night and Ma looks ever so well but says she has no reserve strength.

It`s lovely to be clean and straight again - nice bed to oneself and real live bath every morning. Flossie and William are going over to Beverley tonight to have a look at a house in Lairgate. It sounds rather nice from the description.

I heard from Hartley yesterday. I hadn`t heard for some weeks and was wondering what had happened to her. She says some weeks ago she heard that her boy was "missing" and a few days afterwards that he was killed - the poor girl seems frightfully upset. I got to know her so well during the time I was at Waltham Abbey. It was only five weeks, but we were together all the time. They were awfully happy - just the same as you and I are, so I do feel very sorry for her. I am writing to her tomorrow, but I feel there is really nothing that an outsider can do to help.

11.45 pm. Two of the Runton girls came in, and Mrs Runton, also Nurse Waddington, so I had to leave off. I came to bed at 10.45 but lit my gas fire, got undressed, then sat over it and thought of you until just now. I ought to hop into bed but I felt I must write a little more to you, my sweetheart.

William and Flossie like the Bev. house very much and are taking me to have a look tomorrow aft. It must be a sudden affection they have for me, for they`ve never taken me out before in the world! Leslie Brown (Kathleen Runton`s boy) hopes to get leave the end of July. Arnold Cleminson is not engaged to Mrs Theilmann. Mr Quant said he`d heard about it and wrote and asked Arnold himself (Mr Quant does get to the bottom of things!!) and Arnold wrote back and denied it - so it was all a lousie scandal (Are you shocked at my blinking language?) Colin Marr went past our house tonight in uniform again - he spends the main part of his time with Kathleen Hall (lives next door to us - Major Hall`s (R.G.A.) daughter) and has done so for the last six months - has always been there so the Todds say - more scandal for you! He was out with you, wasn`t he? Jack Ferens is on ten days` leave - home from Bermuda and goes to Catterick next week I think, so you will probably be getting him out before too long. If he is under you you will be able to lead him a dance, won`t you?

It is just midnight so I must turn my fire out and roll in - and think of you again as I go off to sleep.

Sat mg. Just going out to town with Flossie. It has turned fearfully cold the last day or two.

Yours with love, Dora.

ᘍᘗ B.E.F., 26.6.17 12.15 am

My Darling,   It`s midnight and what`s more it`s nearly a week since I wrote to you last. I sent a card today lest you should get the wind up. We are in the midst of "minor offensives". One is going to start in a minute, gas and all sorts of things will be going over. I am quite safe though for the moment as I am a good 30 ft below ground.

The C.O. was bucking about leave at dinner tonight. It might come off soon, and then again it mightn`t. The strafe has just started. I`m going out to see the fireworks.

I`ve been up and it`s nothing very startling, just a few red and green flares, our guns kicking up a terrific row and making the ground tremble like a jelly.

Joy has come out again. I shall be awfully glad to see him again.

I dreamt of you the night before last and had a ripping talk with you.

Yours with love, Cecil.

ᘍᘗ Beech Croft, Tues 26.6.17

My Darling,   I`m glad you liked the photo of Jimmy Raffan. They are bucked with themselves and think that nobody else can possibly be as happy as themselves. You wouldn`t know Emma now - her manner has absolutely changed - dropped her Cambridge views, I think.

We had a letter from Marjorie this morning. They were married at Killybegs on the 12th and had two days honeymoon in Donegal. It seems that Billy Richardson is out on his submarine for nearly a fortnight

and then in for seven days, and out of that time he can only get odd
hours off. Marjorie is living in the little hotel there and they have a sitting room of their own. She says there is another officer`s wife and they
get on very well. She deserves to be happy. She is such a sweet kid.

While I remember - Mrs Maurice Gosschalk (who lives in N. Pk) told
Flossie that Waite was engaged to one of the Clarke girls - they are four
pretty girls who live in Westbourne Av. - cousins of the Kirkella ones, I
think. I know Ena the eldest one best.

I went over to see the house at Beverley on Sat. It is really very nice. It
is in Lairgate exactly opposite Admiral Walker`s entrance. The house is
Georgian, I think, about 80 years old PIC 32. One drawback is that
there is not too much garden, but they might be able to take a piece at
the side with fruit trees in. They have a little greenhouse too - in fact it
is quite old world. If they can get the telephone installed I think they
will have it.

Mother has come round to their getting married in September. I do
wish you could get leave for it. I thought they gave special leave for
weddings. Still, you`ll be over before then - what a joy. I`m simply
longing to see you again.

I expect we shall be fearfully busy till September. Don`t worry about
my VADing, old boy. I`m not going till after the wedding - should like
to, but I don`t see how I possibly can, do you? I shall thoroughly enjoy
going with old Hartley again for next winter.

Bye bye my darling, and come and see me soon.

Yours with love, Dora.

⚹ Beech Croft, Saturday 10 pm, 30.6.17

My Darling,   Your Mother came down to tea yesterday. You
know, I do like her, quite apart from the fact that she is your Mother.
She brought me your letter to read. I rang her up tonight and told her I
had heard again. She hopes your leave will come in August really as the

holiday at Filey would do you so much good. I have been invited too if
you are over then.

Monday morning, 2.7.17. I intended finishing this on Sunday but Mr &
Mrs Elwell came and stayed for tea and supper - then we took them to
Cottingham station. I am to take you over to see them when you are on

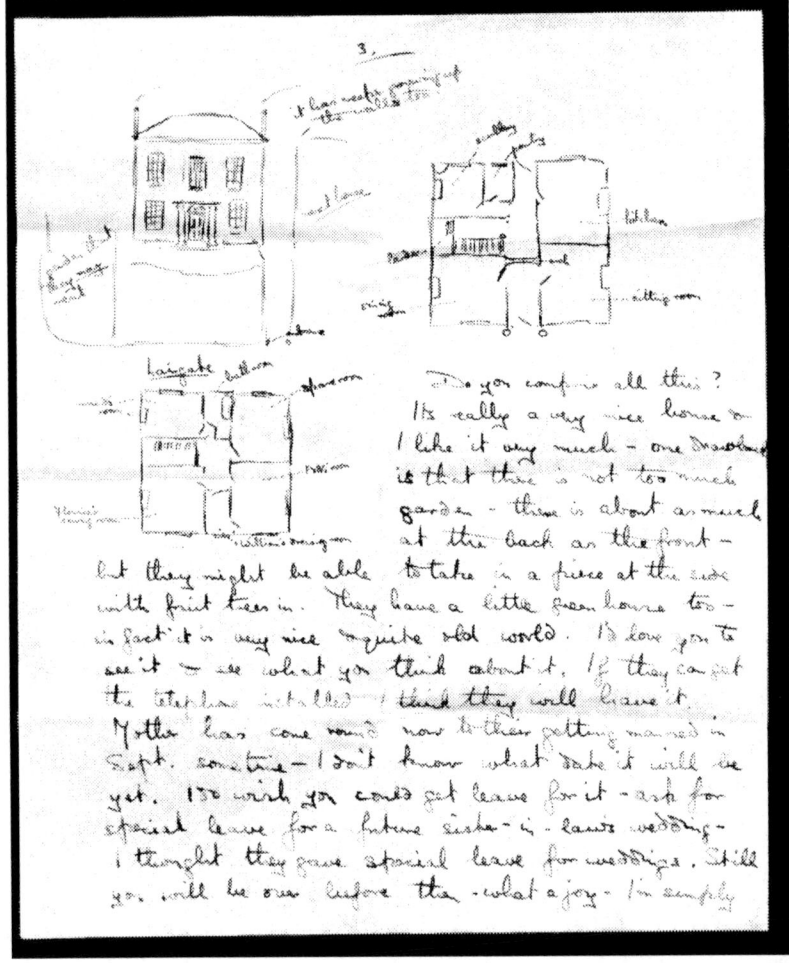

Dora frequently illustrated her letters. Here she explains the layout of her sister's
new house in Lairgate, Beverley

leave so I thought we could go and look at St Margaret`s (that`s the name of Flossie and William`s house) and go and see them too. They are simply full of colour schemes and what they are going to have and what they are not going to have. Mother is just full of it - in fact she talks as if it were her wedding sometimes.

Wilfrid Todd flew over on his way from Newcastle after fetching an aeroplane yesterday. He circled twice over our garden and the Todds` and came very low - nearly on the tree-tops - we waved sheets, etc and we could see him waving quite clearly. We often get RFCs over here nowadays - there`s one that`s always coming - his best girl is the milk girl at the corner of the park and he comes and circles over their farm - serenades her, I `spose!

Yours with love, Dora.

꩜ **B.E.F., 2.7.17 10.20 pm**

My Darling,   We came out of the line this morning, arriving at camp at 5.00 a.m. I had breakfast at 1.0 this afternoon. We`ve had another busy and bad time and have again been let down by people on our flank who said they had reached a place which they hadn`t, with the result that we have 3 officers and 60 men missing. These poor fellows had the Bosche guns of more than two Divisions shelling them for 18 hours and they were buried and blown to bits. It`s awfully bad luck. Capt. Morrill is one of those missing.

Holtby came back yesterday, engaged. I think I shall be handing over to him. I`m going to Le Touquet on the 9th for a Lewis Gun course and am rather looking forward to it.

No, I didn`t know Waite was engaged. I`m awfully glad if it`s true. He`s a ripping fellow. I think Norman Ingleby is going to be married soon.

I wish I could get home for Flossie and William`s wedding.

Yours with love, Cecil.

৫৪৫ B.E.F., 6.7.17

My Darling,   I`m very glad you`re not going VADing again just
yet. It will be a rest for you.

Are you able to get tennis nowadays or has it died down for the time
being? I have been trying to make a football field out of shell-holes
today.

I think I told you that Holtby came back engaged. He`s got it quite
badly. I sleep in the same tent with him. I saw a photograph of his girl
today, and she`s awfully pretty.

The ground is covered with thistles. Bush, my comic servant, put one in
my sponge tonight and when I groused about it said I did it myself.

What do you think of the Russian push? I think it will help the war to
finish in, say, 3 months` time.

Yours with love, Cecil.

৫৪৫ Beech Croft, Friday 6.7.17

My Love,   It does seem wicked that the lot on one of your flanks
should let you down for a second time. Still, it is all over now and you
have come through safely and you will be on your course and then you
will probably get your leave - cheerioh! There is a Mrs Ward who lives
in the cottage adjoining the Todds` garden and whose husband was
killed on the 22nd, I think in the 4th E. Yorks. Capt. Morrill wrote and
told her about it and Miss Walley, the Todds` governess, replied for her
- but before he could receive the letter he must have been killed. She
wrote to ask how he was killed or if it was instantaneous or if he suffered
much, but now that Capt. Morrill has gone she will not be able to obtain
any further accounts of it. I wonder if you know anything about the
man. Mrs Ward is an awfully nice little woman and Miss Walley says
she is frightfully upset and I feel very sorry for her - she is being turned
out of her cottage too, as it is the lodge to the new VAD hospital for
officers on Cottingham Road.

I don`t think I`ve any news at all for you today. Things just go on just the same - in fact, Newland Park gets a bit monotonous. But I`m very busy really: I do all the house-keeping now and Mother doesn`t get up till about 10.30 and Flossie is simply bubbling over with different schemes and planning for their house. They are beginning with painters &c next week, I think.

Flossie saw Ena Clarke in town y`day and she says one of her sisters is engaged to a Waite boy - one that has been wounded, but I don`t know whether it is the one you know.

I owe simply tons of letters - it`s simply chronic. Mother has kept having different people in to tea to see her and that takes up a lot of time in the afternoon. Flossie and I often die for a game of tennis, just an odd set before we hop indoors - but our lawn is in a fearful state - so soft - just like a hayfield after it is cut. I`m sure it won`t be fit to play on this summer, and on the other hand it would mean marking out the whole thing, nets up etc for a very little tennis really as Flossie and William haven`t time at all now they`ve got their blinking house.

It`s nearly 11.30 now - I am going to hop into bed and think of you.

Yours with love, Dora.

ᘜ Beech Croft, 10.7.17

My Darling,   Only time for a scraggy note now - I have been writing to Marjorie Richardson; I haven`t written since she was a Barker.

They have asked me to go on night duty at the VAD hosp. on Cottingham Road about two or three nights every week. I`d like to go really, but Ma and Pa won`t let me. It would only have been for two months or so, so that the other nurses can get their holidays. Rather a swiz, I think.

I hope you have a cheery time in Le Touquet; it`s rather nice to go to a fresh place for a change.

Kathleen Runton`s young man is getting leave in August, he thinks, and he had his leave last Feb - after yours by two months. He digs graves and counts prisoners behind the lines. I think he isn`t very strong.

Bye bye. Yours with love, Dora.

〜〜 B.E.F., 13.7.17

My Darling,   As I have only come to Le Touquet for a short time I am not having my letters forwarded. I had the usual trouble getting here, taking two days to come forty miles.

It is glorious country here. It`s another of the many places we shall have to visit some day. Yesterday afternoon I had a sea-bathe, the first since the war began. I shouldn`t mind having those bathing days at Rydal back again. I remember looking for you forming up in the "crock" ready to march back to Penrhos under the Bug. I could never spot you in the sea though. You used to go out to the boat, didn`t you, and dive into 3 ft of water.

I see that Bob has got his commission in the East Yorks. I wonder if the war will end before he is sent out here. I hope so.*

Leave is still hovering about.

Yours with love, Cecil.

* Cecil to Bob, about this time:

" I was very pleased to see your name in the paper as having been granted a commission in the East Yorks. As you are gazetted to the Territorials you stand a better chance of coming to the 4th Battalion. I suppose you will have joined the third line [Dalton Holme] by this time, where you will wait for two or three months before coming out.

I expect you`ll have some funny specimens of men to deal with nowadays. They`re bad enough when they come out here, `trained`."

ᛣᛣ Beech Croft, Sunday aft. 15.7.17

My Darling,   I hope you are enjoying Le Touquet. I looked it up on the map and find it`s on the coast, so it will be delightful.

Kathleen Runton`s boy is coming on leave in a fortnight`s time. I simply fume inside about it when he had his last leave the beginning of Feb.

Father, Mother, Flossie and I went to Wilton House to tea on Friday. It seemed awfully empty with only three kiddies at home. Harold`s hens seem to be thriving. I think he`s doing jolly well with them and seems to be getting toppingly big eggs.* I think your Mother is going over to Beverley one day next week to see Flossie`s house. Wilfrid Todd had two days` leave during the week and came to see us. I hadn`t seen him for about two and a half years. He is much fatter, and before the war he used to absolutely scorn anyone who got fat and used to run a mile round the park before breakfast every morning!

I`m going to help in the kitchen at the VAD hospital here from 6 to 9 tonight. It`s only because somebody has fallen ill suddenly, but I`m not going to do it again. When one has once worked in the wards it`s a frightful step down the ladder!

I wonder how soon your captaincy will come off. Will your leave come in August, do you think?

Yours with love, Dora.

*Harold to Cecil:

> "We let our hens all over the garden now. 3 came into the house the other day. We have got Cockerel which crows in the morning, I have heard before 5 o`clock in the morning.
>
> We are going to kill a hen soon. I went for a drive the other day and we stopt at a farm. I fell off the top of a haystak 10 feet high and turned a sumersalt on the way down, but luckilly fell on my feet. I got the back of my shoe bitten by a rat the other night when I was in the hen-house. We got an egg 4 inches long the other day and $1^1/2$ inches wide. The hens are just being to lay well now we got 5 eggs yesterday

and 4 today. I am having lessings now. I saw an airship the other day
and it was a big one. It has been fine weather here the last two or 3
days but today was not quit so fine.

   With love from your affectionet Brother Harold."

☟☟ B.E.F., 16.7.17

My Darling,   I go back to the Battalion on Wednesday. Your
letters haven`t reached me yet, which is the only drawback to a jolly
good holiday.

Yesterday afternoon my old platoon sergeant, who has just got a
commission, walked in and I learnt from him that John Ferens was
somewhere about and was going up the line today. I found him in the
writing room, and talked for about half an hour. He`s not coming to
us, I`m sorry to say, but has been posted to the 10th Bn.

I had a most wonderful vision of you on Sunday night. I saw you
perfectly, with the love-light in your eyes, and I spoke to you and kissed
you.

Yours with love, Cecil.

☟☟ B.E.F., 19.7.17

My Darling,   I left Le Touquet yesterday morning. The journey
has been broken at St Pol, and I join the battalion this afternoon.

How is the dugout in your garden getting on? Rather wet and slimy by
now, I should think.

I have meant several times to ask you to send me some more of that soap
you used to send me. I think it`s ripping soap, and it always makes me
think of you when I use it.

Yours with love, Cecil.

℟ Beech Croft, Friday 10.15 pm, 20.7.17

My Darling,   It must be simply delightful at Le Touquet, and I should love to go with you someday.

I think we are all going to Scarborough for Bank holiday weekend about the 4th August. We are going to Red Lea boarding house. It`s right on the front of the South Cliff and has a gorgeous view. If your leave is on then it would be awfully nice - if your Mother wouldn`t mind you being away from Filey for the weekend.

I`ve been writing this in bed and I`m awfully sleepy now so I must drop off to sleep.

Saturday morning. I`ve had a letter from you this morning so I feel extra chirpy. I`ve just rung your Mamma and she`s had one too, both opened by the Base Censor - cheeky man.

They asked me to go to be a scullery-maid at the VAD hospital up here tonight again, but I`ve struck and won`t go this time. A VAD who has worked on the wards is considered to be vastly superior to the scullery VADs. I think I`m doing night duty there in August, but not if you are over.

It was quite exciting here last Mon. afternoon. A friend of Wilfrid Todd`s flew over with their RFC Major. He flew fearfully low over the park and waved to me from the aeroplane and I could see him so plainly. They landed in a field quite near the park to see if it was suitable for an airfield. They want one in Hull but it wasn`t quite wide enough. The RFC Major was awfully young to be a Major and in charge of an aerodrome. Of course, fearful crowds collected from nowhere in the field, but as we knew them we were allowed to be near the machine - and it did look simply delightful.

I`ve been doing some gardening during the week and also framing some pictures with passe-partout. I think I`m going to Beverley this afternoon with Bill and Flossie - help to choose wallpapers or something.

Heaps of love, Dora.

P.S. Flossie is having a little gas oven with a glass door and you can see
your buns cooking - may I have one when we have our little nest? I`ve
read of a lovely job for girls - measuring timber and assessing quantities.
I am writing to Hartley to see what she thinks of it.

ꝏ B.E.F., 22.7.17

My Darling,   An officer went on leave 10 days ago! I am now
second or third on the list, so may be home this year with any luck, and
with great luck in August or September.

I have been officially posted as Assistant Adjutant, Intelligence Officer
and Lewis Gun Officer, so still have plenty of work to do.

I got a letter from you yesterday, posted last Sunday or Monday, and
another today which had been forwarded to Le Touquet.

I nearly got pipped today: a fuse from an anti-aircraft shell came down
plonk at my feet from about 2 miles up. It only missed me by a few
inches.

In your letter today you called Kathleen Runton`s boy her "young man".
It at once made me think of trippers, and Margate, and Blackpool, fish
and chips, and winkles.

I`m sorry Wilfrid Todd`s getting fat. I don`t like fat young men.  I`m
trying hard not to get fat myself.

Yours with love, Cecil.

ꝏ Beech Croft, Wednes. 25.7.17

My Darling,   Many happy returns for the 30th, old boy. Perhaps
you will be here for your next birthday. 24 sounds heaps older than 23,
I think. I wonder if you are older this time than at Christmas.

I have sent you some soap off today, and the nearest approach I can
make to a birthday cake nowadays. I made the red-currant jelly
yesterday too - you may think it`s a bit of a wash-out because it hasn`t

set properly, but it`s not supposed to when it`s made that way.

Our dug-out`s an awful, slimy mess inside nowadays. The pump is out of it so consequently it`s full of stagnant slimy water, and as there are no Zepps to relieve the peaceful monotony it really isn`t much good except as a relic of Zeppy times.

Miss Jones came down yesterday to say goodbye. She is leaving Reckitts on Tuesday and retiring.

Yours with love, Dora.

∞ B.E.F., 27.7.17

My Darling,   I got two nice fat letters from you yesterday. One had followed me to Le Touquet and back.

Capt. Seed got hit a few nights ago when our camp was shelled. He is now in Hospital minus a foot, but very cheery. I rather envy him. He`ll have a good time for the next few months and will probably never come out here again. He`ll have a cork foot, which I believe are very perfect nowadays. He has been out over two years and has not been touched until now, when he gets it walking about on a football field behind the lines.

I will make enquiries about Mrs Ward`s husband and let you know what I hear.

There are millions of earwigs here. They get into one`s bed, one`s clothes, into everything. We moved camp today, and shall be out of the line for a short time.

Yours with love, Cecil.

∞ Beech Croft, Friday 27.7.17

My Darling,   If you come on leave about the 25th you might just be here for the wedding on the 6th. Still, I don`t really mind when you

come, my sweetheart, as long as you come before very long - I am aching
to be with you again.

Mr Rawles has just been in to tea - we knew he was wounded but didn`t
expect him back at his depot at Patrington so soon.

Flossie and William seem to be progressing with their house - painters,
plumbers and joiners etc are monopolising the place at present.

I am looking forward to our hens. I had quite a long dream about you
last night but I seemed to know it was a dream all the time. We were at
Filey.

Heaps of love till I see you. Your own, Dora.

℞ B.E.F., 30.7.17

My Darling,   Many thanks for the birthday wishes and the cake.
I got the cake yesterday and the letter today.

I have got a company again. I expect it will be for "keeps" this time,
unless anything happens to the Adjutant. I have to go into the line
again very soon, and I should think we will be in for about 14 days.
When we come out I really think the Colonel might let me have leave.
It`s 8 months now. I should rather like to get it while my people are at
Filey.

Thanks so much for the soap. The red-currant jelly jar wasn`t smashed.
The salad dressing and the cake turned up today, having followed me to
Le Touquet and back.

Yours with love, Cecil.

℞ Beech Croft, Tuesday 31.7.17

My Darling,   It seems awfully bad luck for Capt. Seed after two
years at the front, still on the other hand I think he is jolly lucky to be
out of it all. Fake limbs, they say, are a marvel nowadays. I saw a man

at Skegness last year playing golf and one would never have known he hadn`t a foot. The man who makes the best false limbs is a German - naturalised Englishman - and he has all the orders for Roehampton where the Tommies who want limbs go. He has sons fighting for the English, but it sounds rather odd.

The earwigs sound awful - they are about the most repulsive looking insects there are. Do sleep with cotton wool in your ears. I don`t think you will for a minute all the same!

Do you know, I`ve had a fixed idea in my head the last two or three days that you`ve got another awful trench raid to do, or another push. It is a horrible thought and I try to squash it every time it crops up. I can`t imagine why I think it because they`d surely never want you to do a second one.

Emma seems frightfully bucked about being married and says she`s never been so happy in her life before, etc etc...absolutely different from the Emma of yesterday. She says I`m to urge Flossie to get married. Hugh Farrell got married on Saturday to the younger Van den Bergh girl - refugees from Antwerp. I`m glad Hilda has passed her matric - she will be a fearful nib at Penrhos next term - head prefect or something I should think.

Cecil, I have dreamt of you two nights together and you seemed so real to me the second time.

Yours with love, Dora.

ॐ B.E.F., 3.8.17

My Darling,   I expect to be seeing you about the 20th of this month. I go into the line tomorrow, and have heard on good authority that I get leave when we come out. I may ask the War Office if there is to be an investiture whilst I am on leave and if so I shall apply to have my Cross presented and then we might get a couple of days in London and go to see "Romance".

We have had a concert tonight in our mess marquee and as the piano is still here there is a lot of noise so I must stop, as I can`t think. I`m just aching for you.

Yours with love, Cecil.

ⱄ **Red Lea, Prince of Wales Terrace, Scarborough, Sat. 4.8.17**

My Darling,   I`m jolly glad you have decided to drop a hint about your leave at last.  If I had been in your place I think I should have done it long ago, but you don`t possess such a cheeky nature as I do. It does seem a shame that you are going into the beastly blinking trenches when I am here at Scarborough. Mother, Mrs Todd and Flossie came yesterday morning with your Mother and five of the kids.

This morning we all went prowling round the old curiosity shops here - I`m frightfully keen on antique furniture, altho` I don`t know much about it.  Pater knows more than I do by a long way.  William comes over this afternoon.  Flossie asked me to go with her to meet him but I should have been bored with them so I`m improving the shining hour by writing to you.

I do hope you will just manage to squeeze Filey in. Florence will love you to go over and criticise the house at Beverley. I tell them both that you and I will learn by their mistakes.

Yours with love, Dora.

ⱄ **Beech Croft, Wed. 8.8.17**

My Darling,   Your letter this morning about leave sounds frightfully exciting. I do hope it will really come off this time. Do be careful in the trenches, and don`t whatever you do get pipped!

We came back from Scarboro` last night. Monday we went to Cayton Bay - it was simply gorgeous and a delightful little spot. Bill Todd came from the Saturday and we had Ma Todd, who is frightfully proper -

however, we managed to survive it. The Crowe girls came over to see us yesterday from Reighton and I am to take you over one afternoon to have tea - we could walk along the sands. They are awfully jolly.

Emma has just written to me in desperation, wanting a maid. She is only managing with one at present.

Don`t catch measles before you come or you will annoy me, Cecil!

Yours with love, Dora.

ᘏᘉᘉ B.E.F., 9.8.17

My Darling,   I haven`t been able to write for the last few days as I have been in the front line, very busy. The Bosche tried to collar one of our forward posts one night, and landed a few bombs right in. We were very fortunate in having no-one hit. The garrison of the post drove the Bosche back with bombs and rifle shots. Three of my men tried to run away and I had to stop them with my revolver. We are having a short rest now in the support trenches before going up again. My servant has just been attending to my shirt, and has killed 17, red, white and black.

Yours with love, Cecil.

ᘏᘉᘉ Beech Croft, 12.8.17 Sunday aft.

My Darling,   I haven`t heard, so I`m hoping the leave isn`t altered. Wire me the train from London and I will meet you - turn up here any time of day or night.

By the way, I am to be the bridesmaid at Flossie`s wedding after all.

I cycled to Beverley and back with the Runton girls and Enid Todd yesterday afternoon and picnicked for tea. I felt a frightful novice - I haven`t cycled for two years since we were at Reighton.

I believe I`ve got a rottenly putrid cold coming. Flossie is revelling in one, so I expect I`ve caught it from her.

Bye bye for another week only. Yours with love, Dora.

ᎧᏅᏅ Beech Croft, 16.8.17

My Darling,   I`m wondering after all if you are starting for home
on the 19th, as you never mentioned leave in your last letter. I feel I
can`t get frightfully excited yet because I`m so afraid it will all be a
wash-out again.

Pater and I have been to see *Intolerance* today - it is a film lasting 3 hrs
and cost half a million pounds, 6,700 performers and 5 yrs to make it.
It`s awfully miserable and a bit "high" too. People seem to be talking
about it so that`s why we went.  It isn`t frightfully artistic either.

Did I tell you I am going to be Flossie`s bridesmaid after all? The
pattern I am sending you is the lining and the flimsy mauve is the dress
itself and the blue is let in under the mauve here and there as I have
pinned it. I haven`t had a really nice new frock for two years so this is
quite exciting.

I`ve been cutting hedges in our front garden this week and it`s getting
to look a little more respectable now.

I often think of the little home we shall someday have and I don`t mind
how tiny it is as long as it is just to our two selves and I shall be there
waiting for you when you get home after being in town all day. I want
you in the evenings more than any other time. Goodbye now, I must
catch the post.

Yours with love, Dora.

ᎧᏅᏅ B.E.F., 18.8.17

My Darling,   The dates have been altered a bit, but I have been
told that I can get my leave on the 29th, so I hope to see you on the
evening of that day. I shall be home for Flossie`s wedding.

We are now in support for a few days. We`ve been having some simply
glorious sunrises here. We have to be up an hour before dawn waiting
for the Bosche to come over, and it`s well worth it for the sunrises. The

trenches have been frightfully muddy. This is my thirteenth day with my clothes on, so you can guess I`m feeling a bit itchy. I killed 11 yesterday, and 2 big ones and a baby today, but I shall have been able to have a good bath in my bucket before the 29th, so your Ma needn`t worry about letting me into the house.

Yours with love, Cecil.

ᘕᘘᘗ Beech Croft, Tuesday 21.8.17

My Darling, I was frightfully disappointed when I got your letter this morning. I was quite expecting you today.

I had an invitation to walk over with you to tea at Reighton and also at Miss Varley`s at Hunmanby, the fiancee of a friend of Pa`s who died. Anyway, I am glad you are coming for the wedding as Queenie and Frank are coming too. You needn`t worry about being frightfully clean either - we can easily sterilise you and carbolise you.

It`s only a week now - pip-pip. It seems too good to be true.

Yours with love, Dora.

ᘕᘘᘗ B.E.F., 23.8.17

Darling, It`s quite certain now that I can come on the 29th. I`m awfully bucked about the sample of bridesmaid`s dress which I got today. You`ll look simply wonderful in it.

I`m having a very cushy time at present. I have eight officers in my company and I let them do the work while I do the foreman stunt.

Yours with love, Cecil.

The bridesmaid's dress Dora wore at her sister's wedding.

(above)

Ouside Buckingham Palace -

Cecil's Father, Dora, Cecil and
his Mother

(right)

Flossie in her wedding dress

A bill for some of the dainties which Cecil ordered from time to time.

PART FOUR:

THE TIME SEEMS TO GO SO SLOWLY

After Cecil`s leave, which ended with the investiture at Buckingham Palace, Dora saw him off at Waterloo...

Hotel Folkestone, Boulogne-sur-Mer, 13.9.17

Darling, I`ve got an empty feeling which in a way makes me feel sick. It`s not sea-sickness or anything like it, just a sadness. I`m horribly miserable about leaving you again my sweetheart, leaving you in body that is; you yourself are here now looking over my shoulder as I write; I can feel you there. I want to put out my arms and hug you, and kiss you again, and it`s partly the knowledge that I can`t that makes me feel sick.

I expect you`re feeling pretty much the same, old girl.

God knows how I long that this War were over, and that you and I were together always.

I left Folkestone about 12.30 and arrived at the above address about 2.45. My train does not go until 11.0 am tomorrow, so I shall get a good rest tonight.

I have struck a very nice room, with a writing table and a little armchair. I am sitting at the table now. My window looks out across the Channel. A gale is coming on from the sea, and it has begun to rain. I think I must have affected the weather. Tonight I shall have a hot bath soon after dinner, and shall read in bed till 10.30. I shall always remember 10.30 to 11.0 each night, as our own particular time.

Your sweetheart, Cecil.

⟪⟫ B.E.F., 14.9.17

My Darling,   I rejoined the Battalion, which came out of the line
yesterday, at about 6.30 this evening. I`m still feeling horribly fed, and
shall do so for a long time to come, until I see you again.

I am quite sure we have come nearer together. I thought we knew and
understood each other as much as was possible the first time, and
although I loved you with all my heart then, my love seems even greater
and stronger now.

It did hurt today, coming up in the train; the country was so beautiful,
and there were ripping little cottages about, and little houses, and I had
to look at it by myself.

Goodnight my sweetheart. Yours with love, Cecil.

⟪⟫ St Margaret`s, Beverley, Friday aft., 14.9.17

My Darling,   I was glad to get your wire and am hoping to hear
that you arrived safely on the other side. After we left you we had
breakfast and then looked at all the shops and caught the 1.30 train. I
snoozed in the train. Missed the connection at Selby and arrived in Hull
about 8 pm.

I never seemed to realise that you had really and truly gone back again
until last night when I was by myself. I felt rotten and missed you so
much - I had a tremendous splash under the bedclothes too. I am sure
we have got to know each other more this time - it isn`t that I love you
more, Cecil, because I couldn`t, but our love is deeper and stronger than
it was, I`m sure.

I`m awfully glad I have been with you in London now - after all, it is an
event of a lifetime. Didn`t I feel proud of my boy when he went into
the Palace and came out again! I felt I was a lucky girl to have a boy
like you.

I`m awfully glad you have seen "Romance" at last and that I was with
you too. I liked it and understood it more the second time.

Here`s some news! Wilfrid Todd came over Wednesday afternoon to see his Ma but she was at Beverley so he telephoned her to tell her he was getting married the next day Thursday (yesterday morning 9.30). Rather a bomb for her, I think. Ma Todd wouldn`t go over for the wedding but I believe her Ma and Pa were there. I think it`s a frightfully risky step to take when they haven`t known each other long - still, it`s their own look-out. Bill seems rather upset about it, as he is responsible for Wilfrid now his Father is not alive.

I am in Beverley today looking after Flossie`s house - they are coming back Tuesday or Wednesday. It has improved since you were here - their bedroom suite is in - some of the living-room furniture and other things too - they have got a lovely comfy settee. It is simply delightful to curl up in. I`m thinking of our little nest today. I like Flossie`s very much, but I shall like ours much better.

Goodbye now, my sweetheart - you have all my love. From your own little girl, Dora.

P.S. Is that too sappy - but I feel it just now.

P.P.S. Please go to the dentist - at once.

༄ Beech Croft, Sunday afternoon, 16.9.17

My Darling,   I am glad you got across the water safely and got a comfy little room. I have come up into my bedroom and am sitting at my desk under the window writing to you. I feel awfully lonely without my sweetheart. I keep thinking about the two Sunday afternoons I have spent with you when you wanted me on your knee and I put my head on your shoulder. I always feel wonderfully happy when I am in your arms Cecil, and when you kiss me. I feel I have your love which means everything in the world to me now. I miss you horribly now that I have settled down at home once more - I keep expecting you to come in and see me. The time seems to go so slowly. I shall be awfully glad when the beginning of November comes and I can get away nursing. In a letter I got from the VAD HQs on Thursday they say you can be drafted abroad after so many months` service in a hospital in England. Would you like me to be sent to France?

I caught the 8.12 a.m. train to Beverley yesterday to let the painters into the house. They have finished all they have to do now and Mother and Mrs Todd go on Tuesday to make up beds, etc., and have stair carpets put down.

I am thinking about you at 10.30 to 11 every night and as soon as I wake up. I have your identification wristlet on at nights - I like to feel it; it reminds me of you.

Your own little girl, Dora.

ൠ B.E.F., 16.9.17

My Darling,   I am settling down and being cheerful and making the best of things and I hope you are doing the same. I have been to Arras today and had lunch at the officers` club there. I nearly came over my horse`s head coming back. We were galloping across some of the country, when we came to a partly filled hidden shell-hole. This evening I have been playing football for the company, and have managed to get both my feet badly kicked, and I can`t get my boots on now.

I suppose Flossie and Bill will have come back by now, feeling very sappy. I think they are very lucky to be able to be married now, but when everything`s over I shan`t be very sorry you and I have gone through the pain of being separated for a long time, although it does hurt hard now.

Yours with love, Cecil.

ൠ Beech Croft, Tuesday 18.9.17

My Dearest,   It was lovely to get another letter from you this morning. Yes, my sweetheart, I still feel horribly sad inside me, because I am wanting and missing you so badly, but I think about all the beautiful days we had together - sitting on your knee with my head on your shoulder and your arms around me. Then there are the thoughts of what is in store for us both when all this is over. I wonder if it will be a greater happiness than we have had during your leave.

Hilda and Mabel asked me to help them to choose the silver wedding present this morning. We went into practically every shop in town and eventually found a silver vase affair. Two names are to be inscribed, and the dates 1917-1892. I feel sure you will like it. Anyway, it was the best we could do in Hull - £6.10.0, and the engraving will be about 7/6. [letter incomplete]

ᘏᘓ Beech Croft, Thursday 20.9.17

My Darling,   Flossie and Bill arrive back today at 4 pm. Mother and Mrs Todd went off at 8 this morning to get everything ready for them.

I have felt much more cheerful and settled the last day or two until today and now I miss you horribly again. I simply can`t settle down to do anything because I want you so badly, my sweetheart. Two big splashes have just dropped on the paper. I know you`ll think I`m an awfully weak and silly kid, but I can`t help it a bit today, Cecil. I think I shall feel better when I can get away nursing.

Hilda and Mabel and I had quite a jolly day yesterday. I forgot to take the key of Flossie`s house so had to get a ladder to climb into her bedroom, only to find her bedroom door locked! However, we went round to a locksmith and borrowed a tray full of keys and managed to find one to fit.

I have sent a parcel off to you today - chocolate cake, flashlight, Bystander and Tatler and the woolly affair that Aunt Yetta made you. She is my great aunt and lives with Frank Willatt`s mother.

Goodbye, my dearest. Yours with love, Dora.

ᗡᎶ B.E.F., 21.9.17

My Darling,   We go up to the line this afternoon. It`s a quiet
part. I got your letter on Thursday and another one yesterday. I have
read them several times and have ached to be with you.

It`s rather sudden about Wilfrid Todd, isn`t it? It`s hardly playing the
game.

I am not putting my big photograph of you on my "dressing-table" but
have got out the one which Harry Quant enlarged. You are giving my
Auntie`s dog a piece of sugar. I think it looks more like you.

I`m not very keen on your VADing in France unless you really want,
because we should probably miss each other when we got leave. You can
do useful work in England. I shall be glad for you sake when you start
again, it will take your mind off waiting.

You don`t stop thinking about me at 11.0 at night just because it is
11.0, do you? I go on till I fall off to sleep. I was thinking for hours last
night.

I had a cold bath this morning in the open. It`s beginning to get a bit
nippy for that sort of thing, and I don`t suppose I shall have many
more.

Yours with love, Cecil.

ᗡᎶ Beech Croft, Sat 22.9.17

My Darling,   I have only time for a scrappy note - have been out
in town this mg - met Hilda and Mabel so took them for coffee and now
I am just going to change for tennis as they expect me at Wilton House
about 3.

I feel heaps more cheerful today and the war news looks more cheerful
too.

Had a note from Marjorie Barker today and she is in Grimsby for a week and wants us to go over - she`s no idea Flossie is married.

Must go now, my sweetheart, so goodbye - life seems worth living today, altho` I wish I could find you at Wilton House.

Heaps of love from, Your little girl, Dora. XX

☿ Beech Croft, Tuesday night 25.9.17

My Darling,   I was so glad to get a letter from you this afternoon - it seemed ages since the last one last Thursday. We had a Zepp raid last night so I felt so dead that I laid down in my room and went fast asleep. I was having a simply lovely dream about you: you had taken hold of my hand and arm and we were laughing and talking and you seemed so real and lovable. Then Mother came in and woke me up and gave me your letter. Whenever I get into bed I think of you, my sweetheart; I think of you puffing your old pipe.

We had quite a lively time last night. The buzzers went at 11 pm. Ma made me get up and we all dozed downstairs and a bomb woke us up at 2.45 am - there were one or two explosions but the searchlights never caught it. They were on until 5 and the relief went at 5.30 but we got rather fed up and went to bed at 4. They have been very near the Naval Hospital and an aerial torpedo went into its garden and broke some windows and the Matron and the Fleet Surgeon nearly got a brick against their heads!

I am sending you some snapshots. I haven`t developed those of the last Sat. at Wilton House yet. I don`t do them myself now as I haven`t had time lately.

Flossie and I saw Hilda and Mabel off to Penrhos again this morning. It reminded me of the times I used to go back. Ma Hovey used to say that our schooldays would be the happiest days of our life but I don`t think so now.

We had a very jolly day y`day - Marjorie came from Grimsby by the early boat and we went out to Beverley for lunch. She likes the house

very much. Marjorie Richardson - swish - looks awfully well, much
better than for some time. She sees her husband for seven days - he
comes up to her about 4 pm and goes at 7.30 the next mg, then he is
out in his submarine in the Atlantic for 12 days.

We met Freda, Enid Todd and Miss Walley in town for tea so it was
quite jolly, except that Enid wanted a pin pricking into her to make her
a little less glum!

I don`t think I shall get a chance of being sent to France now as one has
to serve about six months in a home hospital and I hope the war will be
over by then. I simply couldn`t be in France and know you were on
leave in England. I`d like to have the experience - still, if you don`t
want me to I don`t mind.

Goodnight my dearest. Yours with love, Dora.

∞ B.E.F., Wednesday 26.9.17

My Darling,   I have been busy in the front line the last four days.
We had a good deal of strafing and were lucky in having only two men
hit. I nearly got pipped by a sniper yesterday. I was out in No Man`s
Land in the morning mist and his bullet cracked past my left ear.

We came into reserve last night and are very comfortable. We go in
again soon - but not the front line. After that we are going to have a
rest.

Thanks very much for the cake, lamp etc. We are having the cake for
tea in a few minutes.

We saw the announcement of the Colonel`s engagement in The Times.
It`s very interesting, and we`re frightfully bucked about it.

Yours with love, Cecil.

᷉᷈᷉ St Margaret`s, Friday morning, 28.9.17

My Ownest Sweetest Darlingest Ducksey-Wucksey!!!!
I came here on Thursday to help Flossie to get her house a bit straight -
she is frightfully curious about how I begin my letters to you so I have
written the above for her benefit! Hope it will soak in - and probably
she won`t be so curious in the future!!!

The house is much more finished than the last time you saw it. The
living room is much more livable - huge comfy settee and big arm-chair,
and Bill`s bought a bureau. The spare room is quite comfy to sleep in
too. Some dining-room chairs came yesterday and various oddments
from London.

I have just been talking to your little Ma on the telephone. The girls
arrived safely in Colwyn Bay and Harold is getting on well with his new
governess and has found a double-yoked egg today - I expect you will be
getting another thriller from him soon.

I sent you a rice cake yesterday. It really looked quite "shoppy" when it
came out of the oven so I hope it isn`t biffed much when it arrives.

How do you like the photos outside Buckingham Palace? We all look
rather killing, I think.

Goodnight now, till 10.30. Yours with love, Dora.

᷉᷈᷉ Beech Croft, Monday 1.10.17

My Darling,   I came back from Beverley on Sat. morning and
went down to Wilton House in the afternoon for tennis - it was a
gorgeous day. Mr & Mrs Harvey played and Tommy Dodds. I think
my play was a slight improvement on the frantic and futile efforts I
displayed the last Saturday you were home!

Pater is expecting his Majority in the gazette any day now. He has had a
notice from the War Office about it.

I met Pa this mg and we bought some piano records at Holders. They had a sale and we picked up some ripping ones at 1/- 2/- and 4/- each - good classical stuff too!

I have to meet Miss Stewart who is coming to stay with us a few days - she is Rev C.G. Stewart`s sister - she is rather a nib in the brain line, but not very beautiful to look at. She got her B.A. without ever going to school or college - just being taught by her father.

Goodbye now, my love. I must go. Yours with love, Dora.

ॐ B.E.F., 2.10.17

Darling,   Mother is awfully bucked about the gravy boat your Pa and Ma gave them for their silver wedding. She says she has wanted one like that for a long time.

I`m glad you and Flossie saw Hilda and Mabel off to Penrhos. My schooldays too were my happiest until I became engaged to you, but of course I loved you then in my schoolboy way and used to look forward to Sundays when I should see you in chapel. I used to wonder if it would ever come to what it has. It all seems very great and wonderful to me.

I am in reserve trenches at present, but by the time you get this we shall be well out.

Yours with love, Cecil.

ॐ Beech Croft, Thurs. 4.10.17

My Darling,   We have Mr Stewart`s sister staying with us this week, the one who married Flossie. He was in last night with the Todd girls. Enid was quite sprightly for once.

I have sent off a cake for you today that Mother made. Nellie (Quant) Hemmons` husband has been wounded recently - slightly, in the head and his right hand off. He is in London now and Nellie sees him twice a day. She is really thankful to have him back again and out of danger and to know that he has not to go out again. I know I should be thankful if I were she. One thing I know, if you were to be very badly wounded I should feel sorry I wasn`t married to you so that I could always be with you to look after you better. Still, I don`t think for a moment you will even be badly wounded.

This afternoon we have been with your Mother to the Child Welfare and Food Economy Exhibition at the Guildhall - `twasn`t bad, really - in fact rather interesting. It is supposed to teach poor and dirty people how to be clean and make the best of things and be economical etc, so I hope it will do some good.

Have you got a Cedric Earle a sub. in your company? I spoke to his Ma the other day - I used to go to the same gym class as he and his sister at the Young People`s Institute on Sat. m`gs. I should think I would be about 7 or 8 and he would be about 5 then and I haven`t seen him since!

Yours with love, Dora.

ᘔᘔ Beech Croft, Saturday night 6.10.17

My Darling, Your Mother rang up last night to say that Bob has come home on draft leave and has to leave Hull on Tuesday. Mayfield from Newland Park and Col. Shaw`s other son and someone else are coming out with him.

I heard from you this morning at last after six days. It`s quite an event to get a letter from you nowadays - you must have been kept awfully busy.

It has turned bitterly cold the last two days - hard frost in the early morning - and I have got a blinking chilblain on my left big toe and my left little finger already, so the one on my nose will be arriving shortly. I should expire after the first night if I lived in the trenches - I should be one blinking chilblain all over!

Love and kisses - swishety-swish - from Dora.

P.S. End up your letters with something fresh - they are always the same!

৩৩৫ B.E.F., Tuesday 7.10.17

My Darling,   We are out at rest now, well behind the line. We
moved yesterday in the pouring rain for 10 miles.

I wanted to write to you last night but I was seduced for a game of
bridge, and when I came back the fire was out, and all the fuel gone, and
it was freezing. I slept with my pyjamas and cardigan on over my shirt
and trousers and wore the socks you made for me, and I was still cold.

Your Ducksey-Wucksey letter was very happy in its arrival. As I was
about to open it someone wanted to know how my girl began her letters,
so I showed him.

Goodnight my sweetheart, Yours with love, Cecil.

৩৩৫ B.E.F., Wednesday 10.10.17

Darling,   I got your parcel containing cake and magazines on
Monday. You do make ripping cakes, but I wish I were eating them in
our own home. I hear there are quite a lot of little detached houses at
Hornsea. I asked Grummitt, one of our officers, whose home is there.

I am writing to your Aunt Yetta tonight. I`m afraid I`ve been rather a
long time. The comforter she made has come in very useful lately.

Yours with love, Cecil.

৩৩৫ Beech Croft, Friday 12.10.17

My Darling,   I`ve sent another parcel off for you today, also a
pair of big bed socks to help keep your dear little tootsies warm - they
are a pair of Pa`s as a matter of fact, which he never uses.

The cheeky Base Censor had opened your letter to me - but he hadn`t
crossed anything out, not even the Ducksey-Wucksey!

Dr Blaine inoculated me for the first time on Tuesday last. He said I`ve got 15,000,000 germs - beastly wriggly things inside me. I stayed in bed all day Wed., felt chronic all Tuesday night, but I was alright again y`day.

Wilfrid Todd is having rather a bust-up with his Ma at present. I suppose she is still frightfully mad with Queenie for marrying her boy when she did and has said rotten things about her to Wilfrid and told him never to mention Queenie`s name to her again. So poor Wilfrid has written to Bill and told him he can`t stand it any longer and has written to his Ma never to write to him again as he won`t stand Queenie being treated like that.

Wilfrid is at Grantham doing excessively high flying - so high that he has to feed himself and his engine with oxygen and he got nine days` leave given before he began this so that`s why he got married in it. I suppose Edwin Russell had nine days for the same reason - so he got married to the Pandon girl for it. Since then I`ve heard he has injured his heart or something and has been sent on an instruction job up in Scotland and won`t be going out to France - so they are alright!

All my love, sweetheart. Your own little girl, Dora.

B.E.F., Saturday 13.10.17

My Darling,   I am sorry to hear about Nellie Hemmons` husband losing his right hand, but he is out of it for good now.

You needn`t get the wind up about me just yet, because I`m spending a week or two in hospital. I was playing hockey on Thursday when I slipped and twisted my right knee. In the evening I found three-quarters of my leg black and blue, and my knee the size of a melon. I came to the CCS [Casualty Clearing Station] this morning and am quite comfortable.

I am both glad and sorry that Bob is out here. He has not come in from the base yet. I hope he comes to us.

Cedric Earle is not in my company. `D` Coy owns him, I think - Capt. Monge.

Sorry my "endings up" aren`t more elaborate, but I`m a very simple person you know, and when I say "yours with love" I mean it properly. But here`s an effort.

All my love to my sweetheart from her sweetheart, Cecil.

☿ Beech Croft, Sunday afternoon, 14.10.17

My Darling,   I think I shall rather like house-hunting, just by our two selves. I like Eastgate in Hornsea better than any other part but I believe there are one or two nice little bungalow places near the Mere.

Bill & Flossie (full of married bliss by the way) came over this morning and have just gone back - Bill wants to get some digging done before dark as the garden is in such a frightful mess.

Yours with love, Dora.

☿ B.E.F., Monday 15.10.17

Sweetheart,   Please address your letters to me comme ca:

Capt. C M Slack (4th East Yorks)

49th C.C.S.

B.E.F.

I am very sorry to have to leave my company at this critical time, and just when I was getting to know it too. The day here begins at 5.45 by the orderly waking me up for tea, wash and shave, after which I read until breakfast at 7.30. The M.O. comes round about 10.15, after which my bandages are changed. Lunch at 12.45, tea 4.30, dinner 7.30 is the routine, filled in by reading and making of beds. We are fed very well. I have had roast chicken three times. Now and again a padre is blown in on the breeze, and after gaping a bit, floats out. The sisters are very nice, and so is the doctor, but the night orderly gives me the pip.

Yours with love and lots of these **XXX**, Cecil.

᷒ᷙᷤ Beech Croft, Thursday 18.10.17

My Darling,   It was a surprise when I got your letter this morning
to hear that you were in the C.C.S. Is it synovitis? We had a good
many of those at the Naval Hospital - treated the knee first with opium
and lead dressings for a day or two and then with iodine.

I went to Dr Blaine`s again yesterday for my second inoculation. I
didn`t feel so rotten this time altho` I had a bad night. I went to bed at
10 pm and about five minutes afterwards I saw your face so clearly, but
only for a second while you gave me a kiss - it was so real.

Cecil, I didn`t say I wanted a more "elaborate" ending for my letters -
you silly boy - I said I wanted a change sometimes.

Yours with love (I mean that, old boy, too), Dora.

᷒ᷙᷤ B.E.F., Thursday 18.10.97, 6.45 a.m.

Darling,   The battalion left the neighbourhood yesterday. I heard
the band, but couldn`t get out to see it.

The colour of my leg is changing from black to yellow, and the swelling
has almost gone. The Wesleyan padre blew in yesterday. He`s just like
a piece of suet. He came and sat down on the next bed and just gaped.
I couldn`t very well ignore him and go on reading, so had to talk a bit.
All he said was "yes", "no", "I think so", "perhaps" etc. whilst I did all
the bucking. I didn`t feel very religious about him when he went.

It`s 7.20 now.  I suppose you`re getting up, so I must look the other
way. Goodbye sweetheart, and all my love, Cecil.

᷒ᷙᷤ Beech Croft, Friday night 10 pm, 19.10.17

My Darling,   I was so glad to get your letter to day with your
CCS address.

I know it must be disappointing to leave your company when you have just nicely got it - still, I must say I`m glad you are out of it all for a bit.

12 midnight. The beastly buzzers went at 6.45 pm and the Zepps have been hovering about ever since - we have heard the engines. They were here by 7.20 - have heard about 12 bombs but they must be in Lincs. Mother has been awfully nervous - it will do her a lot of good to get to Nottingham.

The engines have gone away now. Would love to get to bed but I don`t want to miss anything.

We have had Miss Todd and Miss Pallister to see us this afternoon - Miss Todd was quiet for once.

It`s 12.30 now - I expect you have snoozled down into your little cot for the night. Have you got a bird cage over your knee so that the blankets don`t touch it?

Yours with love, Dora.

☊☋ B.E.F., Saturday 5.30 pm, 20.10.17

My Sweetheart,   I keep on aching for you more and more. This continuous lying in bed, with no work to do, gives me more time to "ache" and I expect to go mad in a day or two. It`s just about the time that you`ll be getting ready for me when I come home from work when we`re married. I can see a nice little house, and a nice fire in a cosy dining room, and a table ready for a nice meal, set for two, and such a nice little girl waiting for me - xx. I do love that little girl. It makes tears come to my eyes when I think of it all.

I`m afraid I`ll be getting fat by the time I`m fit again. Last night I had a roast beef-chop, fried potatoes, fresh young sprouts grown on the premises, and a bottle of beer.

Goodnight darling. Yours sappily, Cecil.

🜨 **Beech Croft, Sunday afternoon, 3.45 pm, 21.10.17**

My Darling, I had intended writing to you after dinner but I was reading "The Last Days of Pompeii" which is awfully thrilling. It`s all about Pompeii 18 centuries ago - before it was buried by Vesuvius.

They haven`t got all their pictures up at St Margaret`s even yet! They are really so appallingly slow, but they live in a world of bliss so I expect little earthly things like that don`t worry them at all.

Yours with love, Dora.

🜨 **49th CCS, Tuesday 23.10.17 10 pm.**

Darling, Everyone else is asleep in the ward so I am writing this in bed by candlelight. I expect the sister will stop me if she comes in.

I was allowed to get out of bed yesterday and rest my foot on a stool, and again today. I got two letters from you yesterday via the battalion. The socks haven`t turned up yet. Before I came here I was wearing the other pair you gave me, the ones I was measured for, in bed. There is a hole in one and Bush says he can`t mend it. I don`t wear bed socks in peace time, but it`s cold sleeping in a tent or a hut.

It`s 10.35 now, so I`m going to ponder about something and somebody very wonderful.

xx from your loving sweetheart, Cecil.

🜨 **Beech Croft, Tuesday 23.10.17 noon**

Darling, I expect I shall be going nursing in about a fortnight now, so you must come to my hoppy if that knee of yours doesn`t get better - you know, I hope it doesn`t! I am longing to get away and do something. Hull is frantically deadly in war time.

Your remark about "looking the other way" made me chuckle when I read it this mg - I was just dressing when it arrived, curious to say - I think you are rather a naughty boy, really!!!! I expect I shall have some killing times with you in years to come!! Goodbye now, and don`t forget to wash the back of your neck, even if you are in bed! I hope you are keeping your little moustache the size I like it. Are you?

Bye bye my sweetheart and xxxx bless you. All my love, Dora.

℘ Beech Croft, Wednesday 4.30 pm, 24.10.17

My Sweetheart,   I know just how you feel, sweetheart, in bed all day with nothing to do but think. I always try and make myself do some work - anything to take my mind on to other things, but it`s awfully hard sometimes. That little home of ours seems so far off sometimes, and I think, will this war ever end. I will look forward to the evenings too - we shall have such lovely cosy evenings together.

I have been in town this mg to have a shampoo, consequently my hair is so soft it feels as if it might drop down any minute.

We have breakfast at 8 every morning in Flossie`s bedroom - it is turned into a sitting room now and we light the gasfire. This afternoon I have done the family mending and felt like cussing Pa for having such blinking holes in his socks!

When you said you were so frightfully cold in bed I ordered an extra long sweater to be knitted on our machines for your to sleep in - I am going to send it when you get back to the battalion.

Goodbye my darling - I am thinking of you and loving you just as much as you are about me. All my love, Dora.

℘ 49th CCS, Friday 26.10.17, 7 am.

My Darling,   Good morning, Dora, hope you`ve slept well. I`ve just had a wash and shave, had my bed made, and am waiting for breakfast. Do you still have a cold bath? You`re probably lying in bed funking it.

Yes, it is synovitis I`ve got, and a badly bruised knee. You`re quite right about the lead and opium and iodine dressings. No, I haven`t got a birdcage over my knee.

The padre came in yesterday and bleated a bit, but made up for it by coming again in the afternoon to play chess.

7.30 Just finished breakfast, sausage and egg, both fried. Yes, I`ve been thinking about the home we`ll have. It will have a front door, back door, living room, feeding room, our room, spare room, maid`s room and probably a kitchen, and there must be a fairly decent garden where we can grow our own parsley, and we`ll grow violets and mauve pansies, and bluebells, and if or when we can afford a little two-seater there`ll have to be a shed arrangement for it, unless we keep it in the kitchen.

I can`t think of a new ending at the moment. I think I`ll spend a day thinking some out and writing them in a note-book.

x Yours with love, Cecil.

ༀༀ Beech Croft, Saturday 4.30 pm, 27.10.17

My Sweetheart,   It is just a week today since your last letter was written so I am wondering how you have been getting on.

Father went off to Nottingham this noon so I am all alone until Flossie and Bill come tonight. Your Mother rang up last night to know if I had heard from you.

Miss Walley leaves the Todds on Monday so I expect the family will collapse entirely without her

I have been tidying up generally and have just changed into that warm dark green velvet dress I wore last Christmas and I am now sitting over the fire writing to you and wondering when I shall see you again. I always seem to have to look forward to something indefinite.

Goodbye, my darling - xx for when you go to sleep tonight. Yours with love, Dora.

𝒪𝒴𝒪 49th CCS, Monday 29.10.17 8.10 am

Darling,   Bob turned up last night. His Division is about four miles from this hospital.

I am allowed to get up now and walk a little. The Colonel is in our ward with something wrong with his gut. We have fierce tussles at chess, and at present stand all square, three games each.

The Wesleyan padre has gone to tend another flock. He`s gone to a heavy gun battery and thinks he`s a h– of a brave man.

The sisters who wander about in our ward are very nice. The day sister is a Scotch lassie, and the night one an Irish colleen until a few nights ago when she changed with a nice English girl. You needn`t get jealous about them though.

Your sweetheart, Cecil.

𝒪𝒴𝒪 Beech Croft, Monday afternoon 3.15 pm, 29.10.17

My Darling,   I sent my inoculation papers in yesterday to London HQs and reminded them that I was waiting to be called up.

Pa has come back from Nottingham. Mother goes to the Stewarts at Thirsk tomorrow. I am busy sewing a camisole this afternoon - I am just going to try it, so look the other way! young man!! If you know what a cami is, by the way!

Had quite a nice weekend with Flossie and Bill - made them an apple pie bed on Sat. night, for which Bill nearly murdered me!

Bye bye and be a good boy. Take your medicine when you are told. I shall lead you a life, poor Cecil, and you will say "poor me" in years to come - so after all that will you risk it?

xx sweetheart for tonight, Dora.

𝕺𝕾𝕺 49th CCS, Tuesday 30.10.17, 4.30 pm.

My Darling,   Your letter of the 24th arrived today. The one you wrote the day before hasn`t turned up yet.

I am allowed up every day now, and yesterday I walked 600 yds to the pictures and back.

I have taken the opportunity whilst here of having my teeth attended to. The dentist yanked a piece of bone out of one today.

Yours with love, Cecil.

P.S. I wrote four letters yesterday, a thing I have never done before.

𝕺𝕾𝕺 Beech Croft, Wednesday noon, 31.10.17

My Darling,   I was at Beverley yesterday afternoon. Your Ma, Mrs Baine, Mrs Robert Hall and Kathleen H came over and they all liked the house very much. I did wish we had got our little nest too. I want one more room than you said in your last letter, Cecil. I want a sewing room upstairs like Flossie has. I simply must have one, Cyril - please?xx!!

I have been doing the cooking and housekeeping on my own and haven`t minded so much as when Ma is the boss.  So when I have to look after my own nest I shan`t mind so much after all. I made Pa some delightful soup yesterday.

I simply long to come and talk to you and sit by you and give you a kiss - just one. All my love, Dora.

I do have a cold sponge down every mg - I have a warm bath first though. I shall put a cold sponge on you some morning - when we are married!

𝕺𝕾𝕺 49th CCS, Thursday 1.11.17, 4.45 pm

Darling,   Yesterday and today I have been out for a short walk. My knee`s almost better.

You ask me about the prevailing colour for our living room. I don`t know the mysteries of these things, but light blue or dark blue or mauve, or perhaps orange, or violet, or some other colour.

Love and kisses, darling, from your sweetheart, Cecil.

☙ Beech Croft, Friday 4.15 pm 2.11.17

My Darling,   By your letter yesterday you seem to be much better, toddling about the ward. It will be rather nice having the old Colonel to play chess with.

I haven`t a scrap of news - I feel like a blinking vacuum.  I wish the VAD would buck up and send for me.  I think I told you that Hartley and I want to be in London, but I haven`t told Ma `cause she`d think it dangerous or something silly because of the air raids.

By the way, don`t talk about having "bucks" and being "bucked", Cecil, `cause I don`t like it; it is just as bad to me as "young man" is to you. Do you compris? So you must do as you are told.

Did you know that Capt. Barkworth was killed? It was in last night`s paper.

I`m awfully fed up with life today in fact I feel a positive rebel and a suffragette a dozen times over.  I wonder what you will say to me when we`re married and I feel like a suffragette? It`s awful having a divil inside me.

Goodbye, shall expire soon. A farewell x, Dora.

☙ 49th CCS, Saturday 3.11.17, 1.30 pm

My Darling,   I went for a six-mile walk yesterday to get my hair cut.

I hope the camisole fitted when you tried it on. What colour is it, pink? Why didn`t you send me a pattern? Yes, I know what a cami is. They can be bought at the Army Clothing Dept.

I`m not taking any medicine. If you tell me to take medicine in years to come I`ll swallow it like a lamb. I`d take anything, my dear, if you gave it me. I expect I shall be a very meek and mild husband, and shan`t beat you very much. In spite of the life you threaten to lead me I love you so much that I think I`ll risk it.

All my love, Cecil.

ᘔᘔᘔ Beech Croft, Saturday 1 pm, 3.11.17

Darling,   Have been cooking this morning and made some abso. delish mince- pies. I wish you were here to have one. The divil has gone from me and I feel more or less reconciled for the present to being a potty girl - it`s awfully stodgy being a girl. It gives me the pip pretty often.

I am just going to meet Mother. Pa and Bill have gone with the REs to Brough to shoot on the miniature range. Heaps of love, my sweetheart, I feel awfully sappy today - it makes a big lump come in my throat.

xx from your little girl, Dora.

ᘔᘔᘔ Beech Croft, Monday 4.50 pm, 5.11.17

My Darling,   Mother arrived home on Saturday afternoon and is much better for her holiday. She is going to stay with Flossie tomorrow until Thursday. I am going to turn to the garden tomorrow and begin to clear it all up. Flossie says she is quite fed up with all the afternoon tea parties she is forced to have.

Freda Todd has gone to school today to the convent in Pearson`s Park. I wonder how she will like it - she has never been to school before.

I read in the paper this morning that all soldiers abroad will be given half a pound each of Christmas pudding and the public are asked not to

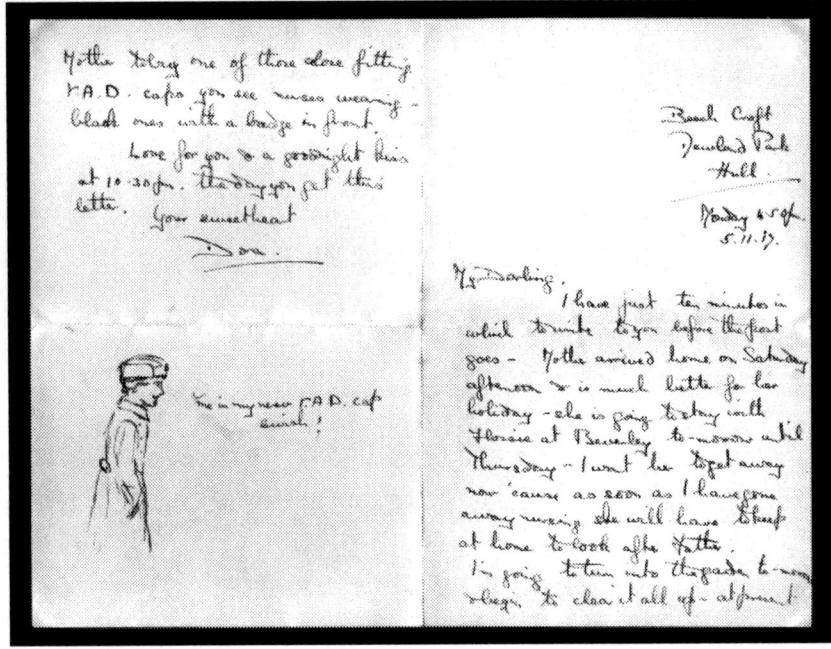

Part of Dora's letter, showing a sketch of her new V.A.D. cap.

send consignments, rather a nuisance when we have already made you a delightful plum pudding!

All the electric lights have just gone off for some reason - but they seem to be coming on again gradually now.

Love for you and goodnight kiss at 10.30. Your sweetheart, Dora.

℘ 49th CCS, Tuesday 6.11.17, 1.45 pm

Sweetheart,   I leave here tomorrow so please address your letters to the battalion again.

Yes, I suppose there`ll have to be a sewing-room affair in our house. Yes, I`m quite keen on gardening. I`m awfully good at sowing potatoes and picking peas, and watering and so on. Weeding is a bit feeding at times though.

It won`t be necessary for you to squeeze cold sponges down my back, because I always have a cold bath before breakfast when I`ve time. I foresee for myself a life of torture. Shall you box my ears too?

Yours with love, Cecil. xxxx

☯ Beech Croft, Wednesday 12 noon, 7.11.17

My Darling,   Your knee seems to be getting on very well - walking six miles too. I telephoned your Mother last night and they had had a few lines from Bob saying he was on his way to the line, so it would be his first time in the trenches - she seemed rather anxious about him too.

You are going to be rather a lamb of a husband - but you don`t need to worry, I shan`t insist on your taking poisonous medicines - but if you need them I shall nip your little nose and make you, Cecil.

The beastly war does seem to hang on horribly - I am quite sick of it and it does make, as you say, our house seem years and years away. I think it would be much nicer to wait till the war is over and you have passed your exam - it is much nicer to go straight to one`s own home than to live in diggings for ages and we shall appreciate it all the more then, and it will make the joy of being together a little greater, don`t you think so?

Yours always with love (that`s a slight variation, isn`t it?) Dora.

☯ Officers` Club, Etaples, Thursday 8.11.17, 3.30 pm.

Darling,   I`m writing to you from the Officers` Club at Etaples where I shall be spending the night. I left the CCS yesterday afternoon, and after the usual slow journey got to Abbeville at midnight. Part of the journey was in a cattle truck whose doors wouldn`t shut but, being an old old soldier I had a blanket and waterproof sheet with me and so wasn`t very cold. I got to this place at 1.30.

I was very surprised and sorry to hear that Capt. Barkworth had been killed. He came out a week or two after our first show. He was wounded on the Somme, and returned about six months ago. He has just had leave. He got his M.C. for good work, and in particular for the day on which he got wounded when we went over the bags, in September last year.

Leave has now been extended to 14 days. I might get mine about next March or April. I`m sorry you`re feeling fed up and suffragettish. I don`t know what I shall do when you feel like a suffragette when we`re married. I expect you`ll stop me smoking in the house.

Yours with love, Cecil.

ᑐᗡᗡ Beech Croft, Saturday 10.11.17

My Darling,   I had a letter from Mrs Stewart on Thursday asking me to go over to Sowerby to help with a Sale on Monday. So here I am in the train - hence the wriggly scrawl.

Yesterday Mother and I went down to your home for the afternoon - all the kiddies looked very well, including your Mother.

I wonder if you could get hold of some more shell cases next time you come on leave, because they would make nice flower vases for our little nest.

I am enclosing you a newspaper cutting about Jack Oughtred - he is in the 1st E Yorks and has been promoted Captain - so he has done well - it is a mistake about his marriage - it is Norman who is expected home on leave anyday to be married. Rottenly stale, I think - two sisters marrying two brothers - don`t you think so?

You are a sausage, Cecil, to say that the war might be over this year,

`cause I`m abso. dead cert. it won`t - and I doubt very much if it will
be next year now - I don`t think for a minute that it will with all this
Italian do and Russia going mad - Lenin in power in Russia seems quite
hopeless when by all accounts he is a paid German.

Always your love, Dora. xxxx

❧ B.E.F., Sunday 11.11.17, 10.30 pm

My Darling,   I got your letter of the 3rd today, forwarded from
hospital. It took me three days to find the battalion which, as you may
have seen from the papers, has been in another show. We had three
officers killed - Barkworth, Drewett and Allchorn - all splendid fellows.
The two latter were in my company, and I am more sorry than I can say
that they are gone. Another officer of my company was gassed. Three
more were wounded.

I`m rather glad, you know, that you wish you were a boy sometimes.
I`m sure we should have been pals if we`d both been boys, but I`m very
glad we`re not.

Love from your sweetheart forever, Cecil.

❧ c/o Rev. C.O. Stewart, Sowerby Vicarage, Thirsk, Yorks, Monday 10.45 am, 12.11.17

My Darling,   I`m looking forward to your next leave now, but
shouldn`t you get 30 days after two years out there?

I got here on Saturday and am having quite a jolly time. Some Jackson
girls who live out in the country came to tea on Saturday and two funny
old maids came in at night - they were killing old fossils: laughed at the
slightest thing.

Later. Went round the market with Mrs Stewart this morning and this
afternoon I have just come in from a walk around the fields with Jack,
aged 9.

I think I shall like Hornsea to live in - it will be lovely having the sea so near and then we shall feel right away from Hull. I hope I shan`t feel lonely during the day when you aren`t there but then I can often come into Hull for the day with you and see people. I shall like the evenings better than any other part of the day though, when you come back and we can have a nice time together in that little sitting-room over a nice cheerful fire. You can sit on one side of the fire and I`ll sit on the other like a nice soggy old pair and never speak a word!!

Goodbye sweetheart, I do love you - my fountain pen is just going out...It has given out now so goodbye, Dora.

🐧 Sowerby Vicarage, Thirsk, Wednesday 5.15 pm, 14.11.17

My Darling,   I am still here - Mrs Stewart asked me to stay till Friday and now she wants me to stay till Monday to cycle over to Northallerton with them on Saturday and I don`t know what to do, so I have written to Mother to tell me.

I went out to tea yesterday and am going out again tomorrow night to some of Mrs Stewart`s friends. The people here are all old who live right in the village - either old widows or old maids. Funny old sticks, some of them and they giggle at the slightest thing - I expect it`s because there is nothing much going on in such a small village. They keep hens here and I fed them yesterday morning. I simply love living in the country - I don`t want to live right in Hornsea nor on the front by the sea. East Gate is rather nice - the part by the old golf links.

The post goes in a minute so I must go. Goodbye, and be a good boy and don`t forget to think about me - goodnight xx darling.

Yours with love, Dora.

🐧 B.E.F., Wednesday 14.11.17, 6.30 pm

My Darling,   I have done nothing since I wrote last except slip about in the mud and bring my company books up to date.

Holtby went to hospital yesterday. I think the assistant adjutant will take his job. I don`t mind, as I would sooner have a company.

I expect we shall be away back by the time you get this letter.

Your loving sweetheart, Cecil.

ᗡᎶᎶ The Vicarage, Sowerby, Friday 16.11.17

My Darling,   I had a letter this morning. I didn`t know about the other officer casualties you had - when I see an E. Yks casualty in the list and don`t know the name I never know which battalion it may belong to.   Personally I think it is a very great blessing you have been away through it all as your coy. has had such a bad time.

That is very cheering news about leave - you ought to be here about the beginning of February. It will be lovely then, sweetheart xx - a twirly feeling of excitement goes down my spine at the thought of it xx!

I am going home tomorrow, Saturday. Mother said I must not stay any longer as it is wartime. Mrs Stewart is going to London on Monday for a few days. A very wealthy parishioner came round y`day morning and said she must come with her - stay at the Hyde Park Hotel and theatres galore - not bad at all is it to have someone take one off for a jaunt like that at a couple of days` notice! It was awfully still last night and I hoped the Zepps would come and wake up all the old maids here, but there was nothing doing!

I`m going to take Jack for a walk early this afternoon and then two more old maids are coming to tea, also an old married fossil too - I might as well tell you there are some potty old bachelors who live here too and from what I have seen of them they are slightly pottier than the old maids.

Goodbye now - I`ll write on Sunday when I get home. xx dearest one, from your Dora.

☯ Beech Croft, Sunday 4 pm, 18.11.17

My Darling,   I got home safely yesterday - the train was $^3/4$ an hour late. I had two hours in York so had a look at the shops and went to the Minster. I got you some sweets at a very nice shop where I had some lunch.

What`s the matter with Holtby - has he got rheumatics? And who is going to be adjutant if you are not?

Bill had to come into Hull for a drill this a.m. so Flossie came with him and got out at Cottingham and walked here and then they cycled back to Beverley about 12.30. They are going to London on Monday - he has some meetings there so she is going to look around. Wilfrid is in hospital there - Millbank or Millbrook - and is to stay there two months for a nerve rest. Queenie has taken rooms quite near and can see him every day.

Kathleen Runton`s boy - Leslie Brown - is coming home on leave in a month`s time and will be here for Xmas - it does make my blood boil when he has only just been here, just a month before you - and he is always at the base too.

I must go and catch the 4.30 post now, and then go and get some tea.

Yours with a kiss, Dora.

☯ Beech Croft, Wednesday 4.30 pm, 21.11.17

My Darling,   Yesterday I went to see Flossie and Bill off to London by the 11.00 - Bill had some paint meetings on and Daddy Runton and two other paint fogies went with them. Yesterday afternoon I did some gardening and cut tons of stuff down. This afternoon I have taken my bicycle nearly to pieces - both wheels off and mud guards - paraffined it all over. I am going to do it up properly, black japan it etc. I haven`t ridden it for about two years so it wants doing up a good deal. Pa is going to buy some new lamps and a carrier so it`s worth it!

Norman Oughtred is married tomorrow to one of the Bentham girls - he came on leave on Monday and has got 14 days, although his sister Mrs Fred Till this mg told me that he had asked for 21 days but didn`t get it. Jack Oughtred was on leave just before the 14 days leave came on - rather a swiz for him.

Love from your sweetheart and a goodnight x, Dora.

ᗕᗐ B.E.F., Wednesday 21.11.17, 9.15 pm

Darling,　　　I got two letters from you yesterday, one dated the 7th, from the CCS. Yesterday I went on a cross-country run. My CSM and I were the hares, and the company followed.

I have hired a large empty room in the village, and am making some tables and chairs for it, and am letting the men have it for reading and writing and cards in the evenings. Have you got any old magazines knocking about? I have also sacked our mess cook and had a big row about some mess kit that has been stolen.

Love from your sweetheart, Cecil.

ᗕᗐ Beech Croft, Friday 23.11.17, 2 pm

My Sweetheart,　　　I am getting on with my bicycle. I have got one coat of black japan on yesterday and am putting another on tomorrow.

Flossie and Bill come home tomorrow. They have seen Wilfrid and Queenie and are not at all struck with Queenie - she was so affected in her manner.

I had a letter from Marjorie Barker yesterday - she is still in Ireland but her Billy has had a bad time in the Atlantic - been forced to dive for a great length of time because of rough seas. The new advance near Cambrai is very cheering, isn`t it?

Goodbye, old boy. I suddenly saw you quite plainly last night when I was just popping off to sleep - it was so nice.

Yours with love and always your sweetheart, Dora.

ᎧᎶ B.E.F., Sunday 25.11.17, 5.20 pm

Darling,   I moved yesterday to a bigger and much more comfortable
mess. There are eight officers in it now. Ruthven has come back from
leave, three new officers have been posted to the company, and the M.O.
and an American M.O. under instruction have joined us for messing.
Another company has come to our village, so we shall be able to get
more bridge etc in the evenings.

It`s turned very cold today, and we had a few snow flakes. I wonder
what you`re doing - sitting on the sofa by the fireside, perhaps. I wish I
were sitting there, with your head on my shoulder.

Goodbye till 10.30, darling, Love from, Cecil.

ᎧᎶ Beech Croft, Sunday 25.11.17, 12.45 pm

My Darling,   Pater had to take his men to Hornsea to shoot for
the day. I haven`t gone to church as Mother didn`t feel up to the mark
this morning but I think I shall rake out the Todd girls for a walk after
dinner.

Heaps of love, Dora.

ᎧᎶ Beech Croft, Tuesday 27.11.17 7.30 pm

My Darling,   I went to the Runtons and Todds last night to ask
for surplus odd books, and Flossie brought me some today - some quite
new Tatlers too. I am making them into two 7lb parcels.

I was busy making you a Xmas cake this mg, then caught the 12.15
train (arriving at the station at 12.14!!) went to Auntie Alice Batty`s for
dinner - and Flossie too - then up to Woodgates to see Marion Ferens
and then to Mrs Holdcroft`s for tea. She was a Miss Storey (dentist).
Flossie and Bill are at the Todds tonight but are coming here to sleep.

Heaps of love from your sweetheart, Dora. xxxx....

ⵏⵗ B.E.F., Wednesday 28.11.97, 5.30 pm

My Darling, Life at present is just one damned thing after another. Parades in the morning, sports in the afternoon, the following day`s programme to arrange in the evening, and the whole intermingled with chits. I have been wanting to write for a pipe catalogue and some boots, but haven`t had time.

Grummitt has been giving me some boxing lessons, but now that we are thoroughly into our "rest" I haven`t time for any more.

Heaps of love from your own boy, Cecil.

ⵏⵗ Beech Croft, 30.11.17,. Friday 7 pm

My Darling, I have got my orders at last! I have to report to Camberley Aux. Military Hospital, Surrey on Dec 12. Hartley goes tomorrow to the same place. Mother and Father don`t want me to go a bit and I believe they think I`m a bit bad to leave them alone, but you know it`s six years since I left school and I have been at home all that time and I feel I shall develop into one of those stodgy girls one sees about town with nothing to keep me mentally alive unless I go and meet some fresh people and learn fresh things. What do you think about it, Cecil? It`s awfully hard to do duty to others and duty to oneself too.

We had Mr & Mrs Hemmons (Nellie Quant) over for the day on Wednesday - he is awfully nice - we did like him. His arm is quite better and will soon be getting his artificial hand. He says what really saved his life was that he knew First Aid so pressed one of the arteries in his arm the whole of the time to prevent haemorrhage. Have you learnt First Aid, because I do wish you would - now is your opportunity, behind the lines with MOs in your mess.

Mother and Flossie want me to postpone going till 1st January so am writing to ask if the job can be left open until then, but if I can`t I shall go. I must catch the 8 pm post now. I did ache for you last night, darling, ever so badly.

Goodnight sweetheart until 10.30, Your own Dora.

෮෬ Beech Croft, 30.11.17, Friday 11 pm

My Sweetheart,   I rang up your Mother tonight and she told
me of the bad news about poor old Bob. They had only had the wire
about half an hour. It really is overwhelmingly sad for them both and
your Mother seemed frightfully upset but is awfully plucky about it all.
She said your Father had just written to you and hoped you would be
able to get over to Rouen to see him. I know now why I was so restless
last night and could not get to sleep.

Goodnight my dearest - I am with you, loving you and thinking about
you all the time. Dora.

෮෬ B.E.F., Saturday 1.12.17, 6.0 pm

Darling,   We are moving again tomorrow. The whole Brigade is
swopping over with another Brigade, rather a silly arrangement really.

I have been arguing with inhabitants about various claims for broken
glass, stolen straw and lost chickens which they say have been done by
our men, and which the men, of course, deny.

Did I tell you I had applied for Paris leave again? I may be going in a
fortnight`s time with Capt. Laverack.

My worthy servant, one Bush, goes on leave tomorrow to Norfolk, and I
shall have to put up with a temporary one. I have had Bush for a year
now. He is a splendid old man, and everyone envies me.

Yours with love, Cecil.

෮෬ Beech Croft, Sunday 4 pm, 2.12.17

My Darling,   So far they have had no more news of Bob, but
Mother seems decidedly more cheerful about him.

I haven`t heard any more about nursing, or whether I have to go on the
12th Dec. or 1st Jan.

What do you think? Wilfrid and Q. Todd are coming to stay at "Carlrayne" [the Todds` family home, across the road from Beech Croft] for an indefinite period. The Dr. thinks "home life" is what he wants so he has got three weeks sick leave. I don`t think they`ll stay longer than a week. Queenie will get tired of their ways of living - there won`t be enough excitement for her, we think.

Heaps of love and kisses, my sweetheart, from Dora.

❦ B.E.F., Tuesday 4.12.17 9.30 pm

My Darling,   I got your letter today to say you had got your orders. Of course your parents are fed about you going, but there are plenty of people whose children have gone off to do their bit and who will never come home again. And then for your own sake I think it would be good to be on your own. I expect you`ll get frightfully independent and will fairly boss me about when I get home.

I`m very sorry to hear the news about Bob. All I know at present is that it is a "serious" wound in the ear. I shall not be able to get over to Rouen to see him. Neither shall I be able to get over to Paris, as we are moving shortly.

Yours with love, Cecil - still badly aching.

❦ Beech Croft, Wednesday 5.30 pm, 5.12.17

My Sweetheart,   It`s awfully cheering about Bob being in Oxford and your parents are more than relieved. You can imagine how anxious they were with a telegram "severely wounded in the ear" - any wound in the head may be mental until one knows for certain. But now Bob has written so it is alright.

We have had Col. and Mrs Bunberry and your Ma to tea this afternoon. He is the C.R.E. for the Humber Garrison. Yesterday we had some officers` wives in and on Monday I was gardening all day and putting in wallflowers.

I got a letter from the VAD y`day to say I must go on the 12th Dec.
Mother seems more reconciled to it.

I am sending your Xmas parcel off tomorrow and am risking a plum
pudding, so to the British Army it is a cake. Please see that the blinking
cooks don`t boil the pudding - it wants steaming for an hour and a half.
If you boil them it takes all the flavour out. Mother has sent you the
chocolates - they are the only kind you can get nowadays.

Wilfrid and Queenie are staying at the Todds and everything is very
sweet and amiable so that`s a good job, although Bill says Wilfrid seems
far from well mentally, frightfully apathetic, takes no interest in anybody
or anything except Queenie. He has 21 days` sick leave and a ground
job in the RFC in England after that, so I don`t know what he wants to
bother about.

Flossie and Bill have come to spend the night and we are expecting Aunt
Alice Batty and Molly for the day tomorrow. Friday Ma and I are going to
Mrs Ferens and Saturday Nurse Waddington is coming for the weekend.

Your Mother has heard thro` a tommy on leave from your company that
you are acting Adjutant and understood you were fighting again at
Passchendaele - or perhaps it was where you had been.

I`m getting quite excited about going away - Hartley went last Sat.

Yours with love, Dora.

ᗺᗻ **B.E.F., Friday 7.12.17 Friday, 9.30 pm**

Darling,   I came back this afternoon from a Cook`s tour of the line.
The C.O., Grummitt, Laverack and I went up. We got shelled a bit up
at the line. A piece hit my helmet.

I forget whether I thanked you for the books. I`m awfully sorry if I
didn`t. The men are very glad to have them.

It will be just a year ago, by the time you get this letter, that you
promised to be my wife. I cannot describe my feelings when I think of

it, or how I have longed and wondered and prayed for years that one day I should have the courage to ask you and that you might love me as I loved you. "Happy" is no description at all. I can`t describe it; it`s like a peep into Heaven.

Goodnight my darling Dora xxxx. Love from your sweetheart, Cecil.

ᗝᗡᗌ Beech Croft, 8.12.17, Saturday 12.45 noon

My Darling, I got your Xmas parcel off yesterday morning and just when I had done it up it weighed over 7lbs so I had to make it into two.

I don`t know Capt. Laverack at all but I believe Eileen Parkin (Dr Parkin`s daughter) knew them. Is he a young or an old bird?

I expect you will be going to Paris almost any time. Tell me all you do and what you see. Please don`t go to the Folies Bergeres this time, will you Cecil. I would really much rather you didn`t - I don`t like to think of you being there. You don`t mind my saying so, do you?

I heard from Hartley this morning. She says there are 100 beds in the hospital but everything is rather quiet.

xx Always your love, Dora.

ᗝᗡᗌ B.E.F., Sunday 9.12.17, 7.30 pm

Darling, You mustn`t get the wind up if you don`t get many letters for the next week, as it is just possible that I may not be able to get any off.

It`s dinnertime now, but I don`t expect anything for another hour and a half as there`s no wood for the fires, which are in the open, it is raining, and all the servants are packing up our valises. There are a lot of minor horrors of the war today. Tomorrow I shall have to rise at about 3.30.

Love from your sweetheart, Cecil.

ᘉᘒ **Beech Croft, 11.12.17, 6 pm Tue**s.

My Dearest,   Just a year ago today, isn`t it?  It doesn`t seem like
it, the time flies so. Will it be very long before I see you, do you think?

It is rotten to think you will be in the line for Christmas - so take care,
won`t you.

I had a letter from the matron at Camberley saying I was not to go until
the 14th as the nurse whose place I am taking does not go until then.

Your Mother has been, and Mrs Todd, also Mrs Taylor, Mrs Leech and
all the Taylor girls - they really are dull. Bob rang up from Oxford this
morning and said his ear was quite healed and has only left a slight scar,
so he will be in Hull for Xmas.

Kathleen Runton`s boy Leslie Brown comes home on the 21st for 14
days - he was only on leave in July, at the end, cuss him - and he is
behind the lines the whole time.

I`m glad you don`t think it selfish of me to leave home - I really was
beginning to think it was too bad, my going away - but I don`t think so
if you think it alright.

Always your love, Dora.

ᘉᘒ **Beech Croft, Friday 14.12.17 In the train, 10 a.m.**

My Darling,   I had two letters from you this morning. I`m glad
I make you more than happy, sweetheart. I knew before I got the letter
that you were having a rough time - I have felt it all this week - so it
shows how near we are to each other. I know you will take every care
but I feel I must tell you again every time.

I am on my way to London now. Your Mother came to see me off - it
was good of her because she has to turn out to meet Hilda and Mabel
this afternoon. Ma and Pa came too. Flossie was supposed to come but
of course missed the train from Beverley.

We are just running through Doncaster now. It is raining horribly - I expect it will be uncomfortable and muddy for you out there. I wish you could come home in the evenings and I could cook you a nice meal and then both sit over the fire.

Goodbye my sweetheart xx. God keep you safely - I am always praying for you.

Yours with love, Dora.

Dora now began her second spell away from home as a V.A.D. nurse, this time in Camberley, Surrey.

PART FIVE:

"DON`T PUT YOUR FOOT THROUGH YOUR SHIRT WHEN WE ARE MARRIED"

Firlands Military Hospital, Camberley, Surrey, Saturday 15.12.17 3.45 pm.

My Sweetheart,   I arrived here safely yesterday. The above is
my proper address. Camberley Military Hosp. is divided into three
different houses in different parts of the town. I live in Firlands with
Hartley and two trained sisters. We have 34 men and have nothing to
do with the other two houses. It is a very easy job compared with
Waltham Abbey. It really was slave work there, but I shan`t get so
much experience as these cases are mostly convalescent. I have signed a
paper today to stay three months, so after that I can get a job with more
serious cases.

I was awfully glad to see Hartley again - we have a room together at the
top of the house but it is frightfully cold up here, but we can go downstairs and sit over a gas fire in the staff-room in our off-duty. On duty
7.30 a.m. - off duty every day from 2 to 3 p.m. and alternate days 3 to
5.30 and 5.30 to 9.0 p.m., and at 9 p.m. we go to bed.

The country is lovely - all pine trees.

It was a fearful job to get a taxi in London. I had to leave my luggage at
one side of King`s Cross and go round to the other to catch one. I wish
I had had you - I don`t like going about London all by myself. Still, I
like being at work again. I do want you, sweetheart. I know you more
now, I love you more deeply.

I don`t like being without my ring - still, I can`t wear it in hospital.
It`s like being without a little bit of you, and I do miss it. I put it on
when I go to bed and try to imagine I`ve got my head on your shoulder
and you have your arm around me and we are both looking at it.

Goodbye, my dearest one, a happy day for you. xxxx for you for Christmas morning!

Always your sweetheart, Dora.

ᘒᘒ B.E.F., 17.12.17

Darling,   We came out of the line last night and this morning we had our first wash and shave for 7 days. I don`t think I`ve been unshaven so long since Ypres.

Thanks awfully for the pudding, cakes, etc and for the purse which I have in my pocket now. We`ve had the pudding tonight. It is, honestly, the nicest one I`ve ever had. A vote of thanks was passed to you by the mess.

We had a pretty cold time up the line. I was fortunate in having a dugout for company HQ which I shared with another company commander. We were very crowded, and buried in one corner was a dead Bosche who strafed `orrid.

However, it`s all over now and we are fairly comfortable in a big draughty hut. It is freezing hard and the fire is out. I am gradually stiffening. I wear your jersey night and day. It`s awfully useful.

Yours with love, Cecil.

ᘒᘒ B.E.F., Tuesday 18.12.17, 6.45 p.m.

Darling,   We only just missed having our hut burned down last night. We had the fire in a tin resting on a piece of corrugated iron; the heat got through to the floor and the wind did the rest.

10.15 p.m. Have just finished dinner, issue of rum, orders, etc. This afternoon I have made another fireplace which works splendidly. I am awfully glad that you are pleased with your new surroundings, and that they don`t work you too hard.

I got Reckitt & Sons` magazine today. I don`t know whether you`ve seen it, but there`s a bit in it by your Pa which I like very much.

It`s 11.00 p.m. now, time for a cold, shivery undressing, and later on dreams of my sweetheart. xx

Yours with love, Cecil.

✆ Firlands, Tuesday 18.12.17, 6.15 p.m.

My Sweetheart,   I seem to have been here ages already. It is my half-day off so Hartley and I went for a tramp over some moors near here. Cecil, you would simply love the country here - gorgeous pine trees all over. We had a slight fall of snow and a fearfully hard frost in the night.

We stayed out for tea today - but don`t think we shall again - as every tea-place absolutely swarms with Sandhurst cadets.

They really feed us very well here indeed - breakfast 8.30 - cocoa 10.15 - dinner 1.15 - tea 4 p.m. and hot supper 7.30 and one of the patients leaves a cup of tea outside our bedroom door at 7 a.m!

The nurses don`t do night duty here as none of them are serious cases - there are two orderlies who come on every night. Hot bath every night - Hartley and I trot off to bed at 9 p.m. and write letters or read in bed and mess around in our bedroom - a nice comfy little room with an attic window - a sort of little turret sticking on to the roof. We have the windows wide open and the breeze on our faces all night.

'X' marks the spot: the attic room at Firlands shared by Dora and Harley.

My hands are beginning to be swollen with the work so my ring will have to say goodbye at night time soon.

The matron is awfully nice but unfortunately is only here for five weeks. She is quite a sport and so decent to us.

Yours with love, xx, Dora.

ᘘᙅ B.E.F., 20.12.17, 8.0 p.m.

Sweetheart,   I have posted today a little Christmas present that I bought in Poperinghe. I don`t know much about these little articles. I`m in fear and trembling that I may have made a mistake.

I have been left behind at the Transport lines whilst the battalion is at the front. We have got a very comfortable place, and a glorious open fireplace and plenty of fuel.

I had lunch and dinner in Poperinghe yesterday with Capt. Laverack, and went to a show in the evening given by the Divisional troupes.

Leave is going very well, and my turn ought to be here soon.

Dinner up! Goodnight darling, till 10.30 and a Merry Christmas. Heaps of love from yours achingly, Cecil.

ᘘᙅ Firlands, Friday 21.12.17, 10.30 p.m.

My Sweetheart,   I`m now adorned in pyjamas and dressing gown writing to my love. The men are getting up a little play for Xmas, but it doesn`t seem a bit like Christmas at all to me.

It is Hartley`s half-day tomorrow so we are going to Aldershot in a motor- bus. I do wish you could come on that course at Aldershot that Holtby came on - wouldn`t it be topping?

Hartley is feeling very fed up tonight - I had been talking about you and said I must write to you tonight, and I think it rather put the cap on things so she has curled up under the sheets - poor kid - I must try not to talk about you at nights `cause it brings back her own boy who`s gone. She`s such a brick generally, but it`s awfully hard for her. I don`t know what I should do if I hadn`t you, my sweetheart.

Always your sweetheart, Dora.

ᘒᘓ B.E.F., Sunday 23.12.17, 6.0 p.m.

Darling,   Your letter of the 18th arrived yesterday. I generally get your letters on the fourth day, sometimes the third. Mine take five or six, I think.

I expect I shall be out of the line by the time you get this, having spent Christmas in a pill-box. I am wondering whether there will be a mutual quietness on the 25th.

We have had two officers mentioned in Sir Douglas Haig`s despatches - Ingleby and Laverack. As they are both friends of mine you see I choose good companions, my dear!

I am living in a cellar or a sewer at present. It`s very low and we can`t stand up in it.

Bush, my servant, having overstayed his leave by one day, has been returned to duty, to my great regret. If he behaves himself I shall probably get him back in a month`s time. He has looked after me for 14 months now.

I hope the camisole reached you safely. Please let me know if it`s all right. There really wasn`t much choice - it was either that or an illuminated card with clasped hands on it.

Goodnight, sweetheart, for a few hours. Yours with love, Cecil.

ᘒᘓ Firlands, Christmas Eve 7 p.m., 24.12.17

My Darling,   You have had a rotten time, old boy and you must be simply starved to death.

I went to the Quartermaster`s to tea y`day - she is awfully nice and lives in the next house to this one. She is a widow - her hubby was something at Sandhurst, I think.

Aldershot was absolutely crammed with khaki, far more soldiers than civilians and a lot of WAACs - I wouldn`t be one for anything; I would sooner be a VAD, although they say they have got rather a bad name in France.

Later, 11 p.m. Hartley came in while I was writing and said the men wanted some music, so I played for them after supper.

I have just read through this - my writing is getting fearfully illegible 'cause I'm always in a hurry - it's a wonder you don't strike. And what tosh I write too!

I feel awfully sleepy, but not a bit sappy - goodbyee. Yours, Dora.

♋ Firlands, Friday 6.45 p.m., 28.12.17

My Sweetheart,   Thankyou ever so much for the camisole. I do like it awfully, and tried it on last night when I went to bed: it fits quite well. I shall keep it for evening dress apres la guerre - it doesn't quite match stiff cuffs and aprons and print dresses. I think it is awfully pretty and you haven't made a mistake about it - although I'd like to know what you know about undies!!?

I got another letter today, written on the 20th. We had presents for all the men on Christmas Day, and in the evening Hartley and I played games with them until 9.30. On Boxing Day we all went to a concert in another house, and last night four of the men gave a sketch, which was quite good. It was my half-day so the VAD cook and I went skating on one of the ponds in Sandhurst grounds. The last time I skated was on Clough Road, towards Stoneferry, and you were there - do you remember?

I had a letter from Frank Sheppardson yesterday (he is a great pal of Bill's, and music master and OTC man at The Leys*). He comes down to Aldershot on the 31st for a month's course. He makes me simply howl with laughter.

Sorry about your old pal Bush. I have got a jolly good orderly at present. He has had trench feet, and slips about in huge shoes, but he sweeps and polishes the floors beautifully. Hartley has given her orderly the sack and got another one.

My chilblains are going on nicely - the one from my nose has disappeared but I have got an awful one on the dangler thing of each ear.

8.30 - later - just had a letter from Ma and she says she feels rather dull without me - I do feel a fearful brute. I do want to put my head on your shoulder tonight, sweetheart. Mother says K. Runton`s boy is on leave now - the louse.

Love & xx - and I like the cami. Your little girl, Dora.

*The Methodist boarding school attended by Cecil`s brothers Norman and Ralph.

⚭ Firlands, Sunday 2.15 pm, 30.12.17

My Darling,   We have just come up from dinner, lit the surgery fire and Hartley and I are writing letters for all we are worth.

I have been here a fortnight already and the time has flown. We couldn`t go skating again after Thursday as a beastly thaw set in and it all went sploshy.

I think the Matron wants the nurses to get a sketch up of our own, so we are going to talk it over at tea today - `twould be rather fun really.

I have had a photograph of Sybil Crowe - she wanted to know how you were. There`ll be no more car trips now - no-one was allowed to motor for pleasure after Nov. 1st.

Things aren`t very busy today so I`ve got plenty of time. Have mended a pair of my lousy socks today. I hate mending socks - I think we`ll both wear sandals when we are married.

Love from. Dora.

⚭ B.E.F., Friday 28.12.17, 10.30 p.m.

Darling,   We went up on Christmas Eve. I was huddled up along-side a pill-box and it snowed and froze, and I was very fed. I got two letters from you on the 26th. One was posted on Dec 14th.

I think tonight is the coldest we have had. I am writing in my British warm, and haven`t got any feet. I expect you`re snugly in bed - I shall be in 10 minutes.

Goodnight my sweetheart. Yours with love, Cecil.

☯ B.E.F., Tuesday 1.1.18, 6.20 pm

Darling,   For once I am warm and able to write comfortably. I got your letter today saying the camisole had arrived. I`m awfully glad you`re pleased about it.

Yes, I remember the time we skated on the Clough Road fields. I came to your house for tea afterwards. I remember Frank Sheppardson at Hymers. He was a prefect when I was a very small, insignificant and naughty boy in the Lower Thirds.

My leave might come through in about six weeks` time, and, on the other hand, it might not.

Your sweetheart, Cecil. Love and kisses.

P.S. Major Jackson sends his New year wishes, and the Padre says he`ll officiate at our wedding if we pay his train fare.

☯ Firlands, Thursday 6 pm, 3.1.18

My Sweetheart,   You have had a rotten time in those beastly blasted blinking trenches - you must be frozen.

I have been awfully busy. On Monday we had the whist drive and we also cleaned out our surgery. As all the patients are practically convalescent the greater part of the dressings are done there. Hartley and I do dressings in turn - one one morning and one the other. But the dressings are nothing here to what they were at Waltham.

I believe I`m getting a bit fatter, Cecil. Hope you won`t stop loving me if I`m a fat dumpling when you next see me, shall you? I`ve got two blobs of ink on a nice clean apron - isn`t it a blinking nuisance?

Heaps of love till 10.30 sweetheart. Your own, Dora.

ᐁᑌᐁ B.E.F., Friday 4.1.18, 11.30 p.m.

Darling,   I`ve struck a very nice comfy billet, a nice bedroom with a nice bed adjoining the mess. My Paris leave has come through. I expect to go on the 6th or 7th.

Major Jackson, I am delighted to say, has got an MC in the New Year`s Honours.

I`m very sleepy, Dora, and I`m going to bed and will write tomorrow.

Yours with love, Cecil. xx

ᐁᑌᐁ Firlands, Sunday 3.45 p.m., 6.1.18

My Darling,   Tea will be here in a few minutes but I`ve just got time to begin my scratch to you. Our men`s concerts aren`t risque - they might be, but the Matron noses into things before hand, I think.

We played a kind of planchette the other night - six of us sat up ever so late with a tumbler, all put our finger on and the electricity makes it move - or the spirit - and it spells out words. I asked it when you would have your next leave and it spelled out March so it remains to be seen. Hartley and one of the sisters went to church this morning - it was simply packed: supposed to be a day of intercession about the war.

I gave Hartley a pipping shampoo last night - I`m quite a dab hand - killed all her chats. I`ll do you some day.

There seems to be a lot in the newspapers about meat being scarce but we don`t feel any scarcity yet, but the Quartermaster gets everything through the Army Canteen so we fare better than other people.*

Till 10.30 - xx sweetheart. Your loving Dora.

* In a letter to Cecil Dora`s mother wrote: "Last week was our first week of meat rations - ours for 3 people cost 3/10 for the whole week. I hope you are still in the land of plenty and no coupons to bother with."

◯𝒱𝒱 Hotel du Louvre, Monday 7th Jan. 1918, 3.30 p.m.

Darling,   Laverack and I arrived here this morning after 20 hours travelling. We have a nice bedroom with a couple of beds and a bathroom attached. I have been saving up for that bath: it`s quite 3 or 4 weeks since I had one.

Love from your sweetheart, Cecil.

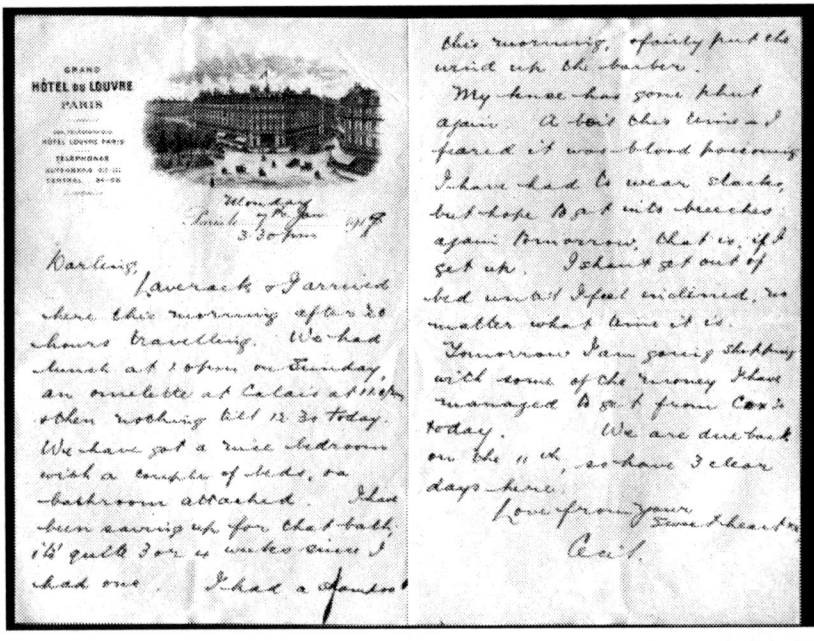

Not only baths - but headed stationery!

ᘐᖆ **Hotel du Louvre, Wednesday 9th Jan 1918, 12.15 p.m.**

Darling,   I`ve just come downstairs after having breakfast in bed.
Laverack and I are having a very good time. We had dinner at Maxim`s
on Monday night, and at Poccardi`s last night.  I`m afraid you`ll be
very fed when I tell you I`ve been to the F.B. after all.  I wasn`t at all
keen but I couldn`t disappoint Laverack without being a killjoy. Last
night we saw quite a good show at the Alhambra and tonight we are
going to the Casino de Paris.

Yours with love, Cecil.

ᘐᖆ **Firlands, Tues. 3.45. p.m., 8.1.18**

Darling,   I had your letter this morning saying you would be going
to Paris on the 6th or 7th - it came through awfully quickly - only posted on the 4th.

The temporary matron leaves in a week`s time and the other one comes
back. She is awfully professional and strict. It`s rather silly in a place
like this so Hartley and I will have to pull our socks up. The sister who
is in this hospital at present worries Hartley and me frightfully. She`s
no good with the men either - they`ve not the slightest respect for her
and they pull her leg and she never twigs. She`s awfully soapy and
slimy too - we don`t bother with the beastly woman. The temporary
matron is a positive gem and frightfully sweet - Hartley and I would do
anything for her.

Yours with love, Dora.

ᘐᖆ **B.E.F., Friday 11.1.18, 10.0 p.m.**

Sweetheart,   We left Paris at 11.30 last night, arriving here at
5.30 p.m. today. We`ve had a ripping time and a good rest. When we
had dinner at Maxim`s we had frog`s legs and they were just like
chicken`s breast.  Another night we had some snails, but I wasn`t very

keen on them. We spent almost all our time sleeping, eating and seeing shows.

I don`t mind you getting a little bit fat, Dora, so long as you don`t get really fat.

10.30. I`m delightfully sleepy, so night night. Yours with love, Cecil.

B.E.F., Wednesday 17.1.18, 10.0 p.m.

Darling,   Have you seen from the paper that our pay has been increased. I get 3 bob a day more - 12/6 instead of 9/6: £54-15-0 a year more.

I`ve got a nice billet here, above the mess.  The weather`s been simply awful for the last three or four days - thunder and lightning, gales, snow, and slush, but it hasn`t been bitterly cold, which is a great deal to be thankful for.

I think I shall dream about you tonight - I`m feeling sappy.

Yours with love, Cecil.xxx

Firlands, Military Hospital, Camberley, Surrey, 18.1.18.

My Darling,   I have been an awfully long time in writing to you but we have been very busy and I have also felt rotten for the last week, like that night before we went to Filey. I felt as if I never wanted to be anyone`s wife - ever.  Don`t be disappointed in me, Cecil, will you, because I simply couldn`t help it.

It`s my half-day today but I have come to bed for it. I have got a stye on my left eye and have fomentations on it.

We had our entertainment last Tuesday and Wednesday. It went quite well and the men said they enjoyed it. I was Cinderella, the Cook the prince and Hartley an ugly sister. We borrowed a stage from the church and had bicycle lamps for footlights. Then we had waxworks. Hartley

was the showman and we dressed up one of the men in an Indian get-up.
We had a VAD scrubbing a Tommy (advert for Pears soap). I was
"Bubbles" - you know that picture - and blew bubbles from a clay pipe.
We had a Tommy chat-hunting in his shirt - shocked Lady Knowles our
commandant - still, it`s only truth brought home! The men roared at it.

I must go to sleep now - it`s 10.30.

Goodnight. Yours with love, Dora.

ᐁᗅᗅ B.E.F., Sunday 20.1.18, 10.0 p.m.

Darling,   I haven`t had a letter from you for eight days and am
wondering what`s up. I got a letter from your Ma yesterday and some
toffee.

Yours with love, Cecil.

ᐁᗅᗅ Firlands, Monday 21.1.18, 3.45 p.m.

My Darling,   I got your letter this morning and the two little
parcels from Paris. I like the tortoise shell pin very much and also the
little bag.

It`s rather nice getting £54 a year more. I shouldn`t mind a rise in my
wages at all but I don`t think I shall get one until I get married.

We`ve got an awful sister as Matron now. At meal times we have to
call each other "nurse" when we always call each other Hartley and
Willie. She is an awful old maid.

We played that game with the glass last night. It said I was weak-
minded, soft and would never develop mentally. We sat up until
midnight so I feel like a wet hen today.

On Sunday we were invited out to tea but at the last minute the cussed
blinking matron made us stay in all afternoon and mend the men`s
shirts. In a bigger hospital one wouldn`t be bothered with cussed little

things because there would be tons of dressings to do. I hate mending
shirts - don`t put your foot through your shirt when we are married, will
you. Still, when I am mending them I swallow all my hate and bring
forth my patriotism! What a game it is!

Heaps of love. You can hug me as hard as you like when you come.
Yours with love, Dora.

⚭ B.E.F., Tuesday 22.1.18, 10.20 p.m.

Darling,   I got your letter yesterday saying why you hadn`t written
for so long. I feel awfully sorry for you. I haven`t felt like that myself
at all and I wish I could be with you to talk to you. I know what helped
you to feel like that - it was my going to the Folies Bergeres when I
knew you didn`t want me to.

I bought myself a present in Paris - a long Meerschaum pipe which I
shall probably break in a week or two.

The Colonel`s leave has come through today. It`s special leave, to get
married, but it`s not public yet. He`s got a month. Major Jackson is
top of the roster now, and I follow him.

Goodnight sweetheart. I do hope you feel alright by now. Your lover,
Cecil. xx

⚭ Firlands, 23.1.18 Wed., 4 p.m.

My Sweetheart,   I had a half-day yesterday and went to
Reading with Sister Cecil. We push-biked to Blackwater and caught the
train. It began to rain when we got there so we went to the pictures,
walked around town, had tea and caught the 6.25 back. We had to
push-bike without head or tail-lamps on our return. I had an old hand
candle lantern with some pink blotting- paper in one side and it acted as
head and tail lamp. However, we got in without running into a bobby.

This matron is turning out a bit better, but we have to mind our p`s and q`s.

I can`t think how to amuse you this time on leave - I`ve got no
weddings or anything like that for you. I`m sorry I`m not at home to
send you any cakes now - cakes in the shops aren`t a bit worth buying
and then it`s so awfully difficult to get provisions of any kind nowadays.
I expect Flossie`s hair will be white with all the worry. She is a louse -
she hasn`t written to me for ages.

Heaps of love and xx from your little girl, Dora.

B.E.F., Sunday 27.1.18, 9.15 p.m.

Darling,   Sorry you don`t like the Matron`s diciplinary [sic]
actions, but perhaps it`s good for you, young woman! I don`t make
holes in my shirts with my feet, so it will be a great relief for you.

We leave our little village tomorrow. We`ve had quite a good time and
the last week has been beautiful Spring weather.

I`m going to bed now. It`s only 9.45, but I shan`t be asleep by
10.30.xx Yours with love, Cecil.

Firlands, Sunday 3 p.m., 27.1.18

My Darling,   It`s a gorgeous day and Hartley and I have brought
chairs outside and are sitting in the sun. I have been printing some
photos that I took of the men last week. One of the patients - an awful
chatterbox, hawker of cabbages in private life! - keeps coming and
talking to us and breaking my thread!

Father thinks the war is going to be over soon now. He has written to
the War Office and told them that unless he can be sent out to the BEF
he would prefer to take up his civilian occupation again and do the
Volunteer job in the evenings as his present work doesn`t give him
enough to do.

Did you know Harry Quant is engaged? A girl about 25 who lives at
Ferriby and is in Reckitts` office - very good at languages and learning

Russian. I believe they are to be married this summer, very quietly. I hope the C.O`s wedding goes off well. Is she a young girl or an old one? All the old men seem to be getting married just now.

Heaps of love and hugs from Dora.

ᘓᘰᘊ Firlands, Wednesday 5.30 p.m., 30.1.18

My Sweetheart,   I haven`t heard from you for five days, so perhaps you are moving again. The guns were going last night so we wonder if the aeroplanes were anywhere near us. Hartley and I often wish they would come - `twould lend a little more excitement to the place. I have heard a rumour that Waterloo Station has been damaged.

Must put a clean cap and apron on now - I haven`t been out of uniform for nearly seven weeks - I haven`t any mufti with me at all.

Heaps of love and goodbye until 10.30, and then xx. Your little girl, Dora.

ᘓᘰᘊ Firlands, Saturday 4 p.m., 2.2.18

Darling,   I haven`t asked Commandant about leave yet - I have to put it through the Matron first (the stinker!) but I think I shall be able to wangle it - shall run away if I can`t. Will it be about the 16th? What about meeting you in London to go up to Hull? Couldn`t you send me a wire direct from Folkestone? I get in at Waterloo and could meet you there - I go from here via Ascot and not via Woking, and that means arriving at a different part of the station.

How could you think it is good for me to be ruled with a rod of iron by this matron! She is coming round to our views more, I think. You spelt "disciplinary" without an s, young man, too!! This stinking Matron has got the Royal Red Cross 2nd class for sticking in this place two and a half years and nursing convalescents only! I heard one Tommy say that if she`s got the RRC he ought to have the VC for being nursed by her!

Bye-byee-ee & xx from, Dora.

☿ B.E.F., Monday 4.2.18, 9.45 p.m.

Darling,   I expect to be home about the beginning of March. I`ve been very busy lately; we`ve been moving every two or three days. I am living in a stuffy little pill-box now, but have been in many worse places. We are having a very quiet time in the line.

I knew about Harry Quant but said nothing, as Father told me as a secret. I think the girl the C.O. married is about 30.

By the way, I expect to be a pukka captain soon. It`ll mean two bob a day more.

Goodnight sweetheart for a few minutes while I look through a few papers and make my bunk tidy.

Yours with love, Cecil.

☿ Firlands, Monday 3.45 p.m., 4.2.18

My Darling,   I`ve got the full fortnight`s leave - pip pip - and am quite wild with excitement! I have agreed to stay on for six months here, but it`s worth it.

Can`t write any more now, old boy - I`m too excited.

Heaps of love and xxxxx...............Dora.

☿ B.E.F., Saturday 9.2.18, 11.30 p.m.

Darling,   I got your letter today saying you had got your fortnight`s leave. I can`t say on paper how glad I am. Please don`t say that it`s a fixed date because I`m not at all certain of coming before the end of the month - Major Jacko`s such a silly old fool for one thing and I daren`t leave him. When I do push off I`ll send you a wire from the boat. If I come via Boulogne and Folkestone I think I get to Victoria about 1.30 p.m. I will push off across to Waterloo and having found out what time to expect a train from Ascot direction will wend my way to the 1st class waiting room and wait. I will first of all though see if there is a telegram for me at the RTOs office at Victoria and also at Waterloo.

The colonel`s marriage has come off, and we got a piece of cake today. His wife was pulled up for driving a car without a licence a few days afterwards and was let off with a light fine and costs only as a wedding present.

It`s midnight now, and I must to bed. Goodnight my love, and heaps of these xx (they`ll be pukka ones soon, won`t they!)

Your sweetheart, Cecil.

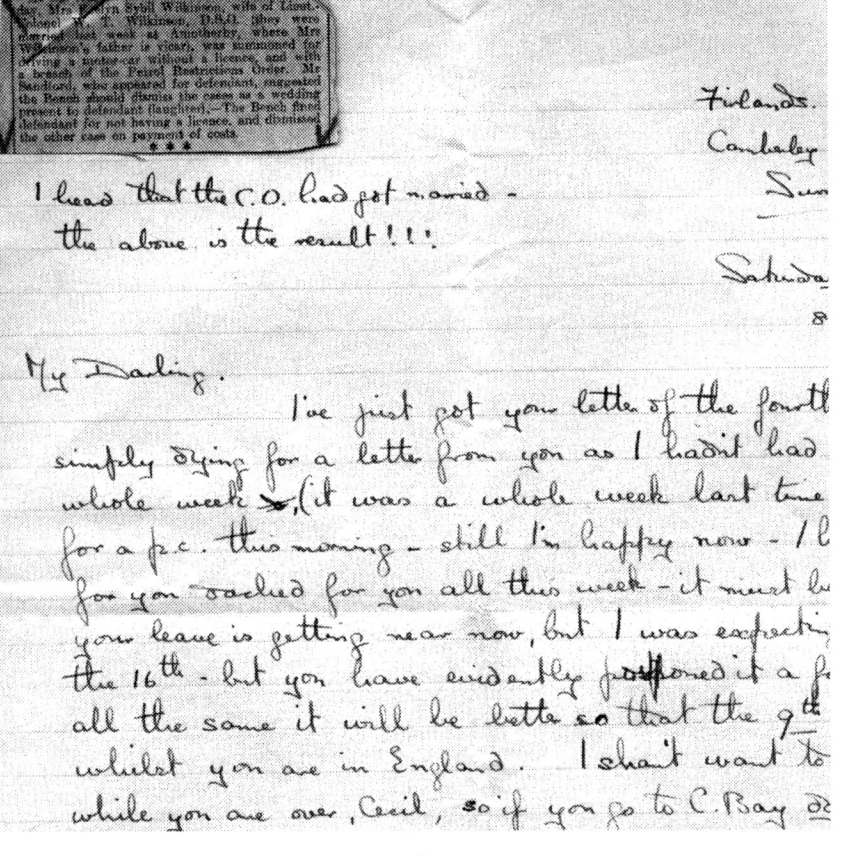

ℭℛℐ Firlands, Saturday 9.2.18, 8.30 p.m.

My Darling,   I`ve just got your letter of the fourth. I
have longed for you and ached for you all this week. I shan`t want to
leave you while you are over, Cecil, so if you go to Colwyn Bay with your
parents do take me with you, sweetheart.

I`ve signed on till the end of June to get this fortnight`s leave, but it`s
worth it - I haven`t told Mother yet.

Saturday 1 p.m. Hartley and I had promised to fetch Sister Sheppard
from "Durley" at 9 p.m. and I felt tired and rolled into a nice hot bath
(aren`t you envious) and rolled off to bed thinking about you, my
darling. I do wish this war were over. I`m so tired of it, Cecil, and we
could be always together and have our little home. In the evening the
Aldershot bus drivers and conductresses came here and gave the men a
concert - an awful wash-out and "high" too!

On Weds Nicholson, Cook Stanford and I went to quite a good concert
got up by one of our nurses - a Curzon girl - relation to the Earl Curzon.
It was very good except for Lady Irene Curzon who sang - simply terribly
- and everyone encored her for pure cussedness.

Sister Sheppard goes for good tomorrow and the real Matron comes
back. Hartley and I are heartbroken. The real Matron is worse than this
Stinking Sister so Hartley and I have decided to pass away quietly during
the night.

It`s a gorgeous day - Hartley, Stanford and Willatt are going for a trot
with Stanford`s dog - a Dalmatian.  Goodbyee - don`t cryee!

I do love you. I`d love to give you a hug xx. Dora.

ℭℛℐ B.E.F., Tuesday 12.2.18, 3.15 p.m.

Darling,   I am sitting in a pill-box which a nice kind German made
for me. It is entered by a small hole at each end and is divided into four
compartments. There are three little bunks in it - two on the floor and

one on top. I repose on the top one and shake dirt down into the Major`s eyes, and when he snores I give an extra shake and fill his mouth and he stops. The bed is a little bit awkward as it`s made of sandbags stretched across from two poles, and in some parts it`s tight and in some it isn`t, and I have to place myself carefully to correspond with the curves.

I get very fed up with life until it darts across my mind that in a few minutes or so I shall be on my way to England and I feel as though I want to bite things and get up and shout.

The weather is wonderful for winter, the mildest we`ve had out here. Tablitz, the American M.O., wonders what all the talk about winter hardships means. We like Tablitz very much. He chews gum, of course, and "guesses" things.

Yours with love, xx, Cecil.

Dora (lower left) at work in the Firlands.

◯◯ Firlands, Wednes. 13.2.18, 5.45 pm

My Darling,　　　　I`m frightfully excited about seeing you again.  My leave isn`t fixed - it`s just when you get yours.  Hartley will push on extra hard with my work so that I shall be able to catch the next train after I get your wire.  I shall be in uniform as I`ve got no mufti with me so don`t miss me or cut me dead!

I had a long letter from Emma today - her hubby is at Blackpool training R.A.M.C. officers and she is with him but expects to go to Italy soon. I`m sending you some more snaps - I`ve got an awfully sappy grin and Hartley is tons nicer than that. How do you like the surgery one? I`m just tying up a stump. The one with the arm off looks like the Venus de Milo really. I expect Ma will be shocked with me for taking such photographs! I got one of the men to click it.

The bell has just gone for a concert, so goodnight my love.

Your own little girl, Dora.

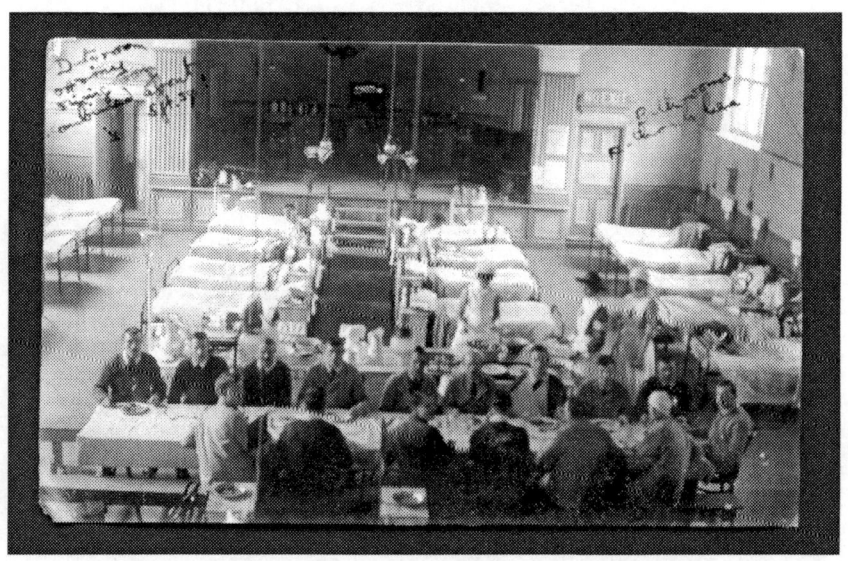

Mealtime on the ward.

Dora (standing) and Hartley outside Firlands.

✎ Firlands, Friday 9.15 p.m., 15.2.18

My Sweetheart,   We have been busy today - had General Sir
Archibald Murray (late of Egypt) round the hospital - he`s in command
at Aldershot - also Surgeon General Bourke and Lord Cranbourne the
A.D.C., who looked an awful weed. Gen. Murray seemed an awfully
nice old bird and talked to us in a fatherly manner!

I`ve had my bath now and am just going to brush my hair and hop into
my bunk. Heaps of xx sweetheart, Dora.

ᘏᙏᘞ B.E.F., Saturday 16.2.18, 11.30 p.m.

Darling,   Just a short note to let you know I still remember you.
I`ve only got one more short tour in the line before I see you again. I
expect to get leave via Calais and may wangle an afternoon boat on the
day prior to my leave, arriving in London about 9.30 p.m. I could then
meet you in the morning and we could have some lunch and go down by
the midday or afternoon train. I`m afraid 9.30 p.m.`s too late for a
theatre, and I suppose convention doesn`t allow it either.

Yours with love, Cecil.

ᘏᙏᘞ Firlands, Sunday 5.15 p.m., 17.2.18

My Darling,   It might be next week that I see you again - it
sounds awfully near when one thinks of it like that. If by any chance
it`s a Sunday or too late to wire, the telephone number is 128
Camberley. I believe we`re on the Aldershot exchange, but I`m not
quite sure.

Mrs Earle`s future daughter-in-law is coming to do my work for me
while I`m away, I think.

Heaps of love and xx. Goodbye my love, Dora.

ᘏᙏᘞ Firlands, Wednesday 6.15 p.m., 20.2.18

My Darling,   I`m living in fear and trembling that leave will be
stopped any day because of German pushes one hears about - it gives one
the pip absolutely.

I get dreadfully excited when I go to bed. There`s only another week in
February now - perhaps in your next letter you will be able to tell me the
date! I`ve got a pink chilblain on my nose and on both ears - the latter
as big as frying pans - so you may get an awful fright.

Your own sweetheart, Dora.

ᐒᐒ **Firlands, Friday 22.2.18, 10 p.m.**

Darling,   I got your note of the 16th yesterday and I hope the turn
in the line is over by now.

You were in the gazette yesterday and are still only acting captain as
long as you are Adjutant - and on lieutenant`s pay. It is a swiz after 3
and a half years of war.

I nearly set myself on fire the other day - I was warming a long roll of
cotton wool over the gas fire when it caught fire and was blazing in a
second and burnt a bit of the chair too - it was quite exciting really.

By the way, I must tell you I`m learning to play bridge. The other
night I was playing with Cookie and Sister and Hartley - I made a little
slam with "no trumps" - playing with dummy! I felt an awful nib!

Goodnight my love - xx, Your little girl, Dora.

ᐒᐒ **B.E.F., Saturday 24.2.18, 9.30 p.m.**

Darling,   I shall be coming along in the next leave allotment in four
or five days` time. I feel quite pleased about it.

We`ve had a rather more strenuous time than usual in the line, and for
the first 40 hours I only got 1 hour`s sleep.  I`ve got a ripping little
room here - the best billet in the battalion. In fact, I`m so comfortable
that I don`t want to come home a bit!

I shall probably let you know today or tomorrow what day I`m coming.

Yours with love, Cecil.

PART SIX:

BUT IF YOU ARE THE ONLY OFFICER LEFT, WHAT HAS HAPPENED TO THE OTHERS?

Calais, 15.3.18, 8.10 p.m.

My Dear Little Girl,   I rang you up at about 2.0 p.m. from Dover, but you were out, so I rang again at 3.30 but couldn`t get through. I only just caught my boat at 4.30 and nearly got landed for a day`s duty at Dover. I am spending the night here, as my train does not leave till 2.30 p.m. tomorrow.

I had a little weep on the train after I said goodbye to you at Farnborough. It`s horrid being parted like this. I have come to this hotel with a fellow who has just got engaged this leave, and he simply hates coming back, but he doesn`t hate it any more than I do. Every time I leave you I hate it more, and I do love you so much. I feel very weepy tonight, darling, but I can`t help it.

Your sweetheart, Cecil.

Firlands, Friday 15.3.18, 6.20 p.m.

My Darling,   I was awfully disappointed to be out when you `phoned this afternoon, but Hartley and I are out between 2 and 3 every day. I got your wire this morning about 9.30. I have felt such a blank emptiness without you near me. How did you get on after I left you at the station? I hated leaving you and felt rotten when your train had gone - I had to wait 20 minutes outside the station for a bus. I got back about 8.30 so Hartley raked me some supper out and I picnicked in the surgery as the staff dinner was done.

If that blinking C.O. doesn`t send you on six months` light duty soon I shall write him a jolly severe chit.

Goodnight my sweetheart - I shall think of the goodnights we had on C. Bay promenade at 10.30

xxx and love for you from Your little girl, Dora.

ᐯᐯ BRITISH OFFICERS` CLUB, Etaples, 17.3.18, 10.0 a.m.

Sweetheart,   I have arrived at Etaples again, and am searching for the battalion. Summer time is in force here, and I am an hour ahead of you. Let me know when your time in England alters.

I think I shall go to Le Touquet and Paris-Plage for a small walk.

Goodbye, darling. Yours with love, Cecil.

ᐯᐯ BRITISH OFFICERS` CLUB, Etaples, Monday 18.3.18, 10.30 a.m.

Sweetheart,   There is no train going towards the battalion today. One of our officers turned up this morning, from a course. We are going to Le Touquet shortly, for a round of golf.

Your loving sweetheart, Cecil.

ᐯᐯ Firlands, Monday 10 p.m., 18.3.18

My Sweetheart,   I`m awfully sorry about the telephone on Friday - it was Sister Smith who spoke, the stinking sister who has turned out to be quite decent and sporting.

I have had a brilliant idea today - to keep rabbits in a hen-house we have here - grow little bunnies and sell them for food. There is a lot of it in the papers nowadays. I`ve ordered a book on rabbits and we are going to get permission. I love rabbits - they are so fluffy and lovable.

I walked to Frimley church yesterday mg with the stinking sister and was on duty for the rest of the day. On Saturday Hartley and I went on a gorgeous walk thro` Sandhurst village and Wellington College grounds (the boys` school). It`s simply huge and absolutely gorgeous. The Leys isn`t in it at all - two of Matron`s boys go there.

I must roll into my nest now - I`m so sleepy. Your little girl, Dora.

ᘓᘍ B.E.F., 20.3.18 Wednesday, 10.0 p.m.

Little Girl,   I joined the battalion again yesterday, getting here in time for lunch. I have the most comfortable billet I have had out here - a large room with a nice big comfortable bed, two tables, a bedroom sofa, carpet on the floor, and a little dressing & washing room attached.

Goodnight, darling. I can`t write or say how I love you - I am bottled up and bubbling over with it. Yours for ever and ever, Cecil.

ᘓᘍ Firlands, Wednesday 20.3.18, 6.45 p.m.

My Darling,   Isn`t it gorgeous weather! I`ve felt like a young lamb all today, and one of the men has marked out the tennis court so we hope to get a game before the weekend. The rabbit hutches are progressing - a one- legged man is making us a couple with all the bits of wood we can pinch when the gardener isn`t looking. We are starting with two pairs, but heaven knows how many we shall end up with!

Hartley goes for ten days` holiday next Monday, so I shall be doing double duty - still, I should rather do that by far than have an extra bloke in. Hartley wants me to meet her for a day in London on her return journey if I can get off for the day.

Goodnight, sweetheart, our time changes to summer-time on Saturday midnight.

Yours with love, Dora.

ℭℛ𝔊 **Firlands, Friday 22.3.18, 5 p.m.**

My Darling, I wonder if you have gone into this beastly German push that the papers say is on just now.*

I have been playing tennis from 2 p.m. to 4 p.m., and I played yesterday too. It`s simply gorgeous and I am hoping to get a good deal of practice and shall give you a good whacking in the holidays.

We have a good rabbit hutch and run made and are now waiting to buy some rabbits. Heaps of love from Your little girl, Dora.

* In a letter to Cecil dated 21.3.18 his father wrote: "According to today`s papers the big German attack has commenced." [The German Spring Offensive had indeed started. The 4th East Yorks, as part of the 150th Brigade in the 50th Division, was involved in the Battle of St Quentin and the Somme, from 21.3.18 to 1.4.18. The only communication Cecil was able to get out during this period was a Field Service Post Card on 29.3.18.]

ℭℛ𝔊 **On 24.3.18 Cecil`s mother wrote to him as follows:**

Wilton House, Mar. 24th 1918

My dear Cecil, It is glorious weather here, and hard to believe that such awful fighting is proceeding in France. From what we have heard today we fear you are in the thick of it. May you have strength for all and be safely kept. It is an anxious time, and we are all wondering what the next few days will bring.

Flossie Todd has been `phoning and enquiring about you. Everybody is very anxious about friends at the front just now. It scarcely seems possible that a fortnight ago we were all having such a good time at Colwyn Bay. God bless and keep you safely, my dear boy.

Your loving Mother, Winnie Slack.

☯ Firlands, Sunday 24.3.18, 12.25 p.m.

My Darling,   I have just two or three minutes to write to you
before the men`s dinner. The summer time bill comes into force this
morning and Hartley and I distinguished ourselves by being late down
for breakfast. I dreamt of you last night and it was so very real - I was
sitting on your knee in my white muslin frock and you were kissing me.

Isn`t this German push wretched - altho` people here seemed to expect
it and don`t think it is so serious. I do hope you are not in it. In
today`s paper Paris is being shelled at a range of 62 miles. I didn`t
know it was possible - is it?

Do take care my darling - I feel awfully anxious. Goodbye, Your little
girl, Dora.

☯ Firlands, 27.3.18 Wednesday, 7 p.m.

My Darling,   I am wondering if you are in the thick of it or still
in that nice comfy bedroom you had when you wrote last Wednesday.
I`ve been frightfully busy since Hartley went off - only off duty for
about an hour each day and during that time I have played tennis with
the men as Matron won`t let them play by themselves..

I had your first letter from the battalion on Monday. I like to know
what your billet is like and then I can just picture you in bed looking like
a little rabbit I should imagine - we have got three rabbits: they came in
yesterday as a present.

Commandant wants us all to be vaccinated again as there is smallpox not
far away. We have a man in now who has boils because he`s been
vaccinated. I don`t want boils and don`t want smallpox so I don`t
know what to do.

Goodnight my darling - a kiss from your own little girl, Dora.

ᏒᎶ Firlands, Good Friday 29.3.18, 10.30 p.m.

My Darling,   It is 10.30 now - just the beginning of our half-hour - but I do wonder what you are doing. I have felt awfully anxious about you and am simply longing for a letter. Practically all the men have gone from a simply huge camp near here. The war news seems to be a wee bit better - but it's pretty bad and I think the struggle must be terrible.

I sent you an air cushion and some soap on Wednesday. I have blown the cushion up and it seemed quite comfy for my old noddle.

We have had another rabbit given us, called Flopsy and we have another called Mopsy and also one called Albert. They are sweet little things and I love them already - I shall never want them to be sold or killed. I think we must keep bunnies as well as hens in that little nest of ours. I have been very busy - gave my orderly who looks after my wards and bed- patients the sack on Wednesday because he didn't polish the floors well enough. I got another one but the old one reported yesterday and cleaned all the windows without my asking him to do them!

The cook's dog was awfully wicked on Tuesday morning and stole the week's meat that was allotted to the staff - consequently we nurses have been living on bully beef. We only get a half pound of meat a week each now and a quarter pound of butter which includes all butter for cakes and puddings etc - still, we thrive quite well on it.

Goodnight, and take care of yourself my sweetheart, Your little girl, Dora.

ᏒᎶ Firlands, Monday 10.45 p.m., 1.4.18

My Sweetheart,   Still no news of you - the battle seems to be worse by the papers. It is just a week tonight since I had your last so you can imagine how lonely I feel.

Hartley comes back on Weds and wants me to meet her in London. I can only get half a day off and then probably the Col. may be coming over to inspect the men - and if he comes I can`t go because he sees all the dressings. The Col. is a beastly nuisance and he`s awfully dull and slow.

The rabbits are going splendidly - we have got Peter, Alf and `Erb, Flopsy and Albert - and two or three more are coming soon. Albert is huge. I`m going to put a dog collar on him and take him for a walk.

I am longing to know what you are doing - it makes me awfully anxious all this waiting and no letters. Do you think the war will be over this year?

It is ten past eleven now so I must roll into bed. I am sitting in pink and white pyjamas writing to you.

Your little girl (xxx) Dora.

ᏓᎶ Cecil`s parents now received Field Post Cards letting them know that he was still alive. His mother replied as follows:

Wilton House, Ap. 4th 1918

> My dear Cecil, We were greatly relieved to receive postcards from you this morning (dated Mar. 24th & 29th) as we were very anxious after reading the news in the papers. The accounts are sickening and heart-rending. Father is looking very worn and weary. He has been very anxious about you.
>
> Goodbye my boy, God bless you and keep you. Much love from, Your affec. Mother, Winnie Slack.

ᏓᎶ Firlands, Thursday 4.4.18, 9.40 p.m.

My Darling, I had a field p.c. from you yesterday dated the 29th and one the day before too - so it was a relief.

Hartley came back last night & I was glad to see her as I was really beginning to feel lonely. I didn`t get to London as we were so busy - filled up the hospital choc-a-bloc.

It is just three weeks ago tonight since I saw you last. I knew you would
have to go through an awful time and that`s why I hated leaving you so
much.

It is only 10 p.m. but I am going to roll into bed now. Goodnight xxx -
your little girl, Dora.

ᴅᏅᏅ Firlands, Saturday 7.15 p.m., 6.4.18

My Sweetheart,   I had a fearful nightmare about you on Thurs
night - woke up and found myself out of bed, howling. I expect you
must have been having a particularly awful time. We got some men in
on Thurs who have been wounded recently and they said it`s awful - I
feel such a long way from you.

I shall want to keep hens, rabbits, bees and a dog in our home - will that
be too many for you?

It`s just post time, so I must fly - it`s dinner time too. Goodbye, my
dear old boy, heaps of love and a nice kiss from your little girl, Dora.

ᴅᏅᏅ On 8.4.18 this brief communication from Cecil arrived at Firlands:

B.E.F., 8.4.18

Darling,   Just a line to let you know I have come safely from 14
days` Hell, and am quite well and fit. I am in command of the battalion
at present and am very, very busy. I am the only officer who has been
through the whole show.

I will write the moment I have time.

Love from your sweetheart, Cecil.

Firlands, Tuesday, 9.4.18, 7.15 p.m.

My Darling,   I only received your very short note this morning,
but you`ve no idea how thankful I was to get it, darling - it`s just a
fortnight since I had a letter. Things must have been more than terrible.

I knew when I said goodbye to you you would be going through
something, but I didn`t think so much. But if you are the only officer
left - what has happened to the others?

There must be a Providence that keeps you safe. I do wish I could be
with you only for a few minutes. I might be a little comfort for you.
You could put your head on my shoulder then. Dinner bell, so must go.

Goodnight my dearest, and God keep you safe, from your own little girl,
Dora xx.

P.S. I am always thinking of you, darling, and I`ve prayed for you too.

Letter from Cecil`s mother, 10.4.18:

Wilton House, Ap. 10th 1918

> My dear Cecil,   We are all full of gratitude to God for again
> sparing your life. Truly it seems almost miraculous that you have
> escaped unharmed through such dreadful dangers. Your letter received
> this morning sends a deep thrill through one.
>
> A further claim is being made for men up to 50 years now, and medical
> men up to 55, ministers and clergymen included.
>
> Bob is at Reading still...training with the R.F.C.
>
> Your affectionate Mother, Winnie Slack.

B.E.F., Saturday 6.4.18, 9.45 p.m.

Little Girl,   It really is very wonderful that I am able to write this
letter. I am the only officer in the whole Brigade who has been through
the whole show. I am unable to give you even an idea of the hell we
have been through. Every day it has been a matter of minutes and inches between capture and worse. My helmet is dented in two places.
Twice I have had to cross 400 yds with bullets churning up the ground
all around me. We have been hunted.

I think the tide is turning. We helped to check it in the end. Our battalion made several counter-attacks, one of which I led myself, and was first in the German trench. I fired 40 rounds into the retreating Bosche at 50 yds range.

I could write sheets and sheets and sheets on what we have experienced had I the time and no censorship. But I have kept a skeleton diary and shall be able to tell you the whole story one day. The C.O. was hit about halfway through.

I am my own Adjutant and up to my eyes in reorganisation, etc. For two days I was in command of the Brigade. There were heaps of your letters for me when I got back. I am awfully glad about your feeling I was so near to you at times, because I had the very same dreams myself - I had you in my arms and kissed you and could feel your face on mine. My dreams were in odd hours during the night and day.

Yours with love, sweetheart, Cecil. xx

ᖴ B.E.F., Monday 8.4.18, 10.0 p.m.

Darling,   We have been moving again today, and have landed up in quite nice billets - too good to last long, I`m afraid.

I am going to try and write a full diary bit by bit of what has happened during our last show.[1] I shall send a copy to you and a copy home, leaving out names and other things which might annoy a censor.

Major Jacko rolled up yesterday and took command, to my immense relief. He hasn`t any kit, poor old man - the Bosche took it all.

I`m awfully glad about the rabbits. I know you won`t want to kill `em, but you`ll have to in the end - there`ll be such heaps of them. I had a boy and a girl one once, but Mother made me give them away.

Poor old Bush got pipped - a nasty cut in the head, but not dangerous.[2] I have got a very good man in his place.

Your sweetheart, Cecil.

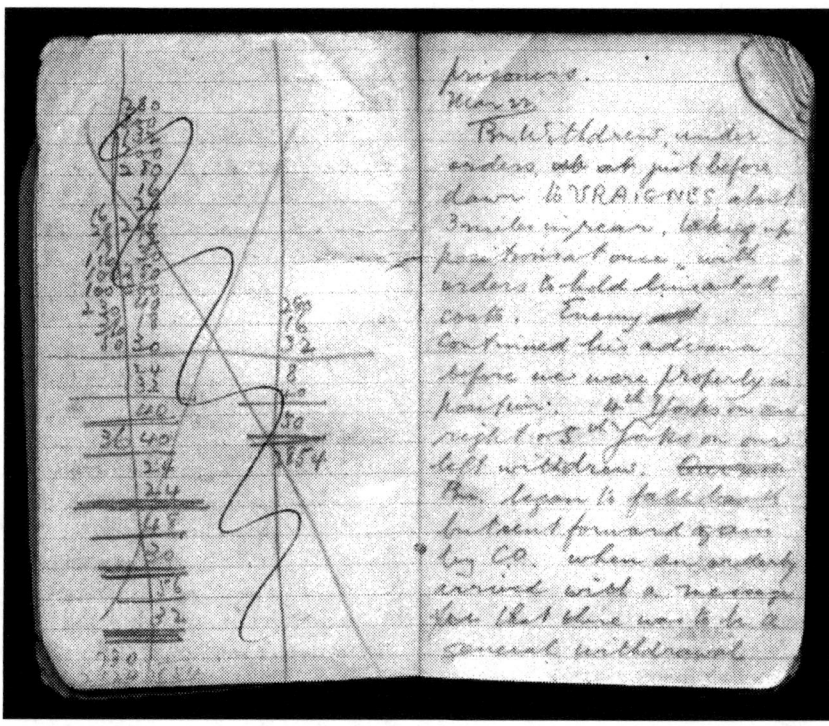

[1]   This he did: lengthy extracts are to be found in *Grandfather`s Adventures in the Great War*.

[2] This undated letter from Pte Bush was later received some weeks later:

> Dear Sir,   I thought I would just write a few lines to you to let you know were I was got to I am got to Blighty I have got a broken nose two cuts on the head one Fractured bone in head the Doctor say it was a close one for me but thank God I am feeling better again and glad of it I thought my number was up.

୨୨ A series of Dora`s letters written at this time failed to reach Cecil; they were returned to her marked "Undelivered", and appear to have remained intact until her daughter-in-law opened them some 75 years later.

ᘔᘓ Firlands, 11.4.18 Thursday, 3.30 p.m. [Returned undelivered]

My Dearest,   I got your letter yesterday telling me what you had been through. Words cannot express what I think. It absolutely bowled me over at first to know what you had suffered but I feel awfully chirpy now when I think of you out of the line. I have been very down at heart the last fortnight because I`ve known you were in the thick of it. I don`t know what I should have done if I hadn`t been frantically busy all day long.

Hartley and I are having a bust in London tomorrow as a great favour from the Matron as we have come up to scratch very well for the old general. Hartley wants us to stay the night at a girl friend`s of hers who is a doctor and has a flat, and come back by the first train for duty 7.30 a.m. But I don`t know whether it can be wangled or not. I`m quite excited about a day`s razzle!

It is tea now, so I must say goodbye until 10.30. With all my love, your little girl, Dora.

ᘔᘓ Firlands, Saturday 10.20 p.m., 13.4.18 [Returned undelivered]

My Sweetheart,   I read in the paper of the terrible fighting that is still continuing - it is very comforting to know that you are out of it.

I`m awfully lonely tonight. I want you here, darling, to cuddle and love and kiss me. I simply couldn`t live without you - it would be just half of me taken away.

Was the C.O. badly wounded? I shall be awfully glad to have a diary of what you have done and it will be a little history to keep of what you have been through.

Hartley and I had a good day in London yesterday. We caught the 10.20 express from Farnborough. We met two schoolfriends of Hartley`s for lunch. We just talked and looked around the shops, and I bought a sweet pale mauve hat and cotton frock to roll in the garden when you come on leave - I look quite a lamb in them.

Sunday morning 7.15. I was too sleepy to go on last night, and the
Sister came in and gassed for about half an hour. The woman bores me
stiff - she is such a worm, but not bad really. Hartley`s friend wanted us
to stay the night but they wouldn`t let us because of the air raids -
frightened we should be bombed. I was fed to the core. You would
have let me stay, wouldn`t you?

I must get up now, darling. Your little girl does love you and want you
so badly. Dora.

ᙣᙦ Extract from an eleven-page letter to Dora from her mother:

Newland Park, 14.4.18

> My dear Dora, It is more than a week since I wrote to you and
> I have four letters from you unanswered, but I have had so little time. It
> is more than awful what Cecil has gone through & I do think he ought
> to come home - his nerves can`t stand much more. If they send him
> again I consider it is more than brutal - but just because he is brave and
> willing they send him. I suppose it would not do for you to write to the
> Colonel, but do try and persuade Cecil to get out of it - somehow. I am
> only truly sorry he is not suffering from shell-shock or nerves.
>
> Mrs Slack got the same little note as you. I will send you the type-
> written copy which they send me, also the other one. Your father has
> brought his typewriter home, so has done them.
>
> Dr Baine says he is full up with the war and says all these politicians
> have been too slow in sending out men - he says he would drown them
> all and men like Cecil ought to be put in Parliament and tell us what is
> wanted...
>
> It`s very wet and stormy, I don`t think the Zepps will come tonight.
>
> Much love from your old Mother.

ᛟᚷ Firlands, 16.4.18 Tuesday, 6.45 p.m. [Returned]

My Darling,   The cook has gone back to her home in Camberley
to sleep and so her bedroom is empty - but it possesses a gas fire. It is
very small - right at the top of the house - but we`ve asked the
commandant to let us have it for a sitting-room and we`ve got it! Pip
pip! Before, we have had to sit in the surgery or in the staff-room where
we have meals - an awful room with a settee in but full of big black cup-
boards - we call it the mortuary - well, we brought that settee upstairs
and put our photographs in the room - you are on the right hand corner
of the mantlepiece and Hartley has her old boy who has gone west on
the other end of it. The couch is just big enough for two comfortably.
I`m up here all alone at present and the gas fire is lit and it`s so comfy -
but yet so empty because it just wants my old boy on the couch, with
me on your knee.

There is awful snow today and it`s frantically cold turning out to see to
the rabbits. We`ve got Albert, Peter, Alf and `Erb, Mopsy, Popsy,
Arabella, Teddy, Ginger and Pickles now.

We haven`t been playing tennis lately, the weather has been so blinking
awful - but I hope it stops the blinking Germans.

Do ask the Colonel or Major Jacko if you can`t be put on a safe job of
something or other - I don`t mind as long as you are safe.

Goodnight my darling, I would love a nice kiss from you now - a nice
long one.

Your own little girl, Dora.

ᛟᚷ Firlands, Friday 19.4.18, 10 p.m. [Returned]

My Sweetheart,   It is just a week ago tonight since I had my
last letter from you - so I`m simply longing and aching for a p.c. even. I
simply detest the thought of your being in it again, my darling.

We are awfully busy now - bigger cases coming in - and I`m kept hard at it all day, but I`m very glad to have such tons of work `cause I should go mad with nothing to do but dwell upon what you are going through. Poor old boy, I wish I could be with you at 10.30 each night for our half-hour to love you and stroke your dear old head.

One of our bunnies has died tonight - a young one called Ginger. I think it was pneumonia. I did hate to see the poor little thing snuff it - but we gave it a dose of chloroform.

Goodnight my dearest. I have to be up earlier nowadays to get all my patients washed and dressed before breakfast. We are sitting over our gas fire - I`m in my pink and white striped pyjamas you may be interested to know. x - that`s a nice long kiss for you.

Your little girl, Dora.

ᖇᖙ Dora`s father now wrote to her at Firlands with news received from Cecil`s father:

Beech Croft, 21.4.18, 4.20 p.m.

My Dear Dora,   Mr Slack has just rung me up - he has heard indirectly from a girl engaged to young Cliffe, an officer in the 4th Yorks (NOT East Yorks) who returned from leave and joined his battalion on the 8th April and was suddenly called on together with the 4th E. Yorks to repel an attack on either the 9th 10th or 11th April. Cecil was in it with a company. There was a mix up of Portuguese Bosche and English. Cliffe went to talk to Cecil who was on his right and just afterwards he (Cliffe) remembered no more: he was gassed and sent to hospital and he has now written to his girl and says in his letter "I wonder what has become of Cecil Slack".

That is all we know at present. It is post time now.

Much love, Daddy.

ᛜᚱᛞ Letter from Cecil`s father:

Wilton House, 21.4.1918

My dear Cecil,   We have been wondering how you have been
faring during the past fortnight as we have not had a line since receiving
your letter of the 6th, but we take it for granted that you have had
another very rough time in the second big push of the Germans. How
you have been able to stand it after the gruelling you received on the
Somme I don`t know.

You have now completed your third year in France. You have seen
much of the dark and hideous side of life and death but you have been
mercifully preserved and we have this satisfaction, that you have worthily
upheld the very best that British manhood stands for.

Several very anxious relatives have asked me if you can give any
information about the following:

2nd Lt G B Petersen, formerly in our office. His mother is greatly
distressed.

2nd Lt F Stephenson - later news is to the effect that he is a prisoner.

Private F A Tiplady 200437.

Private Hanson - I gather his brother has written you direct.

Bob writes quite cheerfully from Reading. He has "busted" one bicycle
and reports that the second is falling to pieces. If he treats aeroplanes in
the same way he will be in for a rough time.

With love from all, Your affectionate Father, W.H. Slack.

PART SEVEN:

"I TOO KNOW WHAT `MISSING` MEANS"

℞TELEGRAM DATED 22.4.18 ex INFANTRY RECORDS, YORK, ADDRESSED TO Mr W H SLACK

> REGRET LT C.M.SLACK 4 EAST YORKS REGT WAS
> REPORTED MISSING 8-17.4.18 THIS DOES NOT NECESSARILY
> MEAN THAT HE IS KILLED OR WOUNDED. INFANTRY
> RECORDS NO. 1 YORK

℞ TELEGRAM DATED 22.4.18, 3.50 p.m. AND ADDRESSED WILLATT, FIRLANDS MILITARY HOSPITAL, CAMBERLEY

> CECIL IS REPORTED MISSING. MR SLACK HAS JUST HAD
> WIRE TO SAY CAPTAIN C M SLACK REPORTED MISSING FROM
> 8TH TO 17TH APRIL THEN THE WAR OFFICE ADDED THIS
> DOES NOT NECESSARILY MEAN HE IS KILLED OR WOUNDED.
> ALEC WOODS WAS MISSING FOR SOME TIME NOW
> REPORTED PRISONER. MR AND MRS SLACK ARE VERY
> HOPEFUL, AND SO ARE WE. WRITING. MOTHER.

℞ No sooner had the telegram arrived - and been passed along the line - than sympathetic notes were being received. Mrs Slack wrote to Dora within hours:

> My dear Dora,   By this time your poor heart will be aching after receiving the telegram from your Mother. We received it at 2 o`clock just as we were finishing dinner, and immediately telephoned your Mother.

> I cannot believe that our dear one is killed. Major Jackson is also wounded and missing, which is worse. Dr Jackson and Will [Slack] are

arranging to get into communication with the Geneva Red Cross and try to get further information.

We hear tonight another officer, Capt. Ruthven is missing also, so it looks as though they have been surrounded, and this makes me more hopeful that they are prisoners.

Many thanks, my dear, for your letter with all details. I went to see your Mother this afternoon. She has been quite upset, but we must all keep up heart. If only his life and senses are spared.

Much love and prayers from, Your boy`s Mother, Winnie Slack.

℞ The following undated note was received from Dora`s colleague at Firlands, `Cookie`:

Dear [Dora] Willatt,   I must just leave you a line before I go to give you my deepest sympathy. I too know what missing means and though I am sure there is every chance that all is well I know what the days of waiting are. I feel for you with all my heart and hope that you may very soon hear the good news you wait for.

Yours, Cookie.

℞ On 22.4.18 Cecil`s father wrote to, Mrs Brealy, wife of the Minister at the family`s Wesleyan chapel:

My dear Mrs Brealy,   Just a line to say that after an anxious ten days the dreaded telegram has just arrived - Cecil is officially posted as "missing". His Battn or Brigade had just gone into rest billets. They were called up on the 9th suddenly owing to the breakdown of the Portuguese. I hear the fighting resolved itself into a melee and I know Cecil`s disposition. He would fight to the end rather than give in, unless it meant the certain destruction of his men. Whatever the outcome may be I know he has done his "best".

I hope you are fully recovered. Yours sincerely, W.H. Slack.

೧೮ On 23.4.18 he wrote to Cecil`s C.O., convalescing in England:

Dear Colonel Wilkinson, I was very sorry to hear from my son, Cecil, that you had been wounded. I trust that you are recovering.

In all probability you will have heard of the unfortunate experiences of the Brigade since it was moved from the southern part of the British line to the Armentieres section. It was only yesterday that we received official information that Cecil was "missing" and that Major Jackson was "wounded and missing", also that captain Ruthven was on the missing list. I would like to take this opportunity of thanking you for your kindness through a period of nearly three years to my boy. When he was at home on leave he spoke to me several times of your splendid services, and of how much he was indebted to you.

Yours sincerely, W.H. Slack.

೧೮ The Colonel`s reply makes interesting reading, for he makes the assumption that Cecil is still alive:

Dear Mr Slack, It is most awfully kind of you to write and give me the news I have been simply longing for. I am so awfully sorry about your son - "Simon" I call him - I somehow can`t believe it. But there`s one great comfort and that is that he is now certain of his life.

It looks as though he is almost certainly a prisoner - and do you know I cannot help feeling almost delighted to think that he is out of that ghastly shambles now. He has always been so absolutely ripping and reliable. I never could trust anyone further than him.

May I offer my condolences to his fiance but, like me, she really and truly ought to be relieved of a considerable amount of her anxiety - if she knew how terrible it`s been in France the last month she would be.

Yours v. sincerely, W.T. Wilkinson.

ᘎᗊᕥ On 24.4.18 Mr Slack wrote to Cecil`s friend Ingleby:

Dear Captain Ingleby,   I received this morning an
envelope addressed to my son which has been returned from the Front,
and which contained documents intended for yourself.

My son Cecil so frequently referred to you that I do not hesitate to write
in order to find out if you can get any information as to what happened
on the 9th, 10th or 11th April. I think I know a good deal of the story
from what I have read in the papers, and also from what I have gleaned
from a Sergeant of the 4th Yorks (not the 4th East, but brigaded with it)
that although on the 9th the Brigade went into action about 1,200
strong, when it was paraded on the 11th there were only 60 present. I
know that one has to discount a good deal of verbal reports.

It is just possible that there are a few of the men who can tell you
something about Cecil, or the last they have heard of him, and whatever
the news may be, good or bad, it will be a relief to have it.

I am, Yours sincerely, W.H. Slack

ᘎᗊᕥ At some stage Cecil`s father had received - or would receive - this letter
from Ingleby dated 16.4.18:

My dear Mr Slack,   I am just writing to let you know as
much as I can about Cecil. We came in for a stunt the very first night
up here and from what I can hear Bttn Headquarters were surrounded
and cut off and I should think it most probable that Cecil was captured
with the others. We hear rumours that Major Jackson was only
wounded, but nothing definite. Anyway, I hope for the best and will
immediately let you know if I hear anything. With deepest sympathy in
your anxiety,

Yours very sincerely, N.W. Ingleby.

℞ Meanwhile fragments of news came in from fellow officers and men of the 150th Brigade, presumably in response to Slack`s inquiries:

copy of letter dated 28.4.18:

> Dear Mr Slack,   ...The last time I spoke to Cecil was about 3.30 on the afternoon of the 9th (our first day of action). We were dug in along the river bank. Of course, I can`t say definitely when Cecil became missing but I think it must have been some time during the 11th as we had a very rough time of it that day and had very hard work to keep our end up. I don`t know anything about his refusing to retreat, but I don`t think they were surrounded on the 10th because I know we were in touch with them on that day
>
> Excuse my pencil scrawl but I write whilst laid in bed.
>
> Yours sincerely, W.A. Cliffe, 2/Lt 4th Yorks R.

℞ Extract of letter dated 29th April from Sgt J.F.W. Westoby, 1/4th E.Y.R. Ward 10 Main, Norfolk War Hospital, Norwich. [Westoby was employed at Reckitts` Canister works.]

> ...I saw both officers [Major Jackson and CMS] on the night of the 9th/10th. We held the Bosche during the day of the 9th through the night till about 5 p.m. of the 10th, when whoever was on our flanks were forced back and we were under fire on three sides. We hadn`t an earthly chance....We had to retire in good order. I saw three officers who got through then - Captain Barr of `D` coy, and Lts Elvin and Cheverton-Brown. We never saw any more of Regimental Headquarters. I think it was Lt Brown who told me they were taken. They were in a shell-hole covered in with corrugated iron during the day of the 10th. We could not get in touch with them; neither Headquarters nor Company runners could get through; it was too hot. I was hit on the morning of the 11th. I cannot see Captain Slack killed. I have faith that he will yet be heard of. There is a lot of doubt as to what happened, and I never saw anyone nearer than we were to Regimental HQ.

ᘔᘓ Dora, too, picked up snippets of information at Firlands and relayed them to Cecil`s father:

"...I have managed to get some news of the Brigade, through a Sergeant who came into hospital yesterday. This Sgt is in the 4th Yorks and was wounded on the 11th inst. The 4th East Yorks and the 4th and 5th Yorks make up the Brigade, as you know.

During the fortnight that Cecil wrote and told us about, they were on the Somme, and on the 7th they came up to Bethune and had very good billets there, thinking that they were on their way to a quiet part of the line, up North. On the morning of the 9th they were suddenly called up to Estares but the Germans took the village late in the day. On the 10th they were relieved by another Division, only to be sent to relieve others who were just hanging on at Neuf Berguin. The following day this Sergeant was wounded, so he knows nothing more about them but they had again had very severe losses and only a few of the Brigade were left."

ᘔᘓ Nellie Hemmons wrote on 30.4.18:

My dear Dora,   I have heard from Ferriby that Cecil is missing and know, dear girl, how helpless and desperate you will be feeling [see her letter of 13.10.17]. I feel I cannot write commonplace words of sympathy but you know how keenly I feel for you during this time of suspense, for honestly I feel it is just that. Cecil has proved himself so full of resources, so capable a soldier that I feel certain he will come through alright.

With all my love, Your sincere friend, Nellie Hemmons.

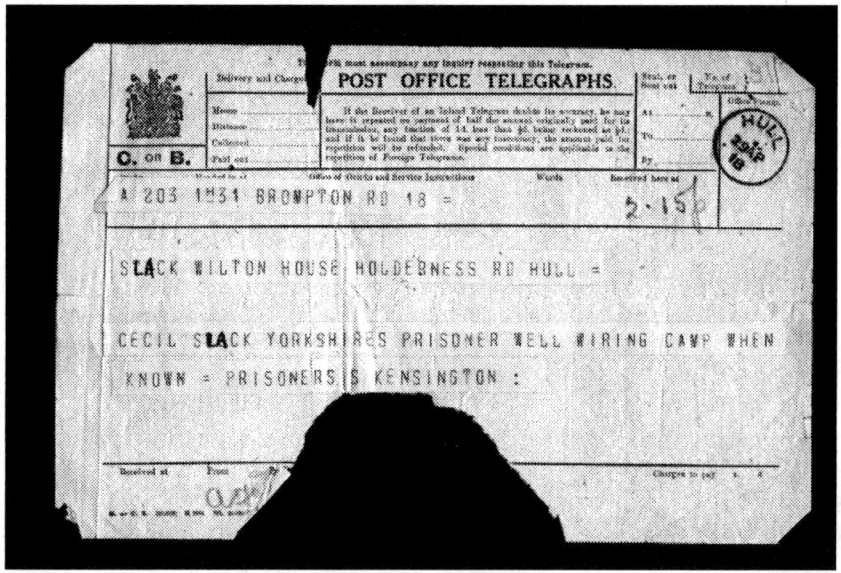

POST OFFICE TELEGRAPHS.

A 203 1ᴹ31 BROMPTON RD 18 =

SLACK WILTON HOUSE HOLDERNESS RD HULL =

CECIL SLACK YORKSHIRES PRISONER WELL WIRING CAMP WHEN

KNOWN = PRISONERS S KENSINGTON :

ᏫᎶ But a week after the telegram announcing that Cecil was missing came the good news the family had been praying for:

rec`d Hull 2.15 p.m. 29.4.18, To Slacks:

> CECIL SLACK YORKSHIRES PRISONER WELL WIRING CAMP
> WHEN KNOWN - PRISONERS S KENSINGTON

ᏫᎶ This was immediately relayed to Dora at Firlands:

Telegram handed in Hull 3.30, 29.4.18; rec`d Camberley 4.18 p.m.

To Nurse Willatt:

> CECIL PRISONER WELL WIRING CAMP WHEN KNOWN
> WILLATT

ᏫᎶ Bill & Flossie added their good wishes...

Telegram rec`d Camberley 11.08 a.m. 30.4.18   To Willatt, Firlands Hospital:

LOVE AND ALL GOOD WISHES TO YOU AND CECIL SIMPLY
DELIGHTED CHEERIO BILL AND FLOSSIE

...as did Tom Ferens:*

rec`d 1146 a.m. 30.4.18   To Slack, Reckitts, Hull:

THANK GOD ALLS RIGHT SEEN RECORD INFORMATION
TAKEN FROM POSTCARD WRITTEN BY CECIL HIMSELF AND
WIRED FROM FRANKFURT REDCROSS FERENS

* the Hull M.P., philanthropist and founder of the city`s University

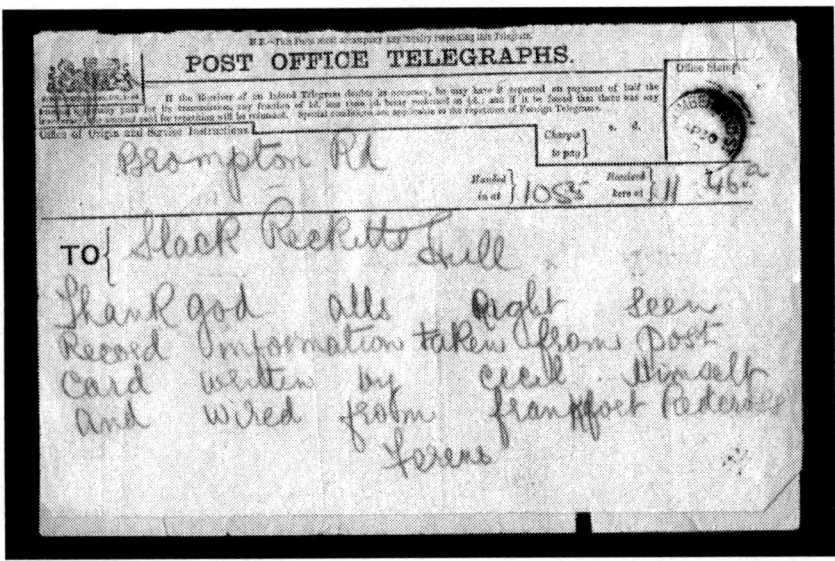

All such news was relayed as it was received:

Telegram rec`d 3.46 p.m.   To Miss Willatt, Firlands:

FERENS WIRES FROM LONDON THANK GOD ALLS RIGHT
SEEN RECORD INFORMATION TAKEN FROM POST CARD
WRITTEN BY CECIL HIMSELF AND WIRED FROM FRANKFURT
RED CROSS WILLATT

℞℘ Telegram rec`d 10.5 p.m. 30.4.18   To Slack, Wilton House:

NAME CECIL SLACK EAST YORKS ON PRISONERS LIST
WRITING RED CROSS

℞℘ Meanwhile Cecil himself had managed to communicate with the Red
Cross, his letter taking roughly six weeks to reach its destination:

To: The Secretary, Red Cross Society, 30.4.18 ["copy rec`d, Hull, June 13"]

Dear Sir,   Can you send me four parcels of food and a small
amount of tobacco to this camp? I should like them at 4 or 5 day
intervals commencing at your earliest convenience. Bread or biscuits,
cheese and tinned meat have preference...

Cecil M Slack, Capt. 4th East Yorks.

℞℘ Cecil`s father now wrote to Dora: May 1st 1918

My dear Dora,   I feel I must write you a few lines as my heart
has gone out to you so much during the past week. You were very
brave.

I enclose a copy of a further letter from Sgt Westoby [below] and in a
day or two I will send you a copy of a long one from Lt Cliffe [see above,
letter of 28.4.18] describing the scenes of April 9th and 10th.

I have had quite a lot of enquiries from people whose relatives were in
the 4th E. Yorks who are very, very anxious. I am telling them that as
Major Jackson and Cecil are safe it is certain that a number of privates
have been taken prisoner.

For the time being the battalion has ceased to exist. If Cecil had got
back to find after 3 hard years the Battn for which he has been proud to
labour had ceased to exist it would have been a great blow to him - I
think it is better to be where he is.

I am Yours affectionately, W.H. Slack.

Letter from Sgt J.F.W. Westoby to William H. Slack

No 10 Ward Main, Norfolk War Hospital, Norwich 15.5.18

Dear Sir,   In answer to your letter of the 14th inst I am very sorry I cannot give you any definite information of Capt. Pollock. If I remember rightly Capt Pollock and your son Capt. Slack fought one of our Lewis guns until the Bosche was within 50 yds or so of them. Your son got away on that occasion but Capt Pollock went to the assistance of his servant and whether he was taken or gave his life during this noble act no one seemed to know.

I am yours very faithfully, J. F. W. Westoby Sgt.

A congratulatory letter now arrived from Cecil`s C.O...

Amotherby Vicarage, Malton, Yorks, 1.5.18

Dear Mr Slack,   I am simply overjoyed about Cecil - I can`t have any other feelings. It is simply splendid to know that whatever now happens his life will be spared. Like so many other people he`s too young to "go under". Now he`ll live to enjoy his life as he should - may I offer my congratulations to his fiancee.

Yours sincerely,

W.T. Wilkinson

...and from Emma Raffan:

Clevelands, Huddersfield, 7.5.18

My dear Dodo,   I was most awfully glad to get your letter and to hear that Cecil is all right. I had been wondering very much about you both. I hope you still have good news, but the suspense between letters must be awful. I now I find it pretty bad from Salonika, and Jim isn`t actually fighting. He has nothing to do but watch Tommies erect tents and sheds. He`s the sort of man who can`t stand inactivity. But I am thankful he isn`t in the front line as he was last time he was out. Yours ever, Emma [Raffan, nee Blamires]

Winnie Slack to Dora: 8.5.18

My dear Dora, Through Lieut. Waite* I have heard that some relatives have risked sending cards and letters to their prisoner relatives in Germany before knowing the camp. He told me of an officer he knows who was a prisoner who received letters and parcels. Mrs Waite has written to her husband and the War Office censored it, then wrote to her saying the letter would be forwarded but advised her another time not to write so much. I am risking a card inside an envelope. I thought you might also. Cecil would be relieved to know that we know he is all right. The official war telegram stating he was a prisoner came yesterday afternoon.

Yours affectionately, Winnie Slack.

*** Dora had apparently written to Lt Waite`s wife, for among the surviving letters is the following, from her**

My dear Miss Willatt, Many thanks for your letter. Yes, I shall be only too pleased if you will send me those addresses you can get for sending bread, and also any other hints you get about writing and little things we could send.

No, I haven`t heard from my hubby yet but you see he was taken on the 12th, that was 3 days after your boy and Major Jackson, wasn`t it? So I might not hear till after you. I was so delighted when I saw your good news in the paper. Yes, I have heard in the same way and had such a nice letter from the War Office. When I have heard from Clem and feel more settled I rather want to try to get to a V.A.D. hospital and try nursing as I feel I must be occupied too, so I wonder if you could tell me how best to go about it. I don`t understand where to apply.

I will let you know when I hear from my husband. Yours very sincerely,

Nora Waite.

ᖇᖴ The first communication from Dora to reach Cecil appears to be this note, dated 10.5.18:

My Sweetheart,   We are all well - am leaving here 26th June. We received wire that you were "missing" on 22nd April and that you were "prisoner" and well in unknown camp on 29th April. We are all very thankful it has happened.

Love and always yours, Dora.

ᖇᖴ **Winnie Slack to Dora:**

Wilton House 18.5.18

My dear Dora,   Just a few lines to wish you many happy returns of the 20th....Major Jackson`s people heard from him yesterday. He is at Rastadt (halfway between Carlsruhe and Baden). He asks for clothing. A letter which he wrote on April 13th has not yet arrived. Evidently Cecil is not at the same camp as we have not yet heard anything.

Yours affectionately, Winnie Slack.

ᖇᖴ **William Slack to Dora:**

Wilton House, 19.5.18

My dear Dora,   May I wish you very many happy returns of your birthday, and that before the next one comes round our Prisoner boy will be back in dear old England.

You may be interested in the following replies to some questions I sent to a Brunswick [Methodist church] boy who is France and who was in the fighting on the Lys:

1 What was the date when Cecil was last seen? Last seen as near as I can say on the 12th April.

2 Who was with him in the shell-hole? Major Jackson, Sgt Major, one signaller on duty and one L/Cpl. I was about 25 yds away in another hole and when I saw it was "all up" I ran, and thank God I got through.

3 Were the enemy then at the back of them? Not quite all round.

4 Was the shell-hole near the river Lys, and had they retired back some distance? We had not retired. Whether the Captain tried to leave the shell-hole or not I cannot say but I was very pleased to hear that he was safe - you see I was right. I thought he would be, but one thing troubled me - whether he would be taken or not.

5 As Major Jackson has been reported a wounded prisoner was Cecil with him or near him? Was Major Jackson wounded early on? The first answers that. The major was with him the last time I saw him.

I had an interesting chat with Lieut. Cliffe who is on leave and fairly well. He told me that when he got back to France the 4th E.Y. was at Essars, just east of Bethune. He went to the billet where Cecil was and found him chatting with Major Jackson. They invited him to mess dinner the next day, but the "attack" made that impossible.

Yours affectionately, W.H. Slack.

⳩ Letter to Mr Slack from a fellow 4th East Yorks officer, 19.5.18: PIC 40

Sir,   I should like to express my pleasure that your son is reported a P. of W. although I know he will hate it and also we miss him immensely especially myself as I have been associated with him for so long.

I happen to be Mess President and it falls to me to square up messing a/cs so I am forwarding his to you and should be glad if you would let me have a cheque for it as I cannot send it to him from this country.

I trust you will be able to do this as there are a lot of a/cs outstanding against "missing" officers and I am anxious to get matters squared before it gets into a hopeless muddle.

Thanking you, Yours truly, Oswald Philip Capt.

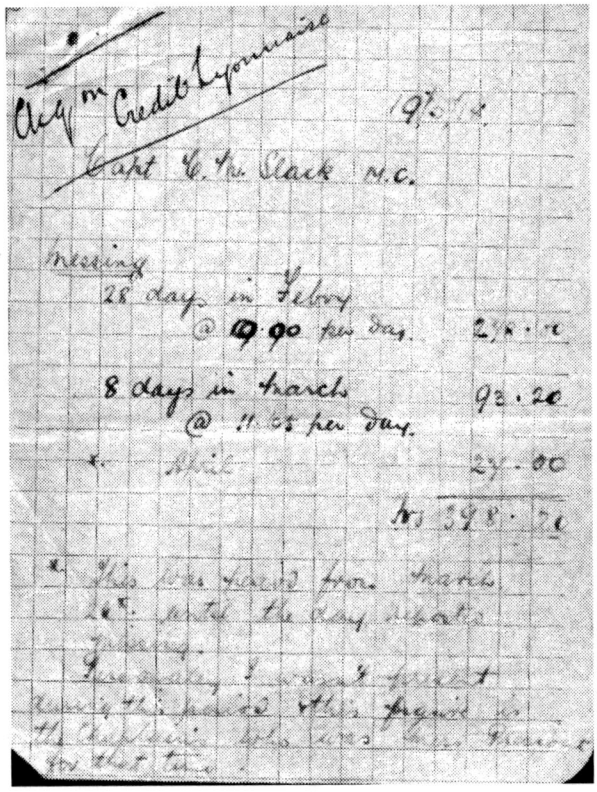

No-one seemed to be offended at receiving this mess bill for the captive - and his father calmly paid up!

ꙮ **Emma Raffan to Dora:**

Bradley Lodge, Huddersfield, 20.5.18

My dear Dodo,　　　　Many happy returns of the day. I only heard yesterday about Cecil. You poor old thing - I am so sorry. But what a comfort it must be to know he is alive and well. Cheer yourself up with the thought that he is at any rate out of the fighting. And after all, the bally war`s got to get over sometime. And I was reading in the paper only yesterday that the Germans haven`t much use for officer prisoners and are only too thankful to get them transferred to neutral countries, so "nil desperandum" Dodo dear.

Poor Rosamund Woodcock lost her brother Geoffrey on April 6th. These bereavements are just terrible.

The best of luck to you old girl, Your affectionate friend, Emma Raffan.

William Slack to Dora:

26.5.18

My dear Dora,   My letters are very poor substitutes for Cecil`s but I think you will be interested in learning that I met this morning Private Morley of the 4th E.Y. He wears the three chevrons and went through the St Quentin and the river Lys attacks. For the latter they started about 850 strong, mostly as he put it "young kids" just out from England - and finished up with about 60. This will probably be the lot Sgt Westoby referred to.

He says he was at one time one of Cecil`s snipers, and would have gone anywhere with him as would all the men, and he added they would do anything for him. He says the new officers they are getting are very different from the old ones, and he is not at all happy about it.

He told me that the last thing he knew of Cecil was that he heard him say he was going to stand by the "old" Major and that he would not leave him.

Colonel Clarke told me yesterday that his son-in-law, Norman Ingleby, is now Adjutant and that he has written to say there is only one officer in the Battn whom he had known previously.

Your affectionately,   W.H. Slack.

PART EIGHT:

"I CANNOT TELL YOU THE JOY..."

Three and a half weeks after receiving the telegram notice of Cecil`s capture, his parents received confirmation in his own hand, by a postcard dated 12.4.18, that he was a prisoner of war in Germany.

ᐁᎧ A second card, dated 23.4.18, was received at about this time:

> My Dear Father and Mother,   Just a week ago today I celebrated a certain anniversary, to the day, in my life by entering this prisoners` camp, and a rather humiliating anniversary too, but one that I am not ashamed of. A party of 5 of us were completely cut off at close quarters, and through no fault of ours. I may not write very often. I have sent you previously a postcard stating that I am well, and have sent Dora a letter-card. At the moment of writing I expect I am still "missing" to you. I now have a reasonable chance of living a full life, and I realise the significance of my present safety. Chocolate, cheese, etc will be welcome.
>
> Love to all, your affec. son, Cecil.

ᐁᎧ Post-card from William Slack to Cecil:

Wilton House, 26.5.18

> My dear Cecil,   We were very pleased to receive yesterday morning the postcard you signed on the 12th April stating you were a prisoner of war and unwounded.
>
> Circumstances prevent writing about many things, but if you are allowed to refer to soldiers who were with you, can you state what happened to Captain Ruthven, Sgt Mjr Foster, Captain Pollock and Lt Wilson. Cliffe called on me a few days ago. He got a dose of gas shortly after seeing

you on the 10th. Private Larter refers to having seen you on the morning of the 12th about 25 yards from a shell hole in which he was.

Directly we hear in what camp you are parcels of food and clothing will be sent.

With love from all, Your affectionate Father, W.H. Slack.

𝕆𝕐𝕆 This post-card was shortly forwarded to Dora by Winnie Slack, who wrote:

My dear Dora,   By the same post as your letter a postcard came with Cecil`s new address. As soon as Mr Slack has seen it we will send it for you to see.

I have posted a letter to him tonight, and this afternoon had a parcel of food sent from Peel House and in the morning am sending underclothing and socks, also through Peel House, as he is sure to need them. Peel House telegraphed to London this afternoon and they cable to Copenhagen about bread, which he will get in three days. Now we must await letters before anything more can be done.

I hurried to Beech Croft with the card this afternoon, and you will probably hear from your Mother before getting this.

Bob expects to be home tonight. I am very tired and feeling a bit sick, as the result of rush and strain.

Your boy`s Mother, Winnie Slack.

𝕆𝕐𝕆 In response, Dora wrote once more to Cecil:

Firlands, Tuesday 28.5.18, 10.30 p.m. [Returned]

My Dearest,   On Sat. your Father received your post card dated the 12th April. I cannot tell you the joy and how thankful I was to see your dear hand-writing again. What you went through and what you must have suffered during your last few weeks in France is more than we can imagine - but we have heard a lot from different sources and people, and I am more proud of my darling than I have ever been before. We have had letters from the Colonel and he feels he has never thanked you for your loyalty and he could never trust any one further than you. Although the thought of where you are is far from pleasant, compared with other great sadness one hears of just recently I am lucky to have my boy alive and well. I know what your feelings would be exactly when you were captured, and I know you are not the man who would have given in had there been any alternative but certain death. We had one week when we knew nothing except that you were missing - I went home for it - I cannot even give you an idea of the agony and suspense I went through - I knew that life was not worth living without you - but that is all over now - but I feel that my love for you now is even stronger than it was before and that it has brought us still more closely to one another.

I am always thinking about you and praying for you - and when you come home you will find your little girl waiting for you exactly the same and just as true to you as when you left her. The meaning in this letter is a thousand times deeper than I have written it - but the space is limited for writing.

Always your own little girl, Dora.

ᘜᘜ Cecil`s first letter to Dora arrived at the end of May:

(Baden) April 17 1918

> Darling,   I hope by the time you get this you will have heard from my people. I sent them a card, saying that I was a prisoner, two or three days ago. Major Jacko, another officer called Thompson, and I were all taken together, after being surrounded. We landed here early this morning. I think this is only a sort of collecting camp, and that we are sent elsewhere shortly. They promise to forward our post to whatever camp we go to.
>
> We cannot write very much, only about 3 or 4 times a month I think. I

have not written home yet, with the exception of the official post card, so will you let them know about me and tell them that any parcels of chocolate, tobacco and tinned or potted stuff will be very welcome. I am comfortable here, but there is nothing at all to do. I understand that things are a lot better at the permanent camps, to which we are eventually sent. It hardly seems possible that so much should have happened since I saw you last. I wonder when I shall see you again, little girl. It may be months, or years but our chances of meeting again are fairly good now. We were taken on the 10th about 4.0 pm. I felt an absolutely hopeless rotter about it, but we couldn`t help it: they were within 50 yds of us and right round us, and we were only 5 strong.

When I get settled down in a permanent camp I`m going to learn drawing and shorthand, and carry on with French and anything else that`s going. I believe there are all sorts of classes, and also football, cricket, tennis. Fortunately I had a few francs on me when I was taken. I have changed this and have been able to buy a ragtime shaving outfit, toothbrush etc from the little canteen here. Will you also ask my people to send me my soft cap, Sam Browne belt, slacks, shoes, socks and sock suspenders and clean underclothing from my kit if it has arrived yet.

I have been allowed to keep my pocket-book, in which I have snap-shots of you. The snap-shot of you giving a piece of sugar to a dog is in my kit, but I have other nice ones of you. Yours with love, Cecil.

ℭⅩ Firlands, 30.5.18 Thurs, 10.30 p.m.

My Darling,   I received your letter this morning - it has taken just six weeks to come. You can imagine my joy: it was just how you will feel when you get this letter of mine. I have a tremendous lot to be thankful for when I hear of all the sadness in homes at the present time. It is impossible to imagine what you must have been through since your leave - when I said goodbye to you it suddenly came over me that something was going to happen.

I have written to your Ma and Pa today about your things - everything has to be sent through Peel House Prisoner of War Fund so I cannot send you any of my cakes. If there are any special things you want, tell me, and I will get them off through Peel House - would you like a box of watercolours - drawing pencils or drawing block? How many letters can you receive a week? Let us know if you get the bread, and you ought to get a parcel every five days. We have had a terribly anxious time about you - I went home for a week - but it is over now and I want to forget it, sweetheart.

Love and always your own little girl, Dora.

Reckitt & Sons Ltd, Hull 31.5.18

✇✇ Winnie Slack to Dora:

Wilton House, 2.6.18

My dear Dora,   Many thanks for letting us see your letters. I have made a note of the various things Cecil requires. His kit has not arrived, so I am having new slacks made and will get new summer underclothing. Two parcels of food have gone, and one will go regularly every 5 days, and officers may receive an extra four parcels a month (called privilege or coupon parcels) which are usually sent by relatives or friends. We have written for the coupons and hope to get the first privilege parcel off this week. Altogether the officers may have 10 parcels of food a month and the poor privates only 6.

Yours affectionately, Winnie Slack.

✇✇ Winnie Slack to Cecil:

Wilton House, 2.6.18 {received by Cecil 26.6.18}

My dear Cecil,   ...Bob has been home for two days. He expects to be sent to a flying school next week. Major Waite`s wife `phoned me last week and mentioned that you and several others were in the same camp as he. Mr Dodds has asked me to send some cigarettes on his behalf, so you will know from whom the next are. How many letters can you receive? Various people want your address, but we do not want you to risk not getting your own and Dora`s letters.

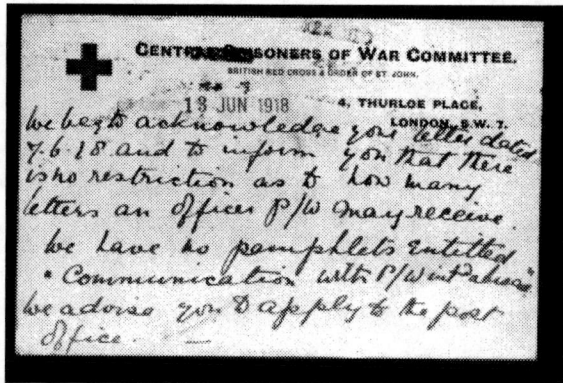

Kitty is to have her tonsils out this week. Ralph looks pale as usual and the hot weather tries him. Hilda and Mabel write in good spirits. Hilda and four other girls who are leaving are keen on taking a cottage for ten days before they come home. They think there is one in the mountains somewhere where an old woman will do the cooking for them. Father and I have not agreed to it yet. Housekeeping is a difficult question for experienced housekeepers at present so I don`t know how five inexperienced schoolgirls are going to manage. At present I am only able to go out at night and Father stays with the children. Having no housemaid I am obliged to stay and help Nellie in the mornings.

Harold`s fowls seem to be on strike at present, or else rats are getting the eggs.

Much love from Your affectionate Mother, Winnie Slack.

℞ Firlands, Wednesday 5.6.18, 9.30 p.m.   2nd letter

My Darling,   I am numbering my letters to you so you will know if you get them all.

Hartley and I leave here on the 26th - three weeks today. We are going fruit-picking in Norfolk we think, but it`s not settled yet. After that I am going to Marjorie Barker`s place at Yarmouth.

I am thinking of taking up a six months` massage course in London about the middle of September. It might be useful. What do you think, Cecil? Nothing is settled yet - I have only thought about it.

I have written to the Colonel to tell him I have heard from you. Your Father and Mother have been absolute bricks through all this. I don`t know what I should have done without them. I was with them nearly all the time I was in Hull for the week you were "missing".

Do you remember two years ago today. It is 10.20 p.m. and I am sure you are lying awake thinking about me now. I think about the future and what we shall do - and about you - my dearest - every night when I go to bed.

All my love, Your little girl, Dora.

ᘒᘓᘙ William Slack to Cecil:

Wilton House, 8.6.18

My dear Cecil,   ...Captain Philip sent me your mess bill which I have settled.

We received a letter from Bob this morning describing his first ride in an aeroplane, including nose dive, looping the loop etc. Jack Forty is with him so they are having a good time.

Bush has been discharged [from hospital] and is going home. Can you give me any information about Ruthven? His people have not heard anything, other than that he was missing at the same time as you were. Do you know anything about the following, as their friends are anxious about them? Gallant, Hanson, Andrews, Ely, Randall, Barrow. Stabler and Sheppard are in hospital but are going on satisfactorily.

We all join in much love, Your affectionate Father, W.H. Slack

ᘒᘓᘙ Rastatt (Baden) 26th April 1918

A scene from one of the POW camps where Cecil was incarcerated.

Darling,   I`m still here, just the same as last time. I have become
an unwilling vegetarian, except for an occasional morsel of meat in the
soup. I`m not grousing, because I think the people here do their best,
and I have my life to look forward to at the end of it all. One cannot fail
to realise that it is not for no reason that a man has been allowed to
come safely through what I have since the war began, and I am now
patiently waiting for the time when I shall do good for the world with
you by my side.

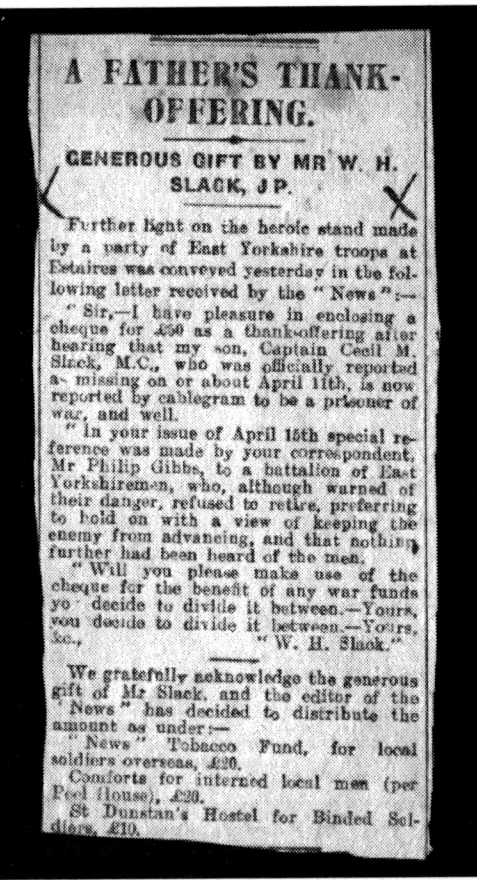

*When news came through that Cecil was safe his father donated £50 to War
funds, to be used at the discretion of the Eastern Morning News.*

The little bit of country that I can see through the barbed wire is very lovely - little hills covered with trees of all shades of green. There is a little village nestling between two of the hills, and nearby is an old castle.

The routine here is breakfast at 8.0, 8.45 or 9.0 when we get sweetened tea - our day`s ration of bread is issued before breakfast - dinner at 11.30, 12.15 or 1.0, when we get a vegetable stew - hot sweetened tea at 3.30, and at 5.0, 5.45 or 6.30 another vegetable stew, and either beet-root, two gherkins, a small piece of sausage, or a spoonful of jam. I was paid 26 marks a few days ago. Today I have been able to buy a small tin of pate de foie gras. Time here is an hour in advance of you. Lights out is at 9.15. Your 10.30 is 11.30 with us, and I am generally asleep then. Would your 8.30 and my 9.30 be all right for our little half hour?

Heaps of love, Cecil.

CXO Firlands, Thursday 7 p.m., 13.6.18   3rd letter

My Darling,   I received your letter of the 26th April yesterday morning. I was hardly expecting one again so soon, so I was delighted.

I am thankful, very thankful, to read in your letter that you are just patiently waiting. What I exist on is that we have our lives before us which we can live together, both trying to do good for the world. We will have our little half-hour at 8.30 p.m. for me and 9.30 p.m. for you as you arranged.

I had seven letters returned to me from France that I had written to you during the last fortnight.

This is a little bit of bell heather from the moors near here - I picked it to send to you when I went for a walk with Matron and Hartley last night. I shall bring you down here some day to this lovely spot.

All my love, Your little girl, Dora.

ᏩᎶ Cecil to his parents: Feldpostkarte, 30.4.18 "rec`d June 14"

My Dear Father and Mother,   I am still at this
temporary camp, hungry and rather limp, but otherwise fit. I believe
that I can make arrangements with the Red Cross to send parcels and
draw from Cox & Co. on my authority. I think all parcels from home
pass through the Red Cross who supplement them to 10 a month - but
this is only rumour. I am writing them - and am also writing Cox & Co.
to send you my pass-book - if it was not in my kit, and should be glad if
you could keep an eye on its workings from time to time. I should like
some of my books - shorthand, etc, sending when I am in a permanent
camp, but not until I write, in case I miss them.

Love to all, your affec. son, Cecil.

ᏩᎶ William Slack to Dora: Wilton House, 16.6.18

My dear Dora,   ...I had a long chat with Private Morley last
Tuesday. He told me he does not know how he got through alive as he
seemed to be more or less lost after Cecil told him and one or two others
that they were at liberty to look after themselves. He says Cecil could
have got away with them, but would not do so, stating that he would
come later on, but he was going back to the shell-hole to stay with the
old Major. He said he knew if Cecil did not try to get away then he
would not be able to do so later and that Cecil really knew it also, but he
was perfectly cool and apparently unconcerned. He seemed to be very
fond of Cecil, and said that he had never known him in the 3 years bully
a man, but that he could get anything he wanted done by coaxing the
men and that if there were any special bit of work involving some risk
the men used to say is Captain Slack going to be in charge, and if so they
were ready to go anywhere with him - that he was always pleased to
explain things to the men which they appreciated....

Yours sincerely, W.H. Slack.

⳩ Firlands, Wednesday 19.6.18 4th letter

Darling, I do hope that by the time you get this letter you are receiving your parcels regularly and in good condition - how often are you getting the bread from Copenhagen, and is it good? I can`t tell you how I long to look after you and cook for you.

Hartley and I leave here next Wednesday for Outwell near Wisbech - near the Wash. It is some sort of fruit-picking, I believe. I have got a pale blue felt hat like a plough boy`s - khaki breeches and long tunic coat to my knees - and a pigtail - so altogether I look rather nice! Nickie [Nicholson] is coming too. You have heard me speak of her - she calls you "Marmaduke" always.

Have you got Major Jacko with you now? Ingleby and Laverack are "missing" since May 27th - I only hope things will turn out alright for their people like they have done for us.

Goodnight, my dearest - I`m always thinking about you and longing for you. Always your little girl, Dora.

⳩ William Slack to Cecil: Wilton House, 23.6.18

My dear Cecil, The last news we had from you was your card dated April 30th....

There is no news yet of Ingleby, Laverack and Hollis. The friends of Waddington and Campbell have had good news.

Hilda`s application has been successful and she will go to Bedford College in October.

Sir James [Reckitt] has fully recovered from his operation and presided yesterday at 85 years of age at a meeting of the company in regard to reconstruction. He makes kind enquiries of you as do a host of friends.

Your affectionate Father, W.H. Slack.

༂ᘏᘐ c/o Mrs Barnett, The Chase, Outwell, Cambridgeshire,

Saturday 29.6.18, 5.30 p.m.   5th letter

My Sweetheart,   Hartley, Nicholson and I left Camberley last
Wednesday and came here the same day. We are working on a fruit
farm here picking strawberries, gooseberries and raspberries. We have
only had two and a half days so far. I earned 9/6 on Thursday and Fri:
I`m so frightfully stiff after the stooping I can hardly walk - it`s
absolute agony!

Hartley (left) and Dora at work on the farm.

We have digs in an awfully nice little cottage and do our own cooking -
but I wish it were you and I here all alone instead.

Love and xx, Your little girl, Dora.

ꙮ c/o **Mrs Barnett, Wednesday 8.30 p.m., 3.7.18** 6th letter

My Sweetheart, It`s just three weeks since I had my last letter
from you so I`m simply longing to hear again - it is the one thing in life
I look forward to.

I haven`t heard any more about Ingleby and Laverack yet. I only hope
they will turn up with you. I can sympathise with people far more now
than I used to - now that I have been through it myself - trouble does
help to bring out these qualities I believe.

We get a halfpenny a pound for picking and Monday was my best day -
I got 7/6. We breakfast at 6.30 and are in the fields at 7. We work
until twelve when we have half an hour to eat our sandwiches, then we
work until 4 and come back to our cottage and cook dinner. Then we
go to bed at 9.

I have heard from the VAD HQs, and they want me to take on more
work at once and I can choose whichever Military Hospital I like - so the
Camberley Matron must have given me a fairly respectable testimonial.

From your little girl, Dora.

ꙮ **Cecil to his parents:**

6.7.18

My Dear Father and Mother, My first and up to the
present only letter was handed to me on the 26th June. It was one
written on June 2nd by Mother, and told me that two food and clothes
parcels had been sent, which rather makes me fear that a number of my
earlier cards have not reached you. The parcel which I drew two days
ago was the clothes one. I have had my present underclothes and socks
on for three months. Our mess now consists of three, the fourth member
having received the boot on account of his dirtiness of person and deceit.

Love to all, Your affec. son, Cecil.

ʊᏕ William Slack to Dora:

Wilton House, 7.7.18

My dear Dora,   ...I received a letter from Private Morley with bad news about Ingleby, but as it is not official I have not mentioned it - you will remember the false report about Cecil. Laverack is a Prisoner of War.

Yours sincerely, W.H. Slack.

ʊᏕ Hesepe, Kreis Bersenbruck, Sunday 26.5.18

Sweetheart,   It is a month since I wrote to you, but this is my first chance, bar a change of address which I sent to my people, and which I expect they forwarded to you. The above is the address of the permanent camp where I am now. I arrived about a fortnight ago with a large batch of other officers. We spent two days and two nights on the journey. The whole time my face and jaws were swollen, and I could hardly eat my scanty supply of food. I am better now and quite able to eat every grain of food I can get hold of. No parcels have arrived yet, but an officer got a letter from England a few days ago. Yesterday I signed a parole card which will enable me to go out for walks, on parole. I hope to do so when I can get something to walk in. My boots have gone phut. Would you please ask my Mother to get me some leather for boot repairs from time to time - about 2 square feet to begin with.

Accommodation here is not very grand. We sit 14 to a table and have been broken up into numerous small messes in anticipation of that wonderful day when parcels will be a reality. I believe our Government still allow me my pay, and on the strength of that I have written to a London firm with whom I have an account, asking them to send me out parcels of food, drawing payment form Cox & Co.

English version of the parole card signed by Cecil at Hesepe.

You will find me a very easy person to look after in later years: plenty of bread and dripping for breakfast, bread and meat at midday, and a good hefty plain meal at night will suffice. Luxuries such as hole-less socks and clean clothes I have become indifferent to. Just feed me and love me and all will be well. I am allowed no more space, so goodbye old girl.

Heaps of love, Cecil.

☙ c/o Mrs Barnett, Wednes 10.7.18, 1 p.m.　　　　　　　7th letter

My Sweetheart,　　　　　　　I received your letter of May 26th last Thurs. By this time you must have received a parcel and letters.

When I get home I am going to the Depot to help to choose your parcels - good solid food, and cheese if I can manage it.

Thursday 7.30 a.m.　I was at home yesterday because of the rain but went out to Wisbech to the pictures. This morning it is still raining.

I made 30/- last week but I can`t make it this week if it continues to rain. It is great fun earning my living and trying to live on it - we just managed it last week. We are leaving here a fortnight today. We are having quite a jolly time and get on splendidly. We have to live in one room and sleep in it. Nickie is the butler, Hartley the housemaid and I`m the fat old cook! The country here is awfully pretty - pretty canals and windmills and a canal running through the village - just like Holland I should imagine.

Love and always yours, Dora.

☙ Hesepe, 5.6.18

Sweetheart,　　　　Just a line or two to let you know I am going on just the same, aching for you and aching for something for my tummy. I went for a short 3 mile walk a few afternoons ago. It was a nice change but I was very exhausted when I got back. I have had to give up my cold shower in the morning - the bread ration won`t stand the strain. I am dying for news of you and I don`t think letters and parcels really can be much longer. It is 2 months now since I was taken....

Love from, Cecil.

☙ c/o Mrs Barnett, Sat. 20.7.18　　　　　　　　8th letter

My Sweetheart,　　　　　I received a p.c. from you yesterday dated 5th

June. I am afraid that at the time of writing you would still have a month to wait for letters and parcels. I was nearly 7 weeks without a letter from you, but you would have to wait 3 months - that 7 weeks seemed years to me.

Father got some leather for soling your boots but Peel House wouldn`t let it go in your parcels, but I hear your Mother is sending some boots out soon.

Last week I only made 21/- because the weather was so bad, but this week I have made 26/-. We have managed to pay our way splendidly.

Goodbye my sweetheart for this week - I am always aching for you as you are aching for me - I often think of the next time we shall meet - how glorious it will be.

Always your little girl, Dora.

ᘔᘯ Now that Cecil was settled, his father`s thoughts turned to the future:

Wilton House, 23.7.18

> My dear Cecil,   ...I strongly recommend you to take up shorthand, as I have plans for your future on your return in which a practical knowledge of it will be necessary...

ᘔᘯ Rastatt (Baden) 12.0 noon 3.5.18

Darling,   I am sitting outside my hut in the sun, having just finished my midday meal and am smoking some wood shavings mixed with a little cigar tobacco. I don`t think I`ve told you yet about my home. It`s a large hut in which about 60 of us live. The bedsteads are in groups of four - two on top and two below. When one man turns the whole affair shakes. I was sharing one with two others, but as they have now both gone to hospital I am getting a more or less peaceful night. I washed my underclothes under the tap yesterday, and feel much more comfortable.

It`s your birthday on the 21st, isn`t it? Many happy returns, little girl,
and I hope I`m with you for the next one.

I shall feel more contented with my lot when I get some real
nourishment into me.

The man in the next bedstead comes from Sandhurst and knows your
hospital. There`s a man in our hut who was in your hospital about Sept.
1916. He was a Cpl Bell then.

Major Jackson is giving a lecture on Finland this afternoon. We are
having quite a number of interesting lectures. I make myself walk at
least [indecipherable] miles a day round our enclosure. I shall do
exercises when I get stronger.

Yours with love, Cecil.

℞℞ Outside Ely Cathedral, Thursday 12 noon 25.7.18   9th letter

My Darling,   I received a letter from you on Tuesday from
Rastatt in which you tell me about Cpl Bell. I will write to Matron to
tell her about him. She is the only one left who was there in Sept. 1916
except stinking Sister Smith - or Calamity Kate, as the men used to call
her.

I left Hartley and Nickie about 10 a.m. They have gone to London and
I am breaking my journey here on my way to Marjorie`s. I am sitting
under a tree on some common ground quite close to the cathedral. Ely
is a very quaint little town something like Beverley.

I am going home on Monday. Marjorie wants me to stay longer but I
must get home to Ma as she is not very well.

I have earned £5.5.7 in exactly four weeks.

Thankyou for my birthday happy returns - I only hope you`ll be with
me next time. I`m 24 - it`s awfully old but don`t feel it.

Love & xx, Dora.

ᘓ Cecil to his parents:

30.5.18 [rec`d 30.7.18]

My Dear Father and Mother,   I am sorry this is not a
letter, but it is my allowance - more next time. This is a new permanent
camp and is not very comfortable as yet. The weather however is
excellent, and each day brings nearer the parcels which will allay the
hunger which has been continuous for nearly two months.

I do not know what arrangements you have made as to parcels, but as I
still get my pay I think I ought to pay for them. I have an account with
Fortnum & Mason, a London firm, and I wrote for a large parcel (25/-)
once a month - but I have only ordered `dainties` such as honey, meat
pies, etc. Will you please send me a pair of boots, my Pitmans
Shorthand, shaving-soap, and a housewife. Sorry to appear greedy.

Love to all, Your affec. son, Cecil.

ᘓ Cecil to his parents:

17.6.18

My Dear Father and Mother,   Yesterday Sunday the
16th June marks a red letter day in my life, that being the day on which
a nine-weeks hunger was appeased. Two loaves per officer arrived from
the Red Cross on Saturday and were dished out on Sunday morning.
Home parcels also arrived for a few, one of whom is on our mess. His
little lot was somewhat mouldy, but we have ably doctored it.

Will you please send me half a dozen razor-blades for a "7 O`clock"
safety-razor, a refill for a McMillan Multiple Ring-Book No 3 (from
Archibald`s in Alfred Gelder St.), a leather wristlet watch strap, a
skipping rope, sponge-bag, sand-shoes and soap.

I shall always remember the commencement of this era in my life. I shall
endeavour to celebrate the 16th June by giving someone a damned good
feed.

Love to all, Your affec. son, Cecil.

ᘯᘓᘆ **Beech Croft, Tuesday 30.7.18**   10th letter

Darling,   It is your birthday today and I have been thinking about
you all the time. Your Mother telephoned this morning to say that you
received some bread on the 17th June - it is glorious to hear that you
have received something at last.

I came home from Yarmouth last Friday as Mother wasn`t well after the
influenza - but she is tons better now and coming downstairs a little. I
went down to your home last evening on my push-bike through
Stoneferry. I did like seeing everybody again and your Mother - it`s like
a wee corner of you.

Cecil Ingleby gets married tomorrow. I enjoyed seeing Marjorie again,
and they have got an awfully comfy house in Yarmouth. Emma
Blamires has got a little girl just a week old.

Goodbye xx, Your little girl, Dora.

ᘯᘓᘆ **Rastatt, 18.6.18**

Little Girl,   Do you realise it is over two years ago since I came
over to Silkstone on leave.

I get a very achy feeling when I walk round the enclosure here and
watch the young cabbages and things sprouting up, and I simply long
for the time when you and I will be able to grow them in our garden.

Remember the 16th June, Dora; it was the day on which a nine-week
hunger was appeased - a red letter day which I shall celebrate yearly.
Two loaves per officer, and in addition Morrison in our mess got 4
mouldy ones which we ably doctored and ate.* Another loaf each
arrived yesterday.

I am awfully pleased with a drawing I have made from a snap of you. I
have framed it. Everyone who sees it admires it.

Goodbye sweetheart. I am always thinking of you. Yours with love,
Cecil.

* Cecil later wrote that the loaves in question were as hard as bricks. They broke them with a hammer, only to find the inside mouldy. They soaked them, squeezed out the green slime, then cooked what was left. He adds that "they were glorious". As to marking the 16th June, he later made a covenant for an annual subscription to Oxfam.

℞ Beech Croft, 10.45 p.m., Thurs 1.8.18

My Sweetheart, I came from Wilton House about an hour ago. The whole family was there except you - Bob is on leave. I did long for you - I always do - it`s the only sort of hunger I have, but it does ache sweetheart. I love seeing all the kids because they all have a wee bit of something like you in their faces.

I had a letter from you this morning dated 18th June. We can`t possibly imagine what you have been going through. It was a tremendous relief to know you had got some bread through at last. Are you much thinner?

Goodnight my darling. It`s 11.30 - I`m going to bed to think of you. xx Your own little girl, Dora.

℞ Wilton House, 3.8.18

My dear Cecil, ...Wilkinson has received a bar to his DSO for his work previous to being wounded.

...Cecil Ingleby was married on Wednesday to Miss Winkley - as you know he lost a leg from the thigh downwards. I am sorry to say there is no news of either Pollock or Norman Ingleby.

...Cliffe has been wounded again rather seriously, a bullet through the right side.

Your own little girl, Dora.

⚬⚬ Hesepe b. Bramsche, 7.7.18

My Darling,   I am at last in touch with England. I got a letter from Mother 10 days ago. It was written on June 2nd. I got one clothes parcel 4 days ago. The socks I was wearing were the ones you measured me for at Silkstone. They are rather holey today after 3 months` wear. Our mess is now reduced to 3, all from our battalion. We kicked out the fourth member. He wasn`t honest over his parcel and was moreover extremely dirty.

We feed at a little table above our beds. We have a supply of crockery and cooking-pots, a trench-fire for which we can collect wood and bog peat; and turns at a range. At the moment we have nothing to cook as our emergency stuff has given out.

I, my clothes and bedding were deloused last week. Whilst my clothes were drying I walked about in my little British warm and a small towel, `boots` and puttees, and must have looked rather a killing little object.

Today is Sunday, and I can picture the people at home just about to sit down to a useful dinner, and a nice book, or a walk, in the afternoon. I shall have soup, a book, and think of a walk with you.

Love from your sweetheart, Cecil.

⚬⚬ Beech Croft, 4.45 p.m., Sunday 4.8.18

My Sweetheart,   I am awfully glad you have at last got your first clothing parcel. Peel House doesn`t know whether a skipping rope is allowed. I bought a box of paints for you, also different grades of pencils and two brushes - a fine one and a bigger one for backgrounds, etc. India rubbers are not allowed.

I am push-biking to Cottingham to catch the 5.50 train to Beverley to Flossie and Bill and coming back by the 10 p.m. train.

Tuesday 11 p.m. I have not had a moment to finish this since Sunday. Bill`s garden is looking lovely - gorgeous sweet peas and cabbages and potatoes and spring onions - there will be keen competition between us in years to come.

Yesterday your Pater rang up for me to go to tennis - dear little Dr. B was there talking hard all the time, and Mr & Mrs Tom Ferens. I arrived home just before lighting up time. I push-bike there always now - over the Garden Village Bridge - it`s tons nearer. I`ve been lucky so far - someone has offered to carry my bike over each time!

Am in bed finishing this. Your old Dora.

✖✖ 5 Southdene, Filey, Friday 9.8.18, 3.15 p.m.   14th letter

My Darling,   I have had a letter from you dated 7th July and you hadn`t yet received food. It must be wretched for you to keep on writing and not hearing from me.

We came here yesterday. Pater and I bathed this morning - it was lovely but rather cold.

Laverack is a prisoner - I think I told you. I sent a parcel off from Peel House on Weds enclosing some of my shortbread and a little Wenslet cheese. I hope you get it.

I have just pulled out three grey hairs. It does worry me having such signs of old age!

Goodbye sweetheart. Your little girl, Dora.

✖✖ Cecil to his parents:

10.7.18

My Dear Father and Mother,   My hand is still shaking from the excitement of yesterday, and the day before, when I drew a supply of food from the first 4 food parcels. On the 8th the parcel cart came in, and on the first packet I looked at I saw my name. Can you imagine my feelings when I discovered yesterday that there were 4 for me? No, you can`t. There were also 3 for

Hatfield, making a total of 7 for the mess. One parcel was from you and 3 from
Reckitts. Gratitude is a very mild word to use. Excitement has kept me awake
for two nights.

Love to all, Your affec. son, Cecil.

P.S. I know of no limit on incoming letters.

ᘓᘔᘓ Winnie Slack to Cecil:

11.8.18

> My dear Cecil,   It was a great relief to us yesterday to receive
> postcards from you acknowledging food parcels....

> Father went to Filey yesterday for part of his holiday. Dora is also there
> with her Mother. We all went for a drive in the afternoon to Burton
> Constable and during this week intend taking seaside trips for the sake
> of the children. Hilda has had a week in bed with influenza. Norman
> went off on agricultural work on Thursday. Hilda goes to a London
> college in October. Cliffe is in an English Military Hospital badly

wounded. No news yet of Ruthven and Ingleby....

Your affec. Mother, Winnie Slack.

Filey, Tuesday 3.45 p.m., 13.8.18   16th letter

My Darling,   I have just been washing my hair and hung it out to
dry on the sands this morning and I have got dozens of grey hairs - it
worries me frightfully to be turning old like this - I shall really have to
dye it with peroxide or cut it short. Heaps of "land" girls and VADs
have their hair cut short nowadays - it`s far less trouble.

10 p.m. Your Pater came in to tea and I have been for a walk with Pa
so now I have come to bed to think about you. I simply ache for you.

Goodnight, my dearest - from your own little girl, Dora.

William Slack to Cecil:

Crescent Hotel, Filey, 15.8.18

My dear Cecil,   I frequently pass the house in which we were
staying in August 1914 and think of the scene when the news came that
we were at war, and again of your decision to be in it. What a story you
could tell of your own history during the four years. Little did I think
that whilst I was sitting waiting for my first meal in 1918 in the above
Hotel I should receive a telegram from Mother announcing the receipt of
your first four parcels of food. I call to mind the joy at boarding school
of a parcel of cakes after the poor grub we used to get but I guess it was
as nothing compared with your satisfaction.

I am making the best of the nine holes with Mr Empson of Rotherham -
and have been favoured with splendid weather. Dora looks very well - I
imagine she wishes the scenes of March last in Colwyn Bay when you
were over could be gone over again here.

With love, Your affectionate Father, W.H. Slack.

ᐁᑫᑯ Filey, In bed 11 p.m., Sunday 18.8.18   17th letter

My Sweetheart,   I started a letter to you on the sand but my
pen sprang a leak so I thought the censor wouldn`t pass ink splodges!

Monday morning 6.30 a.m. The candle suddenly went west last night so
I made up my mind to wake up early this morning. I have Hilda and
Mabel sleeping in my room in another bed. Today we are going to walk
on the cliff tops to Cayton Bay and lunch there and then walk on to
Scarboro` and take the train back.

Your Father was in last night talking about the trips he had had in
Scotland - it must be gorgeous there. I could watch your Father for
hours because he reminds me of you so much in his little ways and
actions. He showed me your p.c. dated 9th July saying you had got food
at last. I simply ached for you. I can`t imagine how terrible it has been
- I think it`s impossible when one has never been hungry. I never
dreamt you would have to go through all this - it never even entered my
thoughts.

Goodbye for today my darling, all my love from your own little girl,
Dora.

ᐁᑫᑯ Filey, Wednesday 9.30 p.m., 21.8.18   18th letter

My Darling,   We are moving tomorrow to one of those cottages
halfway down to the beach - staying there until Sept, 12th. Ma is tons
better and will be stronger for the winter if she is here a good long time
now. Anna is coming to look after us and Pater is going home. Anna is
the old maid Flossie had when you were here - she gave her the push so
she came to us and she is a treasure.

Hilda and Mabel went today and I feel very quiet and dull without
them.

It`s Thurs. morning 7 a.m. now - my candle went suddenly pop last
night so I had to get under the clothes.

All my love xx Your little girl, Dora.

꩜ **3 Sea Bank, Filey, Friday 23.8.18, 10.15 p.m.** 19th letter

My Darling, We have settled down in this cottage and it`s simply delightful - we have all our meals out of doors, including breakfast and the morning sun shines right onto us.

...Goodnight my darling, I`m going to hop into my bunk by the open window and think of you.

Yours with love, Dora.

꩜ **3 Sea Bank, Filey, Sunday 25.8.18, 3 p.m.** 20th letter

My Sweetheart, I am sitting in our little patch looking towards the sea - it`s lovely sitting out here - I`m going to run down the garden in a few minutes and have a bathe with Father before we have tea.

Pater went home on Thursday and came back yesterday - he said he saw in the paper that Norman Ingleby is now officially reported killed since May 27th about. It`s fearfully sad, and I know it will be a blow to you. I saw a letter he wrote to your Pater when he first heard you were a prisoner and he was delighted. He said it was the best piece of news he had had for some time. He wrote that about the 7th of May. I feel so dreadfully sorry for his wife, but she will be glad they had a little bit of married life together.

Goodbye, my darling. Your little girl, Dora.

꩜ **Cecil to his parents:**

20.7.18

My Dear Father and Mother, Today I received your first written letter dated May 26th/28th. and one from Dora and from Mr Philip Reckitt. I got a note from Capt. Ruthven about two minutes before I was taken. It confirmed his previous serious reports and stated the enemy were getting round behind him. Four or five days later I heard from a prisoner out of his company that he had fallen into the enemy`s hands, badly wounded. If no news has been received from him I fear he is dead. Capt. Pollock and I were the last to retreat from a certain wood in our earlier action. He stopped to speak to his servant, wounded in a shell-hole. It was a miracle I got away. If no news has been received from him, I fear he is dead. Reg. Sgt Maj Foster and Lt Wilson`s people will doubtless have heard from them by now. The former was taken with me, and I met the latter at Rastatt. Pte Morley`s tale of my resolve to stand by the Major amuses me. We were caught like rats in a shell-hole and my last few seconds of freedom were occupied in destroying papers.

Love to all, Your affec. son, Cecil.

ༀ Winnie Slack to Cecil:

25.8.18

My dear Cecil,   This morning we received your p.c. dated 20.7.18. I went to see Mrs Ruthven this afternoon and told her what you said about her son. Poor soul, she is still hoping to get further news. It is a terrible strain for her. News has come this week that Capt. N.W. Ingleby is killed. Bob was home for one night during the week. He hopes to go to Manchester next leave and see Roy Brealy who comes on leave on Tuesday. Father is at Sale and expects to come home tomorrow evening. He spent the previous week at Filey. Mrs Willatt has taken a house at Filey for three weeks. Dora is with her. Hilda and Mabel took Ralph and Kitty to Hornsea yesterday. Harold had been sick in the night, so spent the day in bed. Hilda and Flossie are jabbering away on the `phone and have been for the last half hour. Ralph and Kitty seem to be enjoying their holidays and go out in the early morning to meet the milkman and have a ride in his cart.

Much love from us all, Your affec. Mother, Winnie Slack.

ᘒᘒ Cecil to his parents:

27.8.18

My Dear Father and Mother,   Will you please send my
football boots, shorts and a white cotton shirt. The razor you sent me is
a dud, so will you please send me some "7 O`clock" blades toute suite.

The war news seems pretty good. We are allowed to have German
newspapers. I take the Frankfurter Zeitung and endeavour to increase
my vocabulary.

Love to all, Your affec. son, Cecil.

ᘒᘒ 27.8.18, 3.30 p.m.

My Darling,   Your letters are arriving regularly now. The 6th
came a few days ago and I learn that you are earning some honest
pennies, at the cost of an aching back. I`ve got something aching too,
deep inside me.

You ask me what work to take up. I`m awfully glad the Camberley
Matron gave you such a decent report, but I`m sure you earned it.
Perhaps you`ve taken up the work again by now, if you haven`t gone on
the massage stunt. Is massage good for rheumatism, because I bet I`ll
get it hot now, after mud baths in France and Flanders.

You ask if there is anything that I want. I don`t think there is, other
than what I`m getting now. Little things such as brushes, toothpaste ,
etc, but not soap, can be bought at the canteen.

Yours with love, Cecil.

ᘒᘒ 20.7.18

My Sweetheart,   I have been keeping back this letter for three
or four days in the hope that I must be sure to hear from you. My
number was called out on the midday parade today, and shortly

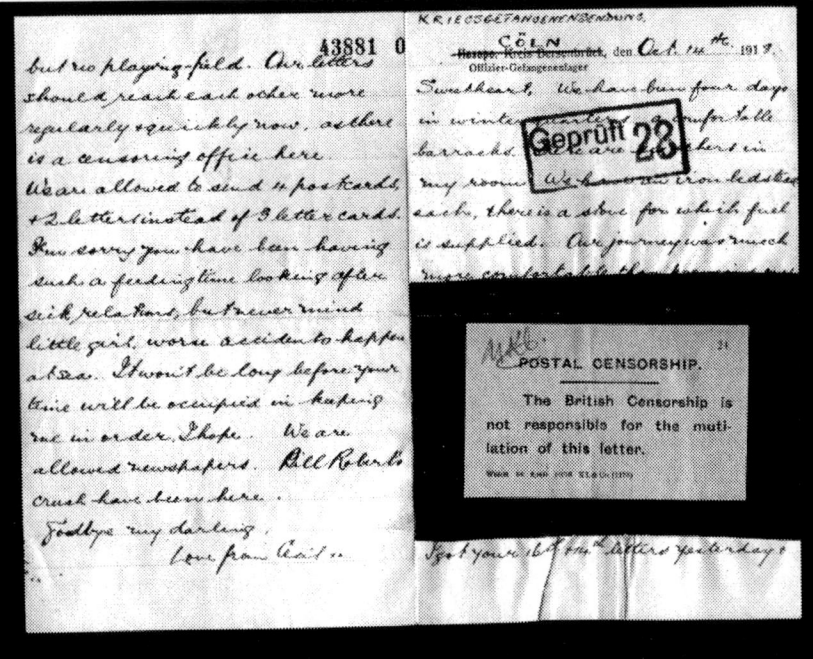

An example of German censorship - and a British disclaimer.

afterwards I got your first letter dated May 30th, one from Father and Mother and one from Reckitts, all first ones. You know how I feel. I drew a very nice cake and some very nice toffee and chocolates from a very nice parcel from your Mother. Please thank her very much. I have received three parcels from Reckitts. I think it is awfully decent of them. Hatfield has had three and Thompson one via Peel House, so we are on our feet again and feeling very thankful to the people at home.

I have bought a deck-chair in which I spend lazy hours with a book and a pipe which nowadays holds real tobacco.

Heaps of love, and kisses, Cecil.

℞ St Margarets, Lairgate, Beverley, Friday 3.30 p.m., 30.8.18   21st letter

My Sweetheart,   I had a letter from you last Tuesday dated 20th July saying you had just got my first letter. You have been nearly three and a half months without a line from me.

I haven`t had a moment to spare since I last wrote on Sunday. On Tuesday I came over here to look after Flossie. She`s not at all well. We want her to come over to Filey but she is so absolutely cussed and won`t come that I am sick of it all. I always get the pip here and feel horribly miserable. I miss you when I`m with Bill & Flossie more than at any other time. At present I feel I`d like to dig a hole and bury myself in it until you come home. However, I`m leaving her for Bill to look after this weekend and going to Filey and I don`t think I shall come back on Monday - her Ma-in-law must come over or she must pull up her socks and look after herself. Cecil, I`m so utterly sick of looking after poorly relations - I get Ma better and someone else begins. I shall have to look after Ma again until after Xmas to see that she doesn`t catch cold, etc but after that I shall get away again - be a WAAC or something, then they can`t call me home. I`m so sorry it`s such a pippy letter but I can`t help it.

Could you write a note to Mrs Norman Ingleby c/o Col. Clarke, Kirk Ella, Nr Hull. She would be so awfully glad to hear from one of her husband`s friends, I know. I hear she has been a splendid brick and worked at Peel House until the day she heard he was killed.

Goodbye my dear one, Your little girl, Dora.

℞ William Slack to Cecil:

Wilton House, 31.8.18

> My dear Cecil,   ...You will be sorry to hear that it is now officially reported Norman Ingleby was killed towards the end of May. Your fear about Pollock is only too correct. The newspapers report "The Captain`s servant who is an exchange prisoner from Germany states that the Captain while carrying him on his back across an open stretch of

country which was being swept by machine gun fire, collapsed and died. The servant after lying by him for four hours was captured...."

Your affec. Father, W.H. Slack.

ᘓᘔ 3 Sea Bank, Filey, Tuesday 3.9.18, 10.10 p.m.   22nd letter

Darling,   I am sorry my last letter to you was so pippy - I feel better again now but I can`t help getting the dumps occasionally. Flossie is better than she was. She wants me to go back to her, but I`m not going. I hate it so....   Your sweetheart, Dora.

ᘓᘔ Cecil to his parents: 8.8.18

My Dear Father & Mother,   Today I got a letter from Dora written two months ago. My latest news is on a postcard from Father written on June 20th....Red Cross lists are continually coming here and they nearly always contain the names of men I know. I saw Ingleby`s and Laverack`s names but I understand that they are prisoners. My parcels, unlike my letters, are coming through regularly. Hatfield`s supply is all right, but Thompson has only received two. We all mess together, so no-one is hard up, and we are looking forward to a cartload for him some day shortly.

Love to all, Your affectionate son, Cecil.

ᘓᘔ Winnie Slack to Cecil:

8.9.18

My dear Cecil,   Your letter dated Aug. 8th arrived this morning. It is strange that Thompson`s parcels are not arriving. I will enquire at Peel House when I go to choose your parcel this week.

Hilda has got her hair up and looks quite the young lady, though she is still the school-girl in ways.

Dora and Mrs Willatt return from Filey this week. Mrs W. is feeling much better for the change. On their return home Flossie and her new husband are going to spend a few weeks at Beech Croft. You will be interested to know that Flossie expects to be a mother in April next. There will be great rejoicings.

Your affec. Mother, Winnie Slack.

◯⋎⋎ **3 Sea Bank, Filey, Sunday 3 p.m., 8.9.18**   23rd letter

Darling,   I have enjoyed the last two days tremendously. On Friday, and again yesterday, I went for a horse ride with old Burr. We had a ripping canter - it`s lovely on the sands. I haven`t been on a horse since I was with Pa at Pocklington in Dec. 1915 and you were at Dalton.

I saw in the paper yesterday that Grummit of Hornsea has been wounded by shrapnel in the shoulder and is now in a London hospital.

Mr and Mrs Stewart and her two kids - Mary and Jack - turned up yesterday evening on push-bikes from Bridlington and are staying till tomorrow. Rev and Mrs were over at Flossie`s wedding, you remember - he has got a church at Bridlington now.

Harold Jarman and Enid Grey are getting married on Wednesday next. I know Enid Grey: she`s very nice, but rather too elaborately dressed always.

I do my hair a different way now - no parting at all and just a bun at the back. I hope you will like it. Bill has got the `flu and is very poorly with it.

Yours with love xx, Dora.

William Slack to Cecil: 10.9.18

My dear Cecil,   Tonight`s paper refers to Ruthven having been awarded the Military Cross, though I am afraid he will never know anything about it.

I met Private Bean recently who said you saved his life and that of his pals when they were in a wood in March and would not have got away but for you calling them out.

Your affec. Father, W.H. Slack.

31.7.18

Darling,   This is my last letter of the month`s allowance. I`ve kept it back in case anything turned up for me.

We are asked not to write too small and to ask our people to do the same to save delay with the censoring. News is pretty scarce as you can imagine - just sleeping, walking, cooking and eating. I find that I can get hold of books for the exam for which I was working before the war by means of a special POW method, and it is possible for the study I do here to be taken into account on return to England. In some camps official exams have been held. This will save some time in swotting after the war.

I am a regular nib at cooking now, though most of it is only a form of heating up. I make excellent porridge and am dead nuts on bacon.

Goodbye little girl, Yours with love, Cecil.

3 Sea Bank, Filey, Tuesday 5.30 p.m., 10.9.18   24th letter

Darling,   I had a letter from you today dated 31st July. I have been riding again yesterday and today, and tomorrow will be my last before we go home on Thursday. It`s just a year ago tomorrow since we were in London, you remember. We had an awfully nice day in Flamborough

last week - the rocks are gorgeous. I brought a live lobster back with us
- it crawled all over the train carriage floor. One girl asked if it was a
fowl!! It was wriggling next morning when I tried to put it in the pan,
so I funked it and called Ma to do it!

Goodnight sweetheart, Your little girl, Dora.

ᏙᎶ William Slack to Cecil: 15.9.18

My dear Cecil,   It is Sunday morning and all are at Brunswick
except myself and the dog. The latter has been whining and crying as if he
were a human being. He becomes quite moody when the children are away.

I wish it were allowed to write something about the world`s events,
though I suppose you get some news of interest as you refer to Red Cross
lists being in the camp. We may hope that recent events have brought
the end nearer and that the day is not very distant when all the Nations
will be at peace.

In a few months time Beechcroft will have a Grandchild if all goes well.
It is rather a long way off so it may be well for you not to refer to it at
present.

With love from all, Your affectionate Father, W.H. Slack.

ᏙᎶ Harold to Cecil, undated:

My Dear Cecil,   I hope you are getting on all right. The hens
are laying very badly. Last month they laid 6 eggs from 20 hens. The
dog is ill he has had to be sent to the vet. We have not had any grapes
this year, we have had a great number of Crab Apples and peaches.

From your Affec. Brother Harold.

ᏙᎶ Cecil to his parents: 15.9.18

My Dear Father & Mother,   We are much better off in
our new quarters than at Hesepe. I am in a room with six others. Coal
and light are supplied; we have tables and chairs. There are no small

messes now. All foodstuffs common in parcels are pooled. Specialities
and dainties we keep ourselves. Cooking arrangements necessitate this,
and I think it will work smoothly . I hear that Norman Ingleby is
officially announced killed. I am very sorry. My books have not arrived,
but I have got hold of a Pitman`s Shorthand and am enjoying myself. I
was on the first walking out party this morning. This is a splendid town.

Love to all, Your affec. son, Cecil.

℞ Beech Croft, Thursday 19.9.18   26th letter

Sweetheart,   Mrs Clement Waite - she was Vera Clarke until last
February - telephoned me last night to know if you were getting your
parcels and how you were. Waite never received any until Aug. 14th,
and he was taken on the 12th April. He is on the Baltic coast and Jacko
is with him. I have asked her down to tea one day next week so we shall
have a lot to talk about. She has been doing a few weeks` motoring in
London and doesn`t know whether to sign on for a year or not.

I brought Flossie from Beverley on Tuesday - we had an awful time with
the dog: it refused to get into the cab or the train and had to be lifted -
it`s a big animal to carry about! He has already succeeded in eating a 2
oz. pat of butter - he can eat things off dishes on shelves and tables but
never breaks a pot!

Did I tell you Cedric Earle was killed - you remember he was wounded
and in London when you were "missing". We saw Mrs Earle - his Ma -
in town and I thought how lucky she was then - but I don`t now.

I made some shortbread for you yesterday and took it to Peel House, also
a Pheasant Pate which they are enclosing in a Reckitts parcel as it
wasn`t allowed in the one I sent.

I want to try and go in for massage after Xmas - in London - I do hate
housekeeping - it`s such a loathsome job.

Goodbye sweetheart, Yours with love, Dora.

ᘔᘓ Cecil to his parents: 21.9.18

My Dear Father and Mother,   We have been given a
young playing-field. So far we have only played hockey with walking-
sticks and a cricket ball but we hope to have footballs etc from a Red
Cross Society.

I am glad to hear that Laverack has been officially reported a prisoner. I
wish I could hear the same of Ingleby.

Love to all, Your affec. son, Cecil.

ᘔᘓ Fragment of undated letter, Cecil to Dora:

...I had an awful nightmare the other night - I dreamt I was married to
someone else. It was horrible. I was just making plans to murder the
person when I woke up. What made the dream worse was that you were
there and just as fed up as I was.

I have found a book of history notes, and find them much more
interesting than when I was at school. Do you remember William the
Conqueror? We learned about him at Miss Keen`s, from the same
book, 17 years ago. I have joined an advanced French course.

Goodbye little girl. Love from your sweetheart, Cecil.

ᘔᘓ Beech Croft, Monday 25.9.18, 6 p.m.   27th letter

Sweetheart,   I have been neglecting you horribly the last five days
- we came home Thursday and I have been most fearfully busy ever
since. Flossie and Bill and Boy (the Airedale dog) come to stay
tomorrow - also their maid - so we shall be a big family once more.

I have been enjoying life - or rather living in the past - by reading some
of your old letters, and it struck me how they have altered since April
10th - you are so matter of fact these days - it was refreshing to read one
of your old ones.

I went over to Wilton House on Saturday. It was pouring with rain so
no tennis, so we all played "sardines" all over the house - it was ripping.
Norman is getting quite talkative these days and of course Harold never
stops, which is rather different from your theory about the men-folk of
the Slack family not having much to say!

Your little girl, Dora.

ᴔ҉ 15.8.18

My Darling,   I have received your 2nd and 3rd letters within a
few days of each other, and shall wait for them now eagerly week by
week.

I received a parcel from your Mother a few days ago. Please thank her.
I cannot write every time, owing to our allotment. I almost know your
three letters by heart.

We have bought a piano for the camp, and negotiations are on foot for a
sports-field. I am doing physical exercises daily and am carrying on with
my cold bath which I now have under one of the pumps. I haven`t any
pyjamas yet and it takes a bit of courage to rush straight from my
blankets to the pump if it`s a bit chilly.

Love from your sweetheart, Cecil.

ᴔ҉ Beech Croft, 28.9.18 Wednes, 10.30 p.m.   28th letter

My Darling,   It`s a joyful day today, `cause I had a letter from
you dated 15 August - the tenth I have received since April.

I am having cold baths in the morning, and then I am doing exercises to
try and keep my tummy down too! So you see you are not the only one!

I do hope you get that sports field - it will make it tons nicer for you.
Why don`t you learn to play the piano now you have one - we could
have lovely times playing duets in years to come.

A note on Capt. C.M.S. was found in the pocket of Ruthven`s returned kit - about the March affair - it makes me realise more and more what you have done.*

Love from your little girl, Dora.

* see following letter.

ᐁ William Slack to Cecil:

Wilton House, 29.9.18

> My dear Cecil,   ...Mr Ruthven sent Mother a few days ago a copy of a note she found in her son`s pocket case in his kit which only reached her quite recently. It is evident it refers to your work following on March 21st and has nothing to do with the April battle as Ruthven was missing on the day you were captured. It reads as follows:
>
> "Captain C.M. Slack, M.C. - Throughout the time the Battn was in action he displayed great courage and determination especially in leading counter-attacks and organising withdrawals; and by his coolness and ceaseless energy he set a fine example to all those under him. On several occasions he held on to positions to the last possible moment, and himself...."
>
> The words omitted need not be inserted, but they refer to something you told us in your letter of April 6th. [they are: "shot down many of the advancing enemy"] It is clear Ruthven had not an opportunity to send the report in - However, you rejoice in your life whereas poor Ruthven has not been heard of.
>
> Waite has written for his golf-clubs and fishing tackle. He must be in a fine place. Your friend the major is at Stralsund.
>
> Your affectionate Father, W.H. Slack.

Beech Croft, Sunday 10.15 p.m., 29.9.18   29th letter

My Darling,   We put our clocks back tonight so it is really only
9.15 now. I am writing in bed - with a hot water bottle. It`s turned so
cold. Don`t be disgusted with me because I have one - I simply must - I
know you scorn them.

We have Mrs Rollit in to see us this evening. Her husband is the man
you went on the musketry course with at Strensall in 1915. She says the
Rollit you know is married and is at Hornsea at present.

All my love to you, Dora.

22.8.18

Darling,

I have received your 4th and 5th letters, the latter being from
Outwell.

The bread, which has now changed to biscuits, is coming through from
Copenhagen....

Your sweetheart, Cecil.

Beech Croft, Wednesday 9.45 p.m., 9.10.18   34th letter

My Darling,   I have dreamt about you the last three nights. We
have been at Filey each time. It seemed so real and I hated waking up
again. Time seems so short when I think I have only been with you for
five weeks since we were engaged, nearly two years ago now - we shall
have a lot to make up for when we see each other again. I often have a
huge heartache for you, my sweetheart.

This is not meant to be a miserable letter, it is only because I feel for you
to such a tremendous extent.

Goodnight x from your little girl, Dora.

ᏋᎩᏓ Beech Croft, Friday 10.15 p.m., 11.10.18 in bed   35th letter

My Darling,   Several of the nurses have got `flu at the VAD
hospital on Cottingham Rd so the Matron rang me up today - simply
beseeching me to go as they wanted help so badly with these nine nurses
being off. So I have to be there at 8 in the mg and have to go into the
flu and pneumonia ward, so I hope I don`t catch either.

I have been in town today with Ma and have been to have a new navy
coat and skirt fitted - it`s a plain tailor-made one, with swishy little
pockets, and I have got a lovely mauve muffler - woollen, all fluffy,
rather like a teddy bear - and then I shall wear a black hat and that will
be all! It`s nothing fluffy for me tomorrow, though: starched cuffs and
stiff apron etc, and a severe look - so I must pull up my socks in the
morning!

Love from your little girl, Dora.

ᏋᎩᏓ KRIEGSGEFANGENENSENDUNG, Coln, 14.10.18

Sweetheart,   We have been here four days in winter quarters, a
comfortable barracks. There are six others in my room. We have an
iron bedstead each, there is a stove for which fuel is supplied.

I got your 16th and 14th letters yesterday and today. The 13th, 15th,
17th, 18th and 20th and the photographs are still missing. By the way,
please don`t peroxide your hair - I wouldn`t like it a bit.

Tomorrow morning I am going out for a walk. Twenty-five may go at a
time. Our turn comes once a week....

Your sweetheart, Cecil.

ᏋᎩᏓ Beech Croft, 16.10.18 Wednesday, 10 p.m.   36th letter

My Sweetheart,   I have been wanting to write to you every
night but have been too tired at bedtime. Then we have been awfully
worried about Gladys Runton. She went to bed a week ago with

influenza and it has turned into pneumonia. She has had a temperature of 107 the last three days. She is terribly ill - in fact tonight it is touch and go with her - the Dr is staying all night. She has caught it at the hospital with nursing influenza and pneumonia cases and this is the result - it`s awfully sad and we feel quite upset about it - especially living next door. I only stayed at the hospital three days - I was nursing the "flu" cases too. On Monday my throat began to feel groggy so I knocked off. I have been doctoring myself since Monday and think I am warding an attack off.

Flossie and Bill have gone home today - I went over to Beverley to get their house in order.

Goodnight, Always your little girl, Dora.

♉ Saturday 9.30 p.m., 7.9.18

My Sweetheart,   No letters have come for me for the last 10 days, but for all that I`ve actually got some news to write about - not very exciting certainly, but something you don`t know. We`ve had 4 events in the Sports! High jump, long jump, throwing the cricket ball, and a relay race between teams from England, Scotland, Ireland, South Africa and America. I ran the quarter mile for the English team, which won. Any apprehensions you may have, my dear, as to my becoming fat, you may do away with, because I won the high jump, clearing 5 ft. I was fourth in the long jump and the cricket ball, both of which followed the relay, which had about outed me.

The war news is pretty useful, but it makes me feel mad to be here, sitting on the place where I always sit, and out of everything.

Tomorrow finishes my week of cooking which we each take in turn. I haven`t had such a bad week, and the people ate quite a lot of what I did. Next week I shall be orderly man and will wash up, set the table and draw tinned stuff, and the following week I become a gentleman of leisure.

I got some pyjamas in a parcel a few days ago. I wore them once - the first time for 5 months - and felt awfully stuffy, and couldn`t sleep. I shan`t put them on again till the cold weather comes.

Our piano has livened us up a good deal. There is one Sowerbutts who is very hot stuff on it.

Heaps of love for yourself from an aching heart, Cecil xx.

ॐ Beech Croft, 19.10.18 Saturday, 9.30 p.m. 37th letter

My Sweetheart, Thursday was a beautiful day in one way for me and not in another. I got your letter of 7th Sept and your photograph - you can`t imagine how I loved getting it - but you have never looked at me so sternly. You look older about the eyes but you are certainly wearing a ragtime outfit! I simply long to turn out your pockets again, they are getting awfully bulgy!

A very sad thing happened on Thursday evening - Gladys Runton died about 7.30 - we had really been expecting it all day but it came as a shock. She had a military funeral today: patients and nurses from the hospital went in the procession. Yesterday morning I started with a temperature and a cough so naturally Mother was very nervous and Dr Baine came to see me. He says I`ve got bronchial catarrh and laryngitis and have to stop in bed a few days. I felt rather rotten, but I feel better today and my temperature is better.

I know just how you feel, my darling, about being where you are when things are moving elsewhere, but do try and bear it and not dwell on it too much. You`ve had your innings, you know.

No more space allowed so I will finish anon. Always your little girl with all her love, Dora.

Cecil, looking 'stern', and Lt. Thompson.

☯ Beech Croft, 21.10.18 Monday, 10 p.m.   38th letter

My Darling,   I`m still in bed and Dr Baine says I have to stay
here yet and have a thorough rest. I can`t imagine what`s made me go
flop all at once. It seems awfully odd to be waited on in bed when I`ve
trotted miles and miles round wards looking after Tommies seeing that
they drink their medicine and don`t pour it down the sink when you`re
not looking! One has to have all one`s buttons on in hospital or they
pull your leg if they get half a chance! I`m quite an old soldier in that
respect now though.

We shall have a lot to make up for after the war, shan`t we? We may
not have many pennies at first, but "Love in a Cottage" will give us a
happy time, won`t it?

Goodnight my sweetheart, Love from your little girl, Dora.

Beech Croft, 23.10.18 Wednesday, 9.45 p.m.   39th letter

My Sweetheart,   I`m still in bed but have been sitting up for about an hour today and Dr Blaine says I shall probably go downstairs on Saturday. I don`t like too much bed - I`d rather be buzzing about.

Pater has taught me to play "bezique" - it`s quite a good game for two. Dr B came to see me again today - bless him. He hasn`t told me to get married lately!

I`m so awfully sleepy I simply must turn over and pop off. Goodnight my darling, I hope you are getting your parcels still. Haven`t dreamt of you lately.

Yours with love, Dora.

Beech Croft, Friday 25.10.18, 9.45 p.m.   40th letter

My Darling,   I`ve been up and fully dressed today, but not downstairs - I`m going tomorrow though. Mother and Father have been out for the day so I`ve been by myself except for Anna to look after me. I felt awfully weak, sweetheart, while I was getting up. I had to keep sitting down and then doing a little more. I don`t know when I have ever felt so weak, really. I do hope you will be careful if you get `flu cases into your camp - if you don`t feel at all well, go to bed and stay there. The Drs say it is the only and the best thing, and just have hot drinks.

Pater and Ma brought me a most beautiful bunch of big grapes - they are simply luscious.

I slept for $2^{1}/_{2}$ hours this afternoon after the exertion of getting dressed this a.m! I might as well be an infant in arms at present.

Goodnight my darling, Love from your little girl, Dora.

∂℞℧ **27.9.18, 5.30 p.m.**

Darling,   I got the snapshot of the fruit-pickers the day before
yesterday. Need I tell you I was delighted to see your picture again?
You look awfully well.

We are allowed to write 4 post-cards and 3 letter-cards a month....

Your sweetheart, Cecil.

∂℞℧ **Beech Croft, Tuesday 8.45 p.m., 29.10.18**   42nd letter

My Sweetheart,   I had a letter from you yesterday. I slept
solidly for two hours in the afternoon - to be woken up with your letter.
It really was very nice, and I had been dreaming about you too - that
you were in Hull again and coming to see me!

I have been to Peel House today and sent a parcel off for you - I`m sorry
I haven`t made an shortbreads this time but I haven`t felt well enough.
I also chose your weekly Reckitts parcel - but I`m awfully sorry I didn`t
put any smokes in - I didn`t remember until afterwards.  Please don`t
be too cross with me. It was silly of me.

Ma and I went to Beverley for the day to see Flossie. I`ve quite decided
I don`t want to live in Beverley - it`s too cramped and stuffy. I
wouldn`t live in St Margarets for anything - although I like the rooms
very much - but it`s rather dismal with so little garden and no fields
near.

My space is up now - so goodnight my darling. Love from your little
girl, Dora.

∂℞℧ **22.9.18**

Sweetheart,   Thank you very much for the paints, pencils and
shaving soap which I received a few days ago. I have taken off my
moustache, but it has grown again quickly and I am attempting a pair of

side-whiskers. I shall not be able to send you a picture of this since it is now verboten.

I see that Cecil Ingleby has been married. I knew Miss Winkley slightly, but I don`t think she will remember me. She was one of a concert party which came to us twice at South Dalton. The Inglebys have had rotten luck in the war - Cecil badly wounded, poor old Norman missing and their sister`s fiance killed. I am awfully sorry about Norman - I wish I could hear that he were safe.

We are living quite well at the moment, but we are trying to get up a little store for the winter weeks when the roads may be snowed up.

Yours with love, Cecil.

Beech Croft 1.11.18 Friday, 8.15 p.m.   43rd letter

My Sweetheart,   I had another letter from you y`day dated Sept. 22nd.

Please do grow a moustache again before you get back to England - in fact you must - and take the side whiskers off too please - so don`t forget, young man! So I s`pose I`ve got to live with that photo you sent me until I see you again - I don`t know how I`m going to do it.

I`m glad you`re putting food by for the winter months - I was hoping you would do. I shall have to look up my French when you get back or I shall be out in the cold when we have our trip to Paris.

Goodnight - xx love from your little girl, Dora.

Beech Croft, Tuesday 5.11.18, 9 p.m.   44th letter

My Darling,   I have had Ma ill since I last wrote - a cold and touch of the `flu, but she`s practically better now. I`m very sorry your Mother has had such a very bad throat and the Dr says she has just escaped something worse so he is taking special care. You needn`t worry because she is practically alright now.

They have asked me to go to work at Peel House - packing up parcels - so I think I might go until Xmas.

I must go and put Ma to bed now and then I have to see that Pa gets a scalding bath - hot milk and aspirins, as he`s got a bad cold too! So I`m busy old boy.

Goodnight darling, Love from your little girl, Dora.

ᗡᙅ Postcard from Cecil received 7.11.18:

> My address is now Offiziergefangenerlager KOLN

ᗡᙅ On 11.11.18 the Armistice took effect. There are no surviving letters acknowledging the fact.

ᗡᙅ Saturday 16.11.18, 8.45 p.m.

> Darling,   Last night I had a glorious dream about you. I had just got out of the train at some funny little wayside station, and you were waiting to meet me. Bill was with you. I gave you two kisses, I can feel my lips on your cheek now, but when I began to speak I woke up.
>
> I haven`t written this month because we had all expected to be home by now. We don`t know when we shall leave this place. It might be any time up to the termination of the armistice. I am almost crying to be with you now that it is so near. Your 24th 26th and 27th arrived a few days ago. I also got a very old one from home.
>
> We are allowed to go out to town as we like between the hours of 9.30 a.m. and 6.30 p.m., on parole, but may not visit music halls, cinemas, cafes, etc. I and another fellow were the first out in the town, and without giving our parole. We were looked at with interest, some timidity, and in a fed up sort of way.

Thompson got a parcel today, and Hatfield got one yesterday, the first since we left Hesepe; we have been in low water again about grub, but I think all`s well now. We got a little bit of wind up during the revolution stunt, but not much. A few of our sentries joined the mob, but the council people kept good order. We had to take the armistice news very quietly though.

Goodnight my darling, my own little girl, Cecil.

ᘺᘺ Letter from Cecil to his parents, written on paper headed "The YMCA with the British Prisoners of War Interned in Holland":

Sunday 24.11.18, 10.30 p.m.

My Dear Father and Mother,   We arrived at Rotterdam today and sail for Hull tomorrow. The journey will take about 50 or 60 hours. From Hull we go to Ripon for explanations, identifications, etc and then home for leave. I expect I shall be able to get home before going to Ripon. We came down the Rhine from Coln, and have had excellent treatment in Holland.*

Love to all, Your affec. son, Cecil.

*Cecil was cutting a long story short here. A few days earlier four officers from the POW camp had packed their cases and gone to the railway station in Cologne to buy tickets to London, only to be told that the lines were damaged and the journey impossible. The result was that the entire camp then pooled resources and chartered a boat to take them down the Rhine to Rotterdam. An overnight stop in Dusseldorf was followed by a warm reception in Holland, where a number of the party were taken ill through over-eating. At Rotterdam they were taken in hand by the British authorities and put on a boat to Hull. Dora and her mother, having heard a rumour that some prisoners were going to arrive but having no idea who might be among them, went down to the dock. It was several weeks before the first prisoners arrived back in England through the more usual channels.

  ᛋᚷ Letter to Dora on similarly headed paper:

Sunday 24.11.18, 10.30 p.m.

Darling,   I expect to be home a few minutes after this letter. We arrived at Rotterdam today and sail for Hull tomorrow. From Hull we have to go to Ripon to tell people all about our being made prisoner, etc., after which I believe we get a month`s leave. If I can break the journey at the little city of Hull, you bet your sweet life I`m doing it. I think my journey across takes two days and one night. I`m feeling very happy; are you?

Love from your sweetheart, Cecil.

  ᛋᚷ Telegram to Slack, Great Northern Hotel, Peterborough, 28.11.18

      CECIL ARRIVED WELL MET BY MRS SLACK AND DORA IS REPORTING AT SCARBORO FOR TWO DAYS. WILLATT.

  ᛋᚷ telegram from Scarborough dated 10.10 a.m., 29.11.18

To Slack Wilton House

Arrive 1.28 today Cecil.

Post-Script

After the war, Cecil resumed his work at Reckitts, eventually becoming Company Secretary. He and Dora were married on 3 September 1919. They had three children who remember them as a devoted, loving couple, but a couple still to an extent living under the shadow of what they went through in the Great War. Relatives recall Cecil occasionally embarking on a reminiscence of his days at the front, only for Dora to tell him "We don`t want to talk about that, dear". Thus it was not until the last years of Dora`s life that Cecil, perhaps to seek distraction from the pain of watching her decline, set about collating and annotating the papers relevant to his war experiences. His diligent efforts produced not only his own excellent book, *Grandfather`s Adventures in the Great War,* but paved the way for the alternative view of the same drama which is portrayed within these pages. Dora died in 1976, Cecil ten years later.